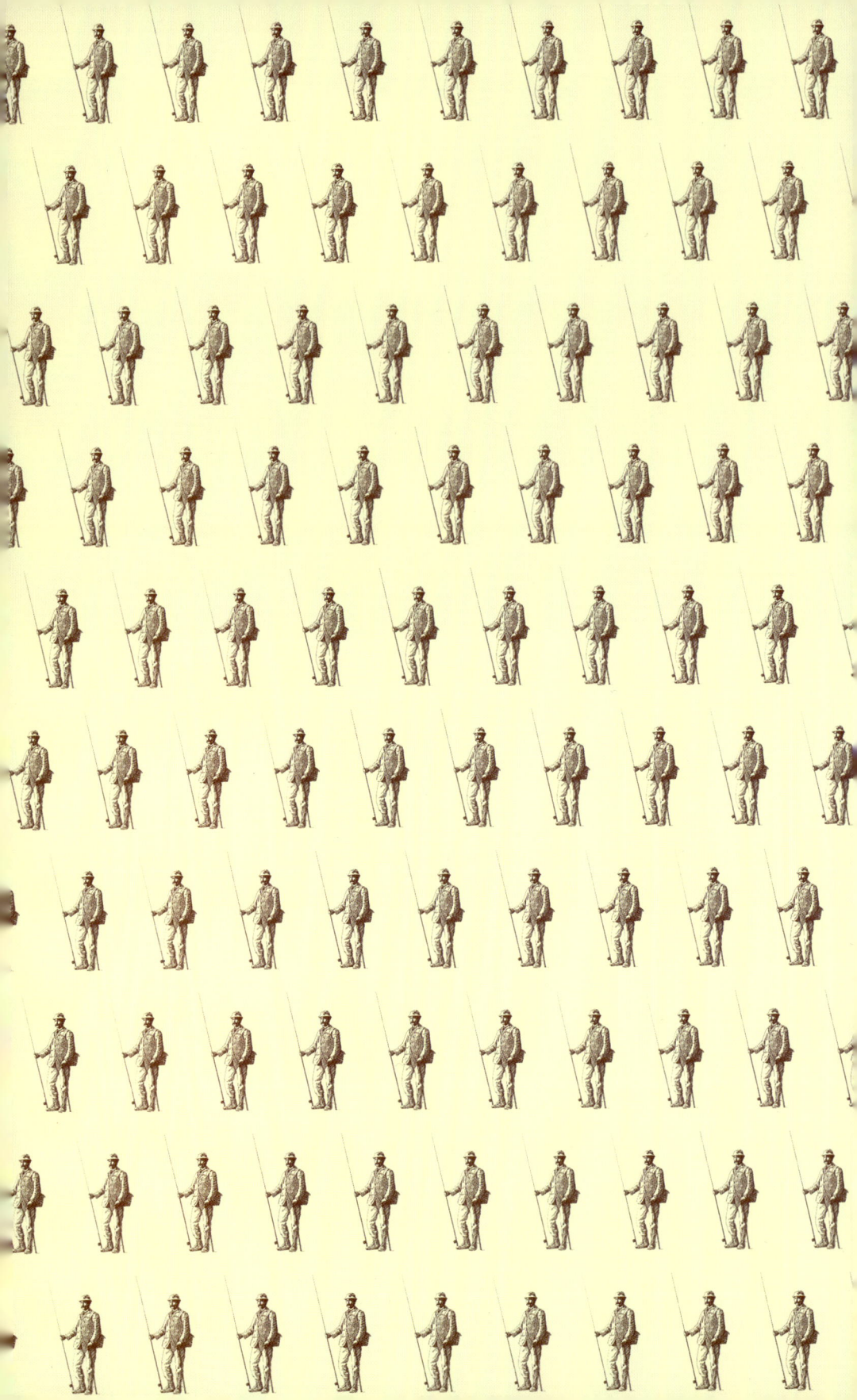

Flyfishing the Welsh Borderlands

Dogsbody (*Harry Powell*)

Fly tied by Jean Williams
Photographed by Terry Griffiths

FLYFISHING THE WELSH
BORDERLANDS

A REVIEW OF FLYFISHING AND FLIES FOR
WILD TROUT AND GRAYLING IN THE RIVERS,
BROOKS AND STREAMS OF THE REGION.

Roger Smith

Coch-y-Bonddu Books
2011

FLYFISHING THE WELSH BORDERLANDS

Written by Roger S. D. Smith

First published by Coch-y-Bonddu Books,
Machynlleth, 2011

Standard Edition
ISBN 978 1 904784 35 7

Collector's Edition
Limited to 250 signed cloth-bound copies
ISBN 978 1 904784 36 4

Flyfisher's Classic Library edition limited to only 30 copies
each containing a Dogsbody fly tied by Jean Williams of Usk
ISBN 978 1 905396 18 4

© *Coch-y-Bonddu Books Ltd & Roger S. D. Smith, 2011*
Flies photographed by Terry Griffiths
Chapter heading illustrations by Will Nickless

Coch-y-Bonddu Books Ltd, Machynlleth, Powys SY20 8DG
01654 702837
www.anglebooks.com

Contents

Cover

The Lion Hotel old fashioned, comfortable

ANGLING HAUNTS

AND

ANGLING HINTS

Appertaining to

RHAYADER

And District.

Being a brief account of the local waters, with a few suggestions regarding flies and other tackle, where to fish, distances, etc.

Topographical, Etc.

RHAYADER—to the Angler—offers facilities almost, if not quite, unrivalled, possessing as it does several miles of free Fishing on one of the best, as well as one of the most beautiful, streams in Mid-Wales. It is within easy reach of the large Midland Towns, either by rail or road.

The River Wye, which divides the town of Rhayader from the neighbouring village of Cwmdauddwr, is at this point of remarkable clearness, free from any trace of pollution, and from Llangurig (10 miles away), flows on to Rhayader amid surroundings of varying beauty, attractive equally to the fisherman and to the artist.

It is well stocked with Trout, of fighting, as well as of edible qualities, which would be difficult to beat. Salmon also ascend to its upper reaches (under favourable conditions) in considerable quantities.

For fuller particulars of the neighbourhood, subjects of interest to the Archæologist or Artist, Walks, Drives, etc., we refer visitors to the Rhayader Guide (obtainable at all booksellers, price 1d.), in which is set out at greater length, and by an abler pen than ours, sufficient descriptive matter to inform the interested.

Our object is merely to speak of the local streams and lakes, and to give a few particulars regarding the same, which we hope may be of some service to visiting Anglers, as well as a desire (of which we make no secret) to effect a little advertisement for ourselves.

Salmon license 5/- the Season

Licenses.

Wye Fishery Board License—Season, 2/6
           28 Days, 1/-
Birmingham Corporation Reservoirs, Streams and
Natural Lakes—
   Daily Ticket, 2/6   Weekly, 10/6
   Monthly, 40/-   Season, £5 5 0

A Wye Fishery License is necessary to fish the B'ham Corp. Waters.

Season opens—Salmon, Feb. 2nd to Oct. 15th.
             Trout, Feb. 15th to Oct. 1st.
A copy of Rules relating to the Birmingham Corporation Waters, together with a list of last season's returns, may be obtained from the Birmingham Corporation Estate Office, South Street, Rhayader.

THE RIVER WYE is free fishing from about three-quarters of a mile below the town to some five or six miles above, with the exception of a stretch between the third and fourth miles. By " free " we mean that it is open water by courtesy of the Riparian Owners—the privileged fisherman will of course appreciate this by care of hedges, closing gates, etc., and will not assume rights which he does not legally possess. To fish it to advantage it is necessary to wade, *i.e.*, wading stockings, not trousers, are necessary.

The best Rod is one from 9 to 10 feet, and a Landing Net with a 4-ft. staff is a " handy thing to have about you," the river best being anything but even. All legal lures are permitted, but as the stream quickly clears after a fresh, fly-fishing is the method chiefly adopted.

The fisherman may leave his hotel and be fishing in three minutes, but he will be wise to take the Llangurig Road (running parallel with the river) for some distance, from which he may strike the water at any point he may choose, so avoiding water which is over-flogged.

THE BIRMINGHAM CORPORATION WATERS consist of four Reservoirs, the nearest being Caban Coch, which is bisected by the Viaduct Carreg Ddu, the upper half of which is known by that name, Pen-y-Garreg, Craig-Goch, and Mynach. The nearest point is four miles from Rhayader, and the farthest thirteen, though the further point—Pont-ar-Elan—can be reached by the old Aberystwyth Road within five miles. Shelters are provided near the Reservoirs, consisting each of a Lunch Room, Stable and Coach House, or Garage. All of the Reservoirs may be reached by excellent new roads constructed by the Corporation of Birmingham.

The Rivers Elan and Claerwen, from which the Reservoirs are fed, also provide excellent sport, and may be fished by ticket holders.

A full account of the Waterworks, with the areas and water capacity of the Reservoirs, will be found in the Rhayader Guide.

A good outfit for the Reservoirs would be—Rod, 10 to 11-ft., strong ; 30 or 40 yards of fairly heavy fly line ; 3-yard tapered cast, the finest part being about 2x (or 3x on calm days) ; flies on hooks No. 10 to 12. Strong boots and a good mackintosh and overalls are almost a necessity (it sometimes rains !)

FLIES.

We approach this question with considerable diffidence—fishermen will not require us to say *why*. However, the flies hereafter mentioned, and a large stock of which we have, carefully tied for us, from our own patterns, have killed for us and our friends in past seasons, and we feel sure that given a trial they will not fail to render a good account of themselves. The list we give is of course not by any means exhaustive, and those set apart for the months can at the best be but approximate. We would suggest their use under such weather conditions as are to be reasonably expected at the seasons given.

With regard to Reservoir patterns, we are confronted with even greater difficulty still, experience having taught us the futility of endeavouring to set apart any particular flies for the months. We have frequently found that given a change of wind or weather, the fly which served us well one day would completely fail the next, a difficulty doubtless not confined to Radnorshire, and one the surrounding of which affords additional zest to the enthusiast, though admittedly exasperating at times.

We have therefore thought it best to class Reservoir Flies into three groups—Spring, Summer and Autumn.

We are aware that there are dozens of other patterns which frequently kill, indeed the fish will some days take almost anything, though against this we have found on other occasions all or nearly all patterns but one persistently refused. Our own plan is to try a couple of the " seasonable group," and if necessary to change until success crowns our efforts, and that is the best advice we can offer to our visitors, although we shall always be pleased to give callers the benefit of our experience up to date.

Stream Flies.

March.—Feb. Red, Cockwing Blue, March Brown, Hare's Ear and Woodcock, Partridge and Orange.

April.—March Brown, Olive Dun, Sand Fly, Blue Dun, Orl, Partridge and Orange, Grannum.

May.—Pale Olive, Pale Blue, Orl, Black Gnat, Peacock, Pratt's Red Spinner.

June.—Hare's Ear Blue, Red Dun, Red Quil, Orl, Coch-y-bonnddu, Pratt's Red Spinner, Pratt's Beetle, Governor, Alder.

July.—Golden Dun, Red Quill, Pratt's Red Spinner, Pratt's Beetle, Orl, Governor, Alder, Evening Blue, Coachman.

August.—Aug. Brown, Sandy Dun, Red Spinner, Red Ant, Orl, Coachman, Pratt's Beetle, Governor.

September.—March Brown, Sand Fly, Partridge and Orange, Hare's Ear and Woodcock, Orl, Dark Blue.

Reservoir Flies.

Spring.—Butcher, Blue Quil, Zulu, March Brown, T. & P. " Favourite," Grouse and Orange, Teal and Red.

Summer.—T. & P. " Enchanter," T. & P. " Favourite," Claret and Mallard, Waverley, Teal and Red, Teal and Black, Victor, Iron Blue (locally known as " Gochenlas "), Brown Grouse, Hump Back, Grey Quil, Coch-y-bonnddu, T. & P. Midge (sometimes kills on warm days to the exclusion of all other patterns—our own careful copy of the natural insect.)

Autumn.—T. & P. " Favourite," T. & P. " Enchanter," Claret and Mallard, Red, Palmer, Orl, Red and Brown.

WEIGHT OF FISH—

Trout in River Wye average 3 or 4 to the lb.
     ,,   Reservoirs   ,,   about 10-oz. or 12-oz.

Salmon Fishing.

The pursuit of the Salmon has been called the millionaire's sport, and on few waters, even where Trout Fishing may be easily procured, has the wielder of the two-handed rod any chance—unless his purse be a long one.

In Rhayader, however, the chief question is one of leisure, or the ability to snatch an opportunity when the river is in fit condition for Salmon Angling. In a rainy season (such as 1907 for instance), the upper reaches of the Wye become well stocked with the " King of Fishes," so much so that it is no infrequent occurrence for the Trout fisher to hook one while striving for the humbler game.

The cost of a Salmon License for the season is the merely nominal sum of **15/-**.

The Rod for Salmon Fishing need not be a very heavy one ; the stream not being very wide, the pools, or " catches," may be easily covered with the aid of a Grilse Rod of 14-ft. to 15-ft.

Flies should not be tied too large. Popular patterns are Jack Scott, Durham Ranger, Fiery Brown, Claret and Mallard, Thunder and Lightning, and Butcher.

CHUB AND DACE abound plentifully in the river **below** the town, and will be found to rise freely to the artificial fly on Summer evenings. They may also be taken on such baits as worms, paste, cheese and wasp grub.

In conclusion we beg to reiterate our wish that the matter we have set forth—although inadequate to do justice to the means for sport which the neighbourhood affords—may be of some interest to the touring Angler. We shall at all times be pleased to give attention to enquiries, and can assure our patrons of our earnest endeavour to supply their needs to the best of our ability.

We cordially wish our readers the Fisherman's Toast—" A Tight Line."

TRIBBECK & PRATT, Rhayader.

Introduction and acknowledgements

It all began on a riverbank in the middle of the grayling season in January, 2008, when Glyn Williams, Secretary of the Worcester Branch of the Fly Dressers' Guild, asked if I would give the branch members a talk on the subject of flies associated with fishing for trout and grayling in our region. This I duly did in the autumn of 2008 and afterwards some members asked if I would be prepared to produce a written account of what I had said.

The resultant forty-five page paper contained my definition of the region together with information gleaned from the eighteen books I had read on the subject, brief details of forty-odd fly-tyers from the region, plus the patterns of 115 flies and a brief look at characteristic features of these flies and the material used in their construction.

I gave this paper the title *In a Class by Themselves*, a phrase from a chapter titled *The Welsh Borderland* in A.G. Bradley's book, *Clear Waters*, in which he states, 'I always think of the streams of the Welsh Borders … as in a class by themselves.' It never occurred to me at the time that this quotation from *The Welsh Borderland* would eventually give me the title of this much bigger project.

At the Grayling Society Symposium in November, 2009, Paul Morgan of Coch-y-Bonddu Books saw a copy of my paper and suggested it might be expanded into a book that would be of interest to the many flyfishers of the region and beyond. *Flyfishing the Welsh Borderlands* is the result. It has occupied much of my spare time over the last two years, I've met many new and interesting people in the pursuit of information, and visited some delightful parts of the country. The number of books of relevance has increased to forty-two, the number of notable fly-tyers and characters has risen to over sixty, and the number of fly patterns to 225! The task, although challenging and time-consuming, has been great fun.

Producing this book would not have been possible without the encouragement and help of a significant number of people. These include: Louis Noble (Dee), Alan Hudson and David Palmer (Ceiriog), Tony Bostock (Severn), Major Stewart Minton-Beddows (Onny), Archer de Haan (Corve), Daniel McDowell and Barney Rolfe-Smith (Teme), Dave Collins, Geoff Franks and Adam Fisher (Wye), Tony Norman (Lugg and Arrow), Patrick Lloyd and John Bailey (Monnow), and Stuart Jarvis, Ron Pomfret, Ron Gover, Nick Brabner, Jean Williams, David Jones-Powell, Paul Bowen and Adam Fisher (Usk).

I am also very grateful to Michael Leighton, Christopher Knowles and Moc Morgan for giving me their permission to use material from their books.

Certain fly patterns within the inventory contained in this book were kindly donated by their originators, and in this respect I especially wish to thank the following for their time and patience: Peter Barrett (Cosmo Barrett's grandson), Tony Bostock, Dave Collins, Ken Glover, Alan Hudson, Stuart Jarvis, Louis Noble, David Palmer, Ron Pomfret and Jean Williams.

A special note of thanks must go to Jean Williams for providing copies of Lionel and Molly Sweet's flies as well as providing the thirty specially tied Dogsbody flies, one for each copy of the de luxe edition.

My thanks also go to fellow members of the Worcester branch of the Fly Dressers' Guild for their encouragement in the project, their companionship on the river, and in particular I take this opportunity to thank Roy McAdam, Glyn Williams, Peter Major and John Bergdahl for their fly-tying skills in the production of the definitive set of flies for the book.

And to many of the aforementioned for their much welcomed contributions to Chapter 2 – contributions which confirm my belief in the unique quality and properties of the flyfishing to be had in the Welsh Borderlands.

My very special thanks go to:

Stewart Johnson for his cartographic and computing skills in the production of the maps.

Paul Morgan of Coch-y-Bonddu Books for his encouragement throughout, and to his colleagues Paul Curtis and Pete Mackenzie for their considerable contribution.

Terry Griffiths, photographer supreme, for the beautiful fly plates.

Louis Noble (again!), for his encouragement, technical authority on fishing, and for kindly writing the Foreword.

Last, but by no means least, I am grateful to my wife, Judy, for supporting me throughout the whole project; for accompanying me on many of the forays into the Welsh Borderlands in pursuit of information; for her forbearance when our house either became overrun with books, paper and laptops, or fur and feather during the fly-tying sessions!

Above all, I hope that through the publication of this book, the flies and the history of wild trout and grayling flyfishing of the Welsh Borderlands will be recognised and enjoyed by an even larger audience in the years ahead.

Roger Smith
Malvern
October, 2011

To all who enjoy fishing the rivers, streams and brooks
of the Welsh Borderlands,
and who realise their true potential, appreciating them to be
'in a class by themselves.'

A.G. Bradley *Clear Waters*

FOREWORD

Flyfishing in the rivers and streams of the Welsh Borders has given me immeasurable pleasure throughout a lifetime of angling. Consequently I am immensely pleased that Roger Smith has assembled this encyclopaedic work on the subject, and delighted that I have been asked to provide this Foreword. I have known Roger for many years, particularly through his work with the Grayling Society, but I also know him as a mountain climber of some considerable repute; he has climbed all over Europe and other parts of the world including the Himalayas. An intrepid character!

As a proud Salopian I have been fortunate to be able to fish many of the waters of the region. However, I now realise that I've only scratched the surface of what is potentially available. To see the wealth of major rivers and tributaries contained within the Welsh Borderlands is quite staggering and something that we flyfisherman should rejoice in – surely it would take a lifetime to get to know them all.

The impressive compilation of information on waters is only one facet of what I consider to be an all-encompassing analysis of what makes the region so important and interesting. In my opinion, nothing has been omitted – we see a wide array of books which hold valuable information on the region, the fishing and fly-dressing characters, a truly impressive collection of pertinent fly patterns and historical notes on the region's fishing.

As if this wasn't enough, we have been given a list

of flyfishing opportunities, materials for dressing the important patterns and to my great delight, a selection of poems relevant to Borderland streams.

As an avid fly-dresser, over recent years I have developed a passion for the patterns of the Reverend Powell, Canon Eagles and Cosmo Barrett, particularly those with reversed hackles, so you can imagine my pleasure at finding so much information and so many original patterns within these pages.

Other publications contain some of this information but this book collates it under one cover – the amount of research that Roger has carried out is extraordinary. Those who know him will understand how his meticulous nature, born out of a lifetime in the field of education, could draw all this wonderful information together for our enjoyment. It is abundantly clear that the creation of this book has been a labour of love, driven by an insatiable interest in the subject.

A commendable feature of this research is the fact that Roger made the effort to locate and visit relatives and acquaintances of some of the great characters. This enabled him to offer a deeper insight than other publications and the text is the richer for this.

An incredibly important point of interest is the inclusion and discussion of so many significant fly patterns of the region, either from a bygone age or from more recent times. It is true that many of these are to be found in other books, but here is surely the definitive collection into which you can delve when attempting to lure the prized trout and grayling from our precious Border waters.

I am writing this Foreword because I believe strongly in the importance of learning the traditions of fishing in our region – successful flyfishing is not just about how technically correct our casting may be, but includes the influences that the past masters can bring to our whole outlook and approach. As a full-time game angling instructor and guide this is something that I impress on newcomers to our sport. I am certain that this book will enhance our knowledge, enjoyment and eventual success.

I am in no doubt that this book will, in time, take its place alongside the major works that Roger has reviewed and that, no matter if you are a keen fisher or collector of fishing books, it will occupy a prominent place on your bookshelf.

Next season, and for seasons to come, my sport will be enhanced as I explore more of the many waters that Roger has brought to my attention.

Louis Noble
Wrexham
October, 2011

Map showing the principal rivers of
the Welsh Borderlands

N

Chester

Dee

Bala

Severn

Newtown

Rhayader

Wye

Tewkesbury

Brecon

Usk

Newport

Chepstow

Scale

0   10   20   30   40   50
miles

Chapter 1

The region, its rivers (and some history)

From Chester in the north to Chepstow and Newport in the south; from Brecon and Bala in the west to Tewkesbury in the east; this is the country known as the Welsh Borders or Borderland, the Welsh Marches or even, as Housman called it, Western Brookland.

The region straddles the border between the mountains of Wales and the river valleys of England. In England it includes parts of Cheshire, Shropshire, Herefordshire, Worcestershire and Gloucestershire, and in Wales, the old counties of Monmouthshire, Brecknockshire, Radnorshire, Montgomeryshire, Merionethshire, Denbighshire and Flintshire. (In modern parlance: Gwent, Powys and Clwyd.)

The principal towns of the region are Chester, Wrexham, Oswestry, Shrewsbury, Welshpool, Ludlow, Tenbury Wells, Leominster, Hereford, Gloucester, Brecon, Llandrindod Wells and Builth Wells, Monmouth, Usk and Abergavenny.

To the trout and grayling flyfisher the region effectively

encompasses the river catchments of the Dee, Severn, Wye and Usk. Within these catchments there are approximately 230 rain-fed rivers, streams and brooks, most of which hold populations of wild trout and grayling.

Writing around 1190, Geraldus Cambrensis (Gerald of Wales) informs us that fish were plentiful in Brecknock, supplied by the Usk on one side and the Wye on the other, each producing salmon and trout; the Wye abounding more with salmon and the Usk more with trout. The Wye also produced a fish called umber (grayling).

The River Dee is rich in myths, legends and folklore and Bala Lake (Llyn Tegid), close to its source, is home to the unique gwyniad, a species of whitefish that is a holdover

Map showing the major rivers, brooks and streams
of the River Dee catchment area

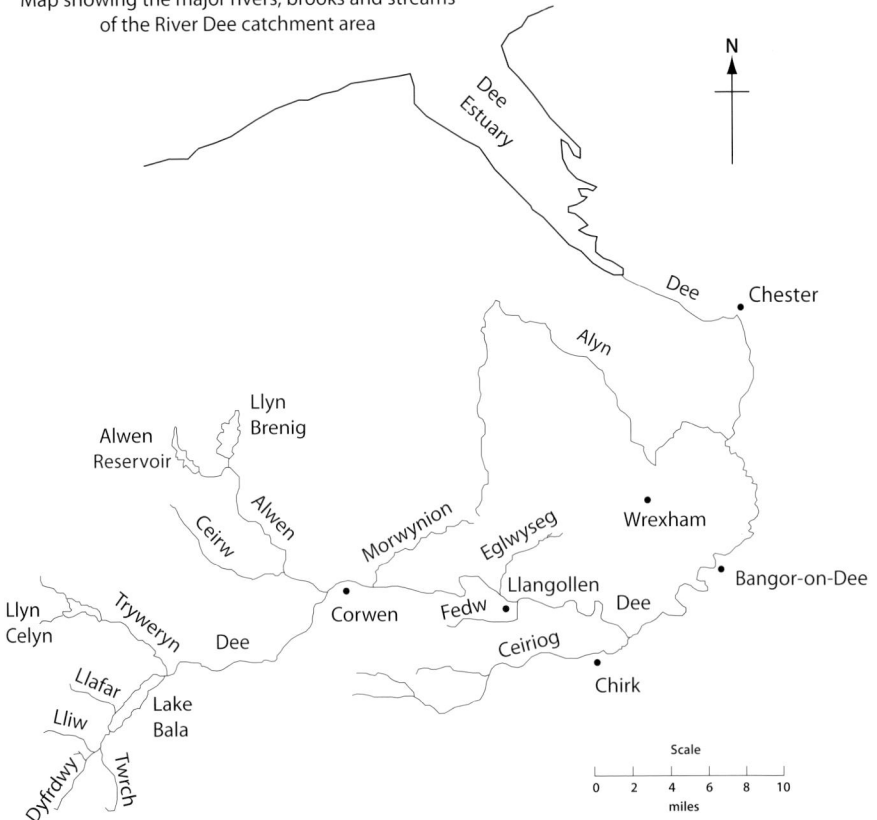

N

Dee
Estuary

Dee   Chester

Alyn

Llyn
Brenig

Alwen
Reservoir

Alwen

Ceirw

Morwynion

Eglwyseg

Wrexham

Llangollen   Bangor-on-Dee

Llyn
Celyn

Tryweryn

Dee   Corwen   Fedw   Dee

Ceiriog

Llafar

Lliw   Lake
Bala

Chirk

Dyfrdwy

Twrch

Scale

0   2   4   6   8   10
miles

from the last Ice Age, first mentioned in literature by Richard Bowlker about 1747.

The earliest reference to trout and grayling fishing on the River Severn appears in 1651 and one of its principal tributaries, the River Teme, is steeped in history and again is mentioned by Richard Bowlker.

The most satisfactory way to look at the history of wild trout and grayling fishing in the region is to examine each river catchment as a separate entity – starting with the Dee.

River Dee (Afon Dyfrdwy)

The River Dee is one of the most interesting and historic rivers in Britain, rich in legends and folklore. Poets have included it in their verses: Milton referring to it as that 'Wizard Stream', while Tennyson called it the 'Sacred Dee' and Charles Kingsley wrote the well-known poem *The Sands of Dee.*

The river is approximately eighty miles long, rising high in the Aran Mountains where it is known as Dyfrdwy Fach or the Little Dee. It is soon joined by two other streams, the Afon Lliw and the Afon Twrch, before entering the south-west end of one of the largest lakes in Wales – Bala Lake. These three streams all hold populations of brown trout and grayling. The lake itself has large numbers of pike and coarse fish, as well as trout and salmon. It may be the only place in Britain where one can fish for grayling in stillwater.

Just below the lake the Dee is joined by the Afon Tryweryn, and becomes quite a substantial river. The river here has always been known for its large and plentiful grayling. An abundance of trout and salmon, in the main river and in the Afon Eglwyseg (Abbey Brook), was reported as far back as the Middle Ages by the Cistercian monks of Valle Crucis Abbey, near Llangollen.

Coracles

The Dee has a centuries-old tradition of fishing for salmon and trout from coracles. The lower river was always difficult to fish from the bank owing to its considerable breadth and heavily tree-lined banks, so the use of such a light and versatile craft enabled fishermen to cover the water.

George Agar Hansard in *Trout and Salmon Fishing in Wales (1834)* gives a vivid description an expert coracle fisher, throwing a short line but covering the most inaccessible water, and negotiating dangerous rapids with ease.

Most Dee coracles were designed to take two people; the attendant who handled the craft, and the fisherman. They were more or less square with sides of approximately 5ft long, and the portion below water level was noticeably greater than that above – thus giving an overall wedge shaped appearance. The frame of the craft was traditionally made from ash laths covered with flannel which was liberally coated with pitch and oil. Later versions were covered in sailcloth and painted with bitumen. The finished article weighed 30lb to 40lb and was, of necessity, portable. Skilful fishermen not only covered considerable distances but also made large catches of salmon and trout. There are many tales of large salmon towing the coracle through the water before coming to the gaff.

Major problems

The most significant occurrence to affect the fishing potential of the river over the last century and a half has been the impounding and diverting of its water to supply the Shropshire Union Canal and, more significantly, to provide a reliable and adequate supply of wholesome water for the burgeoning cities of Liverpool, Birkenhead and Birmingham during the massive changes associated with the rapid industrialisation of the mid-1800s.

In 1804 Thomas Telford completed a sluice gate on Bala Lake which in turn guaranteed adequate water lower down the river at Chain Bridge near Llangollen for the Shropshire Union Canal. The combination of controlled flow from Bala Lake and the construction of reservoirs Llyn Brenig, Llyn Alwen, and later Llyn Celyn, enabled reliable flow levels to be maintained without seasonal fluctuations, working on the principle that water released higher up the river could be extracted lower down in closer proximity to the cities.

The construction of a fish hatchery at Maerdy on the Afon Alwen in the 1960s was an important factor in maintaining stocks of salmon and trout on the River Dee and throughout Wales. In recent times the hatchery has pioneered the propagation and conservation of grayling, gwyniad, and even freshwater mussels.

Fly patterns of the Dee

Over 20 fly patterns have been developed specifically for the Dee and its tributaries and among them are few noteworthy examples that have gained wider importance. These include the following:

– The *Bangor Duster* and all its variants.

– The *Ceiriog Spinner*, devised by Alan Hudson for use on the Ceiriog.

– *Coltman's Duster*, a reversed-hackled fly made popular on the Ceiriog.

– The *Cul de Canon*, a relatively modern fly developed by Gwilym Hughes when competing in the 1998 International.

– The *Feather Duster*, with its ingenious cork underbody for flotation.

– The *Grey Duster*; a famous general-purpose dry fly, collected by A. Courtney Williams with its origins on the Afon Alwen.

– C.V. Hancock's *March Brown*; a most successful wet-fly pattern.

– *Y Diawl Bach*, now internationally famous; originally the handiwork of Dewi Evans of Bala.

River Severn (Hafren)

The River Severn is the longest river in Britain and historically has acted as an important barrier between various invading forces and the resident Welsh. Nowadays, whilst still acting as a notional boundary between England and Wales, the river is known for its tidal bore, its magnificent bridges and (less widely known) as the supplier of water to the cities of the Midlands.

Piscatorial history recalls that the main river has always had a fine reputation for its coarse fish, and for salmon. It is to the tributaries and upper reaches of the main river that one has to go to find early fishing records of trout and, particularly, of grayling. During the nineteenth century the River Teme, with its tributaries the Corve, Onny and Clun, was recognised as one of the best grayling rivers in the whole of Britain, and became a very popular with anglers.

The Severn catchment has a rich literary history of flyfishing. The earliest reference is by Barker in 1651 who states that 'there is a fish in my Countrey called a Grayling, which swimmeth in the gallant river of Severn ... the bait must be either a small artificiall or a natural flye.' Richard Bowlker, in the 1749 edition of his *Art of Angling*, included *Fishing Stations in North Wales*, recording trout and grayling fishing locations on the Severn, the Clywedog, the Banwy and the Tanat. Samuel Taylor also made reference to fishing locations on the Severn, Teme and Tanat in 1800. References were made by Davy in 1828 and Francis Francis in 1867 to the grayling fishing on the River Teme, in the Downton Gorge and Leintwardine district.

Major problems

The regulation of the flow of the River Severn has been a key feature in its history and this in turn has affected the fishing. The flooding of the valleys in the construction of Lake Vyrnwy

Map showing the major rivers, brooks and streams
of the River Severn catchment area

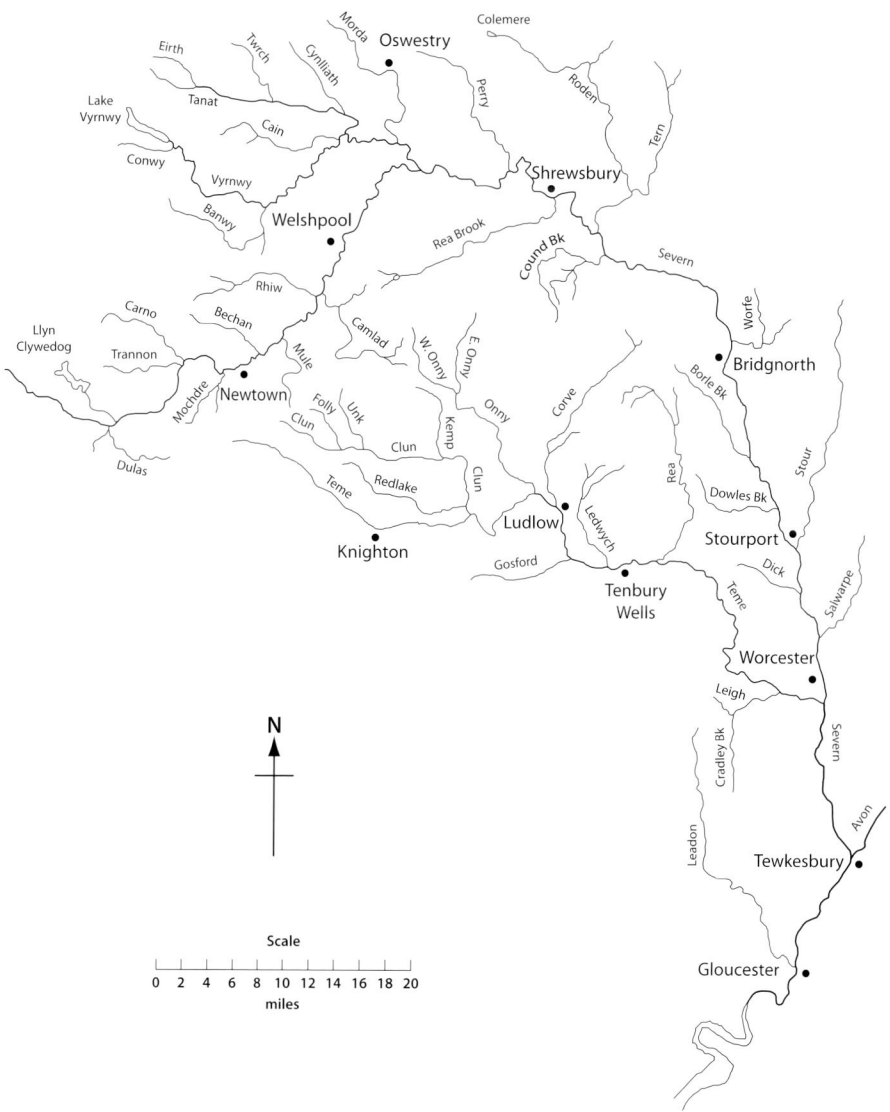

Eirth
Twrch
Cynlliath
Morda
Oswestry
Colemere

Lake
Vyrnwy
Tanat
Perry
Roden

Conwy
Cain
Tern

Vyrnwy
Shrewsbury

Banwy
Welshpool
Rea Brook
Cound Bk
Severn

Rhiw
Worfe

Carno
Bechan
Camlad
W. Onny
E. Onny
Borle Bk
Bridgnorth

Llyn
Clywedog
Trannon
Mochdre
Newtown
Mule
Folly
Unk
Clun
Onny
Corve
Rea
Stour

Dulas
Clun
Kemp
Clun
Dowles Bk

Teme
Redlake
Ludlow
Ledwych
Stourport
Dick

Knighton
Gosford
Tenbury
Wells
Teme
Salwarpe

Worcester

Leigh

N

Cradley Bk
Severn

Leadon
Tewkesbury
Avon

Scale

Gloucester

0 2 4 6 8 10 12 14 16 18 20
miles

and Llyn Clywedog naturally changed the local habitat and removed spawning grounds for trout and salmon. To meet the needs of the cities of the Midlands, the extraction of water from the lower reaches of the river (close to Bewdley) varies and in order to maintain sufficient volume within the main trunk of the river, variable amounts of water are released from the reservoirs in the headwaters. This released water is often much colder and less oxygenated than naturally expected and this in turn will affect the quality of fish and the fishing. In common with the other rivers of the region, acidification due to coniferous plantations has affected fish stocks. The ongoing and future management of the Hafren Forest is a key feature to the survival of the river.

Fly patterns from the river

The history of fishing has thrown up many unique and colourful individuals and the Severn and its tributaries have contributed many such characters. It is interesting to note that the river and its tributaries hold some key features in the development of artificial flies.

In 1863, a group of twenty-five fishermen formed the Leintwardine Club on the stretch of the River Teme between Leintwardine Bridge and the Downton Gorge. The club, one of the oldest in the country, is still thriving today and owns one of the few fisheries that are definitively marked on Ordnance Survey maps. The development of the Grasshopper fly by members of this club and the method by which it was fished, is graphically recorded by Francis Francis.

One of the earliest flies designed for a particular river, in this case the Severn, was the March Brown recorded by Bowlker in his 1746 *Art of Angling*.

The famous Red Tag or Worcestershire Gem, dating from 1850, has its origins on the banks of the River Teme and is thought to be the handiwork of a Worcestershire gentleman, Mr Thomas Flynn.

The Teme valley in the area around Ludlow and Tenbury has, over the years, been the nursery for a number of significant fly patterns including: Ted Coombes' Blue Variant and March Brown; Ludlow postman, Mr Brookes, with his Brookes' Fancy; Herbert Grant's Murderer (which started life as Grant's Indispensable); Walter Sanders' patterns, the Sanders' Special and the Silver Twist; Austin's Gold and Austin's Silver.

A few local patterns were developed in response to the creation of Lake Vyrnwy, notably Gordon Forrest's Claret Coch-y-bonddu, Michael Leighton's Golden Duck and York's Special.

A noticeable feature of flies used on the upper reaches of the River Severn was that they were all very heavily hackled.

No historical review of this area would be complete without reference to the Rev. Edward Powell of Munslow. His legacy to the sport is phenomenal, not only through the sheer number of flies he created (twenty-seven are featured in Chapter 3), but he is also remembered for the tenacity and skill with which he fished them.

Contemporary initiatives

In common with the other rivers of the region, moves are being made to try to improve the quality of the ecosystem of the rivers, and several initiatives are in place. The Teme Catchment Fisheries Association has been the forum for clubs, syndicates and riparian owners for a number of years, and more recently the Severn Rivers Trust was formed. The purpose of this trust is to preserve and care for the Severn catchment by protecting threatened species and endangered habitats, campaigning for cleaner rivers and educating as many people as possible in the process.

River Wye (Afon Gwy)

The River Wye has always been one of the country's most famous salmon rivers with access to fishing principally in the hands of riparian estate owners and syndicates. Local flyfishers were occasionally able to wet a line, principally for grayling, in the period outside the salmon season. Over the years, brown trout and grayling fishing undoubtedly have played second fiddle to the salmon fishing.

It is notable that, historically, it has been the tributaries of the Wye that have supported the major wild trout and grayling fishing sites. The Monnow, Lugg and Arrow, Llynfi,

Map showing the major rivers, brooks and streams of the River Wye catchment area

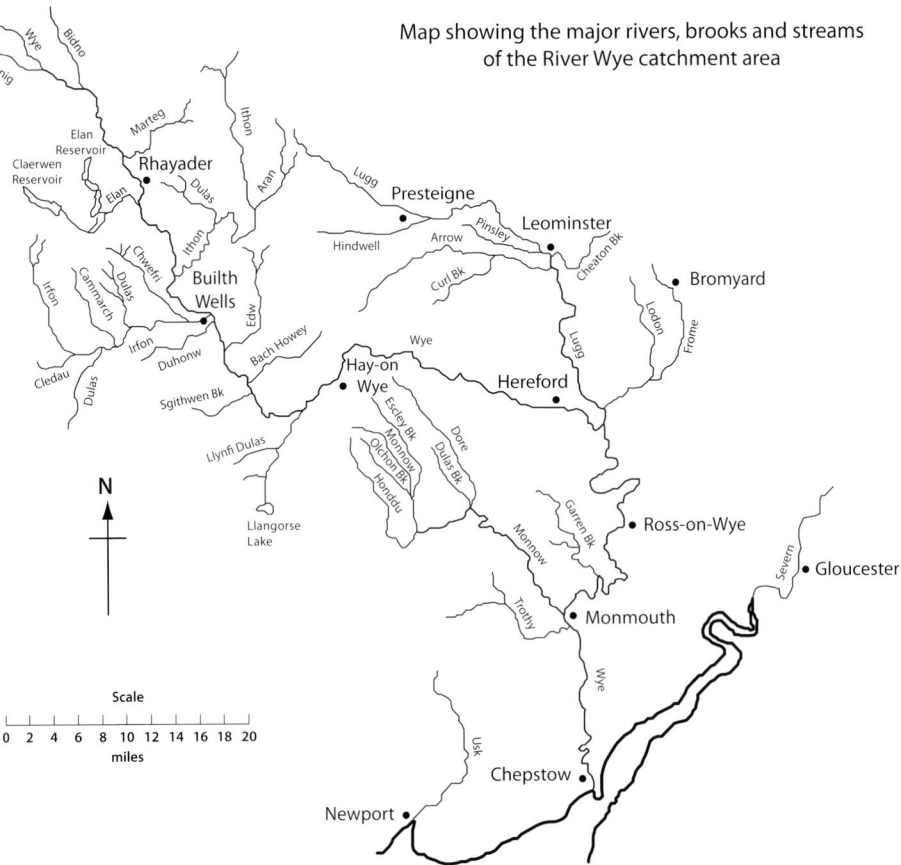

Wye
Bidno
Tarennig
Elan Reservoir
Marteg
Claerwen Reservoir
Rhayader
Ithon
Elan
Dulas
Lugg
Presteigne
Aran
Irfon
Cammarch
Chwefri
Dulas
Ithon
Builth Wells
Hindwell
Arrow
Pinsley
Leominster
Cheaton Bk
Bromyard
Lodon
Frome
Curl Bk
Irfon
Duhonw
Edw
Bach Howey
Wye
Lugg
Cledau
Dulas
Sgithwen Bk
Hay-on Wye
Hereford
Llynfi Dulas
Escley Bk
Monnow
Olchon Bk
Dore
Dulas Bk
N
Llangorse Lake
Honddu
Garren Bk
Ross-on-Wye
Severn
Gloucester
Monnow
Monmouth
Trothy
Wye
Scale
0 2 4 6 8 10 12 14 16 18 20
miles
Usk
Chepstow
Newport

Edw, Irfon and Ithon and the upper reaches of the Wye itself, above Builth Wells, all have a rich piscatorial history.

Wye tributaries and history of the upper river

The earliest reference to trout or grayling fishing in the Wye catchment was made by Samuel Taylor who, in 1800, made specific reference to trout and grayling on the Wye, Trothy, Lugg, Monnow, Irfon and Ithon. Later, in 1834, Hansard makes general reference to the fishing on the Wye, Irfon, Llynfi, Elan and Eddwy, with specific reference to Aberedw (Edw), Builth Wells (Wye), Llandrindod Wells (Ithon), Michael Church (Arrow) and Presteigne (Lugg).

The quality of the brown trout and grayling on the tributaries has always been of a high standard as verified by Ward Lock's 1933 *Red Guide*. This guide mentions the Trothy as a good trout stream, and the Monnow as 'a river of rapid streams … over a rocky bed, hence it is essentially a trout river, but grayling having been turned into it, they are ousting the trout.' It recognises the Lugg as one of the largest feeders of the Wye and 'for either trout or grayling no better river could be fished.'

Next in importance to the Lugg, the guide mentions the Arrow, especially for its trout, the flavour of which, apparently, is superior to that of fish from other rivers and streams connected with the Wye.

Higher up, the Irfon has been fortunate in having two well-known, highly-recommended, fishing hotels which are affectionately referred to by Gallichan in his books. The Cammarch Hotel is situated at the confluence of the Irfon and Cammarch rivers in the village of Llangammarch Wells and has four miles of fishing on the Irfon. The hotel's waters have always been renowned for their grayling.

Nearby, the Lake Country House Hotel and Spa has seven miles of fishing on the Irfon and this hotel's waters are again well known for their winter grayling.

The Upper Wye in the vicinity of Llangurig for years has had the reputation of holding good stocks of trout and grayling, with the The Clochfaen Historic Sporting Estate having piscatorial links stretching back well over 500 years.

Major problems

In common with the other rivers of the region, a major impact on fishing has been the impounding of water. Although the Wye itself has not been dammed, significant quantities of water have been impounded in the Elan and Claerwen valleys giving rise to an area colloquially known as the Welsh Lake District.

Five sizeable reservoirs, Claerwen, Caban-Coch, Garreg-Ddu, Pen-y-Garreg and Craig-Goch were constructed between 1890 and 1950 to supply Birmingham with piped water on a daily basis. One effect of their construction was to reduce the salmon, and, to a lesser degree, trout, spawning grounds.

Today the River Elan provides a useful venue for winter grayling fishing when the main river is in spate, since its flow is governed entirely by 'controlled release' from the reservoirs. However, it is also noticeable that very little of the riverbed gravels remain and so trout spawning is restricted thereabouts.

The other problem common to upland rivers is the acidification of the watercourse caused by the coniferous forest plantations on the moorland slopes. The Wye valley did not escape this problem and there are extensive coniferous swards bordering the upper Irfon, the Afon Bidno and Afon Tarennig valleys, all of which may affect the fish stocks of the upper Wye itself.

Fly patterns from the river

It is really quite surprising that there are only a limited number of trout and grayling flies having their origins in the

Wye catchment. They include:

– A *Black Gnat* devised by Thomas Thomas of Llangurig for use on the upper reaches of the river.

– The *Bloody Mary*; a fly of unknown origin which was designed for use on the Elan Valley Lakes.

– The *Cochen-las* was the handiwork of Rhayader-based Ned Hughes, again for use on the Elan Valley lakes.

– The *Hereford Alder* and the *Willow* are the only two surviving Canon Eagles patterns of which we have details. They were developed on the banks of the infant Monnow from his family home in the Longtown area.

– *Barrett's Bane* and *Barrett's Professor* are two well-known and highly successful patterns developed by Cosmo Barrett and his brother Bruce when they lived in Presteigne.

– The *Polo Nymph, Fisherman's Curse, Grizzly Mayfly, Peter's Peril* and *Pheasant Tail* were all created by Peter Flint who took over the Barrett's business in Presteigne.

– The *Hereford Pheasant Tail* and *Border Mayfly* were tied by James Evans for use on his local River Lugg.

Contemporary initiatives

Concerns over declining stocks of salmon and trout led to the formation of The Wye Foundation in 1995, after which a full survey of the upper river and its tributaries was made. The results indicated that there were several problems within the catchment, including barriers to migration to spawning grounds and pollution caused by sheep dip and excessive grazing damage. Overshading was also identified as a concern.

In 1998, the Wye Habitat Improvement Project was begun and initiatives to improve the health of the river have continued apace ever since. In 2002 the Wye and Usk Foundation was formed.

Meanwhile, in 2003, The River Monnow Project got under-way with the aim of improving the capacity of the river to support wild trout, grayling and other wildlife.

Similar projects have been undertaken in the Lugg and Arrow river catchments in order to improve the habitat for fish and other wildlife.

All these initiatives are held together under the Wye and Usk Foundation umbrella and the signs are that some improvements to fish habitat have been noticed during the last fifteen years.

River Usk (Afon Wysg)

The River Usk is renowned for its salmon and brown trout and noted for its lack of grayling. The river has been fished since ancient times and the earliest references are those made by Samuel Taylor, Robert Lascelles, Sir Humphry Davy and George Agar Hansard. It has always been known as an early-season river, with prodigious hatches of March Brown. Sadly these hatches are now in decline and have become merely a part of the river's rich history.

Throughout the length of the river the fishing has predominantly been in private estate ownership, with only the towns of Usk, Abergavenny and Brecon offering fishing to all comers. This situation still holds true today.

Major problems

In the late nineteenth and early twentieth centuries there were four major problems which influenced the quality of fishing on the river:

Until the turn of the nineteenth century netting and fish trapping with 'putts' and 'putchers' were prevalent near the mouth of the river. However, in 1898 the netting rights were included in the sale of many of the Welsh estates belonging to the Marquis of Worcester. This sale included eight castles and twenty manors, as well as the rights to net the tidal waters of the Usk. The Usk Conservators took the opportunity to

Map showing the major rivers, brooks and streams
of the River Usk catchment area

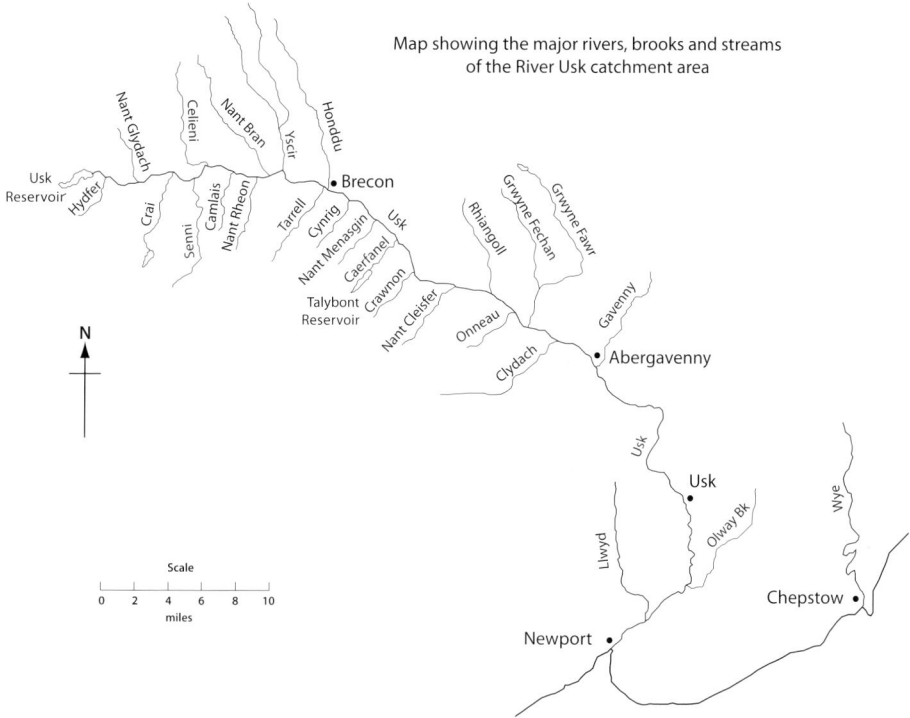

Nant Glydach

Celleni

Nant Bran

Yscir

Honddu

Usk
Reservoir

Hydfer

Crai

Senni

Camlais

Nant Rheon

Tarrell

Cynrig

Nant Menasgin

Caerfanel

Crawnon

Usk

Nant Cleisfer

Onneau

Clydach

Rhiangoll

Grwyne Fechan

Grwyne Fawr

Gavenny

• Brecon

Talybont
Reservoir

• Abergavenny

N

Usk

Usk
•

Olway Bk

Llwyd

Wye

Scale

0   2   4   6   8   10
miles

Chepstow •

Newport •

take control of the netting rights and limit the number of nets operating on the river. As a result, by 1902 only a restricted number of nets remained in operation. Fortunately most of the Bristol Channel putts and putchers were near Porton and Goldcliff, higher upstream than the mouth of the Usk.

Secondly, during the latter part of the nineteenth century, pollution in the River Llwyd, the lowest tributary of the river, played a major part in the decline of fish stocks. The tin and coal mining industries high up this tributary discharged untreated waste into the main river, thus adversely affecting migratory fish. By the beginning of the 1900s these industrial activities started to decline. However local authorities remained primary culprits, discharging untreated sewage to such an extent that, in 1902, the Llwyd was described as being 'little better than an open sewer'.

Thirdly, the lack of protection of spawning beds for salmon, as the result of the removal of weirs on the tributary rivers by landowners, resulted in a habitat favouring brown trout in the upper reaches of the main river and the demise of the stocks of salmon. This led to antagonism between upper and lower river fishery owners in a brown trout versus salmon conflict. The lower river owners realised that the salmon spawning beds lay in the upper reaches and they alleged that the upper river owners, content with their brown trout, did nothing to protect the salmon. Indeed, in some cases they were thought to encourage the taking of spawning salmon in order to use their eggs for the production of 'salmon paste,' an irresistible bait for trout.

And lastly, water extraction and capture, common features in the history of all four rivers of the region, have also played their part in the Usk valley. The construction of the Brecon Canal, linking Brecon and Abergavenny to Newport on the Severn Estuary, took place from 1795 to 1800. Throughout the nineteenth century the canal was supplied with water from the main river and, in 1899, a notable year of drought, the river ceased to flow altogether over the weir in Brecon, with the subsequent death of thousands of fish. As a result, a public meeting was called to oppose the canal company extracting so much water, much of which, it was noted, was not just for the canal but was also for sale to local authorities lower down the river.

There were plans, made public in 1895, to develop a massive reservoir (the Cray Reservoir) by damming the river upstream from Sennybridge in order to supply London's water needs. Fortunately these plans never came to fruition and the fish stocks in the river were spared. Sixty years later, in 1955, a smaller reservoir (the Usk Reservoir) was constructed very close to the source of the river, high up in the Brecon Beacons. This reservoir holds a stock of native brown trout that are supplemented with stocked brown and rainbow trout.

Fly patterns of the river

Set against these problems it is interesting to record the changes and developments of the trout fly patterns over a similar period of time. It has been recorded that, in 1968, the Brecknock Museum in Brecon held a case of flies labelled 'Old Usk Flies'. Within the case were flies that apparently resembled those listed as white and brown moths by Richard Bowlker in 1746. Sadly my own research has revealed that this case of flies is no longer in the museum.

A significant change in fly patterns is noticeable in the latter half of the nineteenth century when Usk-style patterns based on the Scottish fly introductions and referred to by W. H. Lawrie in *English and Welsh Trout Flies*, emerge.

An undisputed fact throughout the history of Usk trout fishing is that it is an early (or spring) river and the flies of successive periods reflect this fact, for example: March Brown (or Cob) patterns from Richard Bowlker in 1746; Acheson in 1850; John Henderson in the 1930s; Leslie Peters and Major J.D.D. Evans in the 1960s – with Grannom patterns from Acheson c. 1850; Harry Powell in the 1960s; Lionel Sweet in the 1970s; Dave Collins in 2008 and Louis Noble in 2010.

Other early season patterns include the traditional Usk Light Blue; Usk Dark Blue (Leslie Peters); Usk Naylor (Mr P. Naylor); the traditional Usk Purple; and Stuart Jarvis's Bastard Adams, and Grouse and Gold must not be overlooked.

Places that merit a visit

There are several places worth visiting with links to the piscatorial history of the Usk – it may be a reflection on me that the three I've chosen to highlight are all licensed premises!

The King's Head Hotel in Usk town dates back to 1588 and has a room dedicated to the life and times of Lionel Sweet, the former owner of Sweet's Tackle Shop. The room is filled with items of tackle, flies and photographs, all of which tell tales of a former age of piscatorial plenty.

The Bridge End Inn in Crickhowell not only has fishing rights on the river but also houses some wonderful items of old tackle, flies, lures and photographs.

No visit to the valley would be complete without making a visit to Gliffaes Hotel, a short distance north of Crickhowell. The hotel has three very fine beats on the river reserved for its guests, and has angling artefacts and memorabilia in virtually every room.

Every afternoon a table in the hotel is loaded with the legendary Gliffaes tea, a magnificent spread with an endless supply of sandwiches, scones with cream and delicious cakes. What more can the visiting angler ask after a few hours on the river?

Chapter 2

An introduction to flyfishing the Welsh Borderlands

Arthur Bradley's assertion that the rivers of the Welsh Borderlands are 'in a class of their own' is likely to be supported by anyone who has ever fished them. So while this is not intended to be a 'how to' book, a couple of accounts, memories and tactics of a few flyfishers from the area (starting with my own) may be of value to visiting fishermen.

I spent my teenage years serving my flyfishing apprenticeship, with split cane rod and silk line, on the upper reaches of the River Kennet. There then followed a long break before, in the early 1990s, I picked up a fly rod again, this time a state-of-the-art carbon fibre affair with lines to suit every occasion. I am eternally indebted to Roy McAdam for encouraging me at this time, not only to fish once more, but also to tie flies and join the Worcester Fly Dressers. Finding suitable river fishing close to my home in Malvern proved to be a challenge: one that naturally took me into the Welsh Borderlands. At this time I joined the Gamefishers Club, which had more than ten miles of stream and river fishing in the region, and I was truly hooked once again.

While serving my time as Chairman of the Worcester Fly Dressers in the mid 1990s, I managed to secure some stretches of the Leigh and Cradley brooks for members to fish, and I'm delighted to say we still have access to these local beats and the enduring sport they've provided over the years. As if this wasn't enough, I was then invited to join a small group of friends who had fishing on a delightful two-and-a-half mile stretch of the River Edw, a tributary of the Wye. It was through this group that I started to learn about the fascinating history of the flies and flyfishing of the region. More recently I've become a member of the Pheasant Tail Fly Fishers, a club with about five miles of flyfishing in the Borderlands, and have also taken on the job of Area Secretary for the Grayling Society. Fishing in the Welsh Borderlands has become a significant part of my life and I trust will remain so for many years to come.

The waters of the region are, in the main, spate-streams: rain-fed watercourses flowing through mountain, moorland, forest and farmland on their inexorable journey to join one or other of the four principal rivers of the region – the Dee, Severn, Wye or Usk. They are subject to the vagaries of weather, and their water levels oscillate from chocolate-brown and bank-full to gin-clear and thin. Over time the scouring effect of the ever-changing water levels has carved deep channels, with high banks that make casting a fly quite a challenge. The width of the watercourses varies from broad, shallow rippling stickles, to narrow slow-flowing deep pools – some remarkably deep. Each stream or river has its own particular character or personality – so much so that streams in adjacent valleys can be entirely different in nature to their neighbours.

On the whole these rivers support healthy populations of wild brown trout and grayling whose food source is truly catholic, comprising many aquatic insects and crustaceans, supplemented by terrestrial offerings that fall from the extensive canopy of vegetation.

Fishing alone in these quiet places you may be lucky enough meet a foraging otter, one of an increasing population on Border streams. Red kites and buzzards will be spiralling overhead, with wagtails and dippers hunting insects at the water's edge. You may even catch a glimpse of the orange and blue flash of a kingfisher going about its fleeting business. Being close to, almost at one with, nature, is part and parcel of the Welsh Borderlands flyfishing experience.

Apart from the supply of food, there are several other important factors that affect the growth and populations of fish, aquatic invertebrates (insects and crustaceans) and vegetation of a stream.

The pH of the water has a profound effect as below pH 6.5 (acidic) and above pH 8.5 (alkaline) it is known that fish growth is impaired. The underlying geology has a direct bearing on the pH of rivers and it is significant that much of the Welsh Borderland region has non-calcareous underlying rocks – thus tending to the acidic end of the scale. Also the peaty uplands yield acidic water with low pH that in turn restricts the growth of waterweed and both insect populations and diversity. There are though, some parts of the region that have rivers that flow over limestone including the upper Teme and sections of the Clun, which naturally show rather different characteristics.

Riparian agricultural practices also influence the ecology of the rivers greatly. Water abstraction for crop irrigation can decimate the flow and thus the life of a river, and algal blooms and the choking of watercourses by weed are caused by excessive use of artificial fertilisers. Pesticides can be a problem too, killing species that trout prey on and other beneficial organisms – 'collateral damage' to the original targets.

Trout (and to a lesser extent, grayling) are remarkably territorial – individual fish fiercely guarding small pockets of the streambed and, in so doing, monopolising the food supply thereabouts. Also fish like to have a safe haven to which they can retreat when threatened in any way. These bolt holes are usually in the deeper or more inaccessible places – instream trailing root systems of trees are particular favourites in the smaller waters that I fish.

Seldom do I actually spot fish directly in these waters and usually it is the rising of a fish that indicates its presence. It's also the exception rather than the rule for me to be able to cast to a regularly rising fish. More often than not, I find myself casting to where I believe I've seen a rise, and not infrequently I cast to where I think a fish may be lying. Working out where the fish are likely to be lying, reading the water and being proved right is, I believe, one of the intrinsic attractions of flyfishing in the Welsh Borderlands.

To further my own understanding of these waters I have read extensively about rivercraft – that unique combination of being able, firstly, to read the water; secondly, make careful observation of insect life; thirdly, to know where fish are located; and then lastly, to use appropriate tactics to catch them. These four key factors coalesce into the amalgam of instincts, sensations and experience we know as flyfishing.

Happily, for most of us the understanding of these four factors requires a lifelong and usually most satisfying apprenticeship!

In order to put all this into practice, I think it is beneficial to put oneself in the place of the fish and try to see things from its unique perspective. It is widely understood that the most important sense a fish has is its ability to detect shock waves through the water using its lateral line (a sort of extended ear). Next in importance is sight, with the circular visual window above and in front of the head, where both eyes detect images in a form of binocular vision. The senses of smell, taste and pain are thought to be less important – they are not well developed in most fish's nervous apparatus and so play less significant roles in the survival stakes.

One of the important things a fish must do to survive is to place itself in a position to gain best advantage of the food trundling past in the current – a 'conveyor belt' usually referred to by flyfishers as the food lane. This is essentially the path taken by the bulk of the floating, sinking and totally drowned material, both useful and useless, that is carried by the current. It is often indicated by a stream of bubbles on the water's surface and generally follows the line of the fastest current. To the fish what is interesting about the food lane is that it brings food – insects, dead, dying or doomed, as well as newly hatched and emergent forms. Remember always though, that fish will not usually lie in the food lane itself, but in a quieter current to the side of it and always in sight of what is on offer.

Welsh Borderland streams and small rivers are characterised by having a successive alternation of pools and riffles. Classic pools start at their upstream end with a neck (the point where water enters) then a stretch of even current in the body of the pool, followed by the tail through which the water makes its exit. It is usual to find an upstream and downstream shallowing from the body of a pool towards its neck or tail, and it is worth remembering that these are favourite locations for fish. Pools are also frequently associated with a bankside projection such as a tree or a rock. The current strikes the bank just upstream of these projections where, over time, it has scoured out a small pocket in which floating debris collects. Water then spills from this pocket past the projection where, on the downstream side, it forms a larger, deeper pocket. From this larger pocket, water slips downstream into the body of the pool, making a distinct food lane.

Over the years I have noticed that trout often lie in the eye of these pockets as well as in the slacker water beside the food lane as it flows into the body of the pool. Grayling however, tend to lie in the stretches of faster running water.

When I'm fishing I try to keep reminding myself that fish will station themselves where there is an availability of food, sufficient oxygen in the water, safety from predators or proximity to a safe haven and, most important of all, where they will expend the minimal amount of energy. I've also realised that trout show some seasonal changes in locations. In early season, when they are still recovering from spawning, the fish will lie in moderate flows, where they pick up food and shake off parasites and gain strength. As the season progresses they move to stronger currents, establish their territory, and by high season all parts of the stream are more or less populated.

For what it's worth I share with the reader some of the tactics I've adopted over the years in my quest to optimise my chances of catching Borderland fish. There is nothing new here, just a few honed practices that I find work well for me.

Before putting a fly anywhere near the water I always try to spend time watching the water and observing any insect activity. I find that this can be quite difficult to do when fish are rising, as in these situations I am tempted (like most of us I suspect) to get on with fishing.

Next is my approach to the water – I always wear chest waders, usually with knee-pads, since I never know just how deep I'm going to have to go and I find that the ability to kneel in comfort is absolutely essential. I always try to keep as low a profile as possible when approaching likely spots and keep an eye on my shadow, making sure it is not cast over the water's surface. I always carry my trusty homemade hazel wading staff on a retractable lanyard. It serves two main purposes: as a third leg when wading, and as an extra-long arm when retrieving flies from overhanging vegetation. I also carry a metal cup-hook that can be screwed into the top of the staff to retrieve flies from way beyond arm's reach and for really stubborn entanglements I also have a length of thin cord that attaches to the staff and can be used to lasso offending branches.

I find that a combined leader and tippet length that is the same as the rod length works best for me. On most of my favourite stretches there are very few opportunities to practise the traditional backcast and I spend much of my time flicking or even catapulting my fly onto the water.

Seldom do I have more than a few feet of flyline out of the rod tip – irrespective of whether I'm nymphing or fishing a dry. I usually carry a lightweight net on a retractable lanyard attached at the top of my back, where it's conveniently out of the way.

I tie my own flies and find that my flybox for these waters contains a selection of the patterns which have, over the years, given me most success. The contents are a real mix of the old and the new. The sub-surface flies include: Gold-head Pheasant Tail Nymphs with brown partridge hackles (size 12 – 16), a weighted spider-hackled Hare's-ear Nymph (size 14) and my own shrimp pattern (size 12 or 14). To imitate emerging flies I use either a Superpupa (size 12 – 14) with fawn, olive, grey or black body and hackle or an F-fly (size 12 – 14). For surface flies, I carry Baby Sunfly (size 14), Dogsbody (size 12 – 14), a mayfly (Mike Weaver's pattern in size 12) and a selection of reverse-hackled flies with black, brown and olive bodies (size 14 –16). For a fall of beetles I use a black foam beetle pattern (size 12 or 14) and I also carry a deerhair sedge pattern (size 12) from which I frequently suspend nymphs 'New Zealand-style'.

So much for my own techniques and tactics – here are a few other accounts of the rivers and the sport to be had in the Welsh Borderlands from some flyfishing companions and local experts. All of them reflect their own experiences of the type of flyfishing encountered in the region; each of them different in their own way, but then fishing the region is always unique.

Tony Norman, Pembridge, Herefordshire

I have farmed here at the Leen, on the banks of the Arrow for forty years. I came here passionate about fishing – I now find myself passionate about the river. I have lived within fifty yards of the river, been boating on it, been frightened by it, surrounded by it, fished in it, camped by it and have come to be absolutely fascinated by it.

I rarely fish the river these days though. Just occasionally, perhaps when we have a barbeque, I will take the old rod off the garage wall, still with the Grey Wulff that was on last year and have a few casts. I can't guarantee it, but I can usually have two or three trout wrapped in layers of wet Telegraph on the hot grid within twenty minutes. I just love it. The fish join the rabbit we have shot, together with the steak and the other stuff.

My sons (who now farm the Leen) are part of this, and so are my grandchildren. I was particularly pleased that one grandson, Freddie (with the help of a worm from the garden), caught his first trout just outside the house while still in nappies!

Hopefully they will go on to care for 'their' river and get as much fun out of it as I have had.

Glyn Williams, Little Comberton, Worcestershire

I had a Welsh father and have an English mother, so I guess I have been 'on the border' between the two all of my life and my fishing experiences mirror this.

My great love is the Welsh Dee where I have spent countless hours catching many fish and learning much about patterns and techniques in wonderful surroundings. Sadly I had to move away from that locality some time ago.

I've now lived in Worcestershire for twenty years. At first I thought that I was in no-man's-land – with little good fishing close by. How wrong that proved to be. Once I had plugged into the local grapevine, courtesy of the Fly Dressers Guild, I began to realise what was on my doorstep and through friendships made along the way, I have enjoyed many great days in good company sampling the delights of our Borderland streams and rivers.

Why do I enjoy these waters? Well, many reasons spring to mind, but I guess it is the amazing choice I have at my disposal that is so attractive. If I want to brave broad, powerful water I look to the Wye – such a fabulous system with all of those enticing tributaries, and home of enormous fish. Or maybe a creepy-crawly day in high summer, flicking terrestrial patterns under the trees on the Corve might appeal. Or the anticipation of the appearance of the early olives on the Usk. I have all of this at my disposal and count myself a lucky man. (I must confess also to a feeling of being at home when I cross the Border west into Wales – the *hiraeth* calling, perhaps?)

Of course, one particular love of mine is the grayling and we are well served in that respect (with the exception of the Usk of course). This really makes my flyfishing season a twelve-month affair. We are so lucky to have the grayling and they are a great indicator of the quality of our streams. Wading those gravel runs in late autumn to outwit sipping grayling with tiny flies is just about as good as it gets.

Did I mention the stunning scenery? Deep river valleys, with dramatic, breathtaking views to the Welsh uplands, abundant wildlife, little traffic, solitude, plus those typically Borderland pastures with hidden twisting streams wending their way quietly on their journey to join the main river.

Although my fly boxes might indicate otherwise, I confess I do not overburden myself with patterns on most of the smaller streams. All I would say is that the older I get, the smaller the patterns I fish. This is mainly due to time spent sampling insect life on stream and the realization that many of my fly patterns were considerably bigger than the real thing. Netting the surface film has demonstrated graphically what fish are picking out which is often hardly visible to the naked eye. Once I began to have success with these tiny slips of flies, my confidence in them grew and grew. I have had some of my very biggest fish on tiny flies and providing the tackle is balanced to complement them, I fish with assurance.

Finally, I must mention the part that the Wye and Usk Foundation has played in allowing anglers to access so much delightful fishing in our region. I believe that The Severn Rivers Trust will soon afford even more access to more and different rivers and I thank both organisations for that. If anyone is not certain what to buy me for Christmas, then a book of vouchers always proves very acceptable!

Roy McAdam, Malvern, Worcestershire

In days gone by we travelled north and south on the M5 for our trout fishing, leaving home at the crack of dawn to miss the commuters – the big reservoirs of Bristol or the East Midlands were where we were most likely heading. Then I stumbled across The Gamefishers Club – its roots in the city but its fishing out west of my home – in Herefordshire, Shropshire and the Borders. The journey to this fishing seemed more in keeping with field sports somehow – yes, there was still traffic, but the pace was slower and more sympathetic to the surroundings, with roads, railways and rivers drifting in and out of Wales, into England and back again.

Under the bridge I go, I have just passed the 'Welcome to Wales' sign and there's my goal for the day – the River Monnow (even the name sounds fishy). I park at the field edge and peer upstream. Fish are definitely moving –not many, but some very confident risers. The mayflies are on the wing. I hurriedly put up my rod and select a fly recommended by James Evans in his book *Small-river Fly Fishing for Trout and Grayling*. It's a Border Mayfly, a strange dressing of two double hackles fore-and-aft, and a great fish catcher. There are high red clay banks plunging towards the river with occasional riffles and pools. (Thigh waders were the norm in those days – no breathable chest-high jobs then!) I make my way along the bank towards where the river flows between the legs of the bridge. The fish are still rising. I slither down the bank, grasping at saplings to slow my descent, until I'm at the water's edge. Far too deep to wade, I peer in – nothing – and then in the shade of the alder, I spot what was feeding. It's not the usual seven-inch fish – no, this is a monster which must be twelve inches long or more. Then a second, even bigger fish rises. Then I notice several more beauties, cruising perhaps a foot down, each one in turn leisurely drifting up to engulf a struggling mayfly. This is what flyfishing is all about. Crouching at the foot of the high bank I pull out a few feet of line and work it out of the tip ring, only able to manage a kind of flick to get the fly out. I target a fish about four yards upstream. After a couple of attempts I land the fly just upstream of the fish, heart in mouth I watch … nothing. I recast. Yes! A reaction … a slow cruise up towards my fly, then close inspection and then disdain, the fish on its way to pastures new. Several similar experiences later but try as I may – traditional up-wing, wet fly or nymph, stationary or twitched – nothing! Ages spent flicking this, that and the other at these super fussy fish to no avail.

What an experience! These splendid fish obviously only showing when the mayflies are up – the rest of the year, they are presumably down on the bottom, or holding in the deepest pools, super-suspicious of any artificial. They've learnt what it takes to live and grow to become such splendid creatures.

I return to the car fishless, but feeling privileged to have been part of the spectacle of these magnificent fish in such beautiful surroundings.

Dave Collins, Moccas, Herefordshire

As a young lad in the 1950s my love affair with fishing began on the River Derwent and the Trent and Mersey Canal south of Derby, trotting and ledgering for roach and perch. In those days, although the fishing may not have been of the best and the angler was pretty useless, the fishing bug was well and truly caught.

Just a few years later, when the family moved to Bridgend in South Wales, I sold what little coarse fishing tackle I had and bought an Alcock's Popular split cane three-piece rod, together with a green silk line. What followed was my first taste of fishing with a fly, and I was soon catching trout and the occasional sewin from the River Ogmore, all within walking distance from my new home. Wow, now I really was hooked! This old rod, now retired to hang on the wall, also did duty some years later on annual excursions in May to fish the waters of the Wharfe at Kilnsey, where a trout or two occasionally took sympathy on me and obligingly took my ill-presented flies. Then, about fifteen years ago, I began fishing on the Longford and Trafalgar Estate waters on the Avon, south of Salisbury. I also started fly-tying at about that time. Although I still fish there, a few years ago, in anticipation of the not-too-distant qualification for the bus-pass, my wife and I moved to West Herefordshire and the middle Wye – the culmination of a long-desired return to a quieter land of hills and rivers.

Now with the Wye on my doorstep, the River Dore just over the hill, the Escley and Olchon Brooks, the Honddu and the upper reaches of the Monnow all little more than half an hour away to the south and west, what more could one want? Well, maybe the Lugg and Arrow not far away or the upper Wye and the Usk only forty-five minutes away – wonderful fishing, in local waters of all shapes and sizes.

While fly hatches are reputed not to be what they were years ago (the March Brown hatches of the Usk are largely a thing of the past), the diversity and abundance of fly life on the rivers, brooks and streams of this part of the Welsh Borderlands is still very healthy and more than adequate to sustain good fish populations.

Large dark olives tempt the first trout and grayling of the year to the surface, and encourage the angler to float his imitation over them, even though these lunchtime hatches can be infuriatingly short-lived. April, of course, sees prodigious hatches of grannom on many of the waters, which has led me to develop some successful pupa-emerger patterns particularly for the Wye. While I'm no entomologist, I attended a river-fly workshop some years back and am involved in a local invertebrate sampling programme. I just can't resist trying to find out what fish are eating!

April and May see the arrival of large flies like false March Browns, large brook duns, olive uprights and, of course, the truly striking Yellow Mays, all of which are usually present in sufficient numbers to be worthy of imitation. Yellow May hatches can tempt trout and chub to behave much like trout chasing mayfly on a chalkstream, although they typically ignore the Yellow May duns and instead aggressively feed on emergers. Yellow May emerger patterns are lethal and here on the Wye I've developed one of my own, which fish will move a long way to take – just as they will with the natural. Others though will just sip it.

As spring merges into summer, smaller olives and pale-wateries begin to dominate, together with huge populations of mini-caddis on some waters, including parts of the Usk and, again, all are well worthy of imitation. With gnats, midges, sedges and terrestrials added to the mix over the course of the year and, depending on the water, abundant shrimp populations, there is a huge diversity of life in these waters – more than enough to keep the flyfisherman and fly-tyer busy all year round, the amateur entomologist scratching his head and, above all, to get fish feeding. With grayling present on many of our local rivers and streams, the fishing season extends right into winter when the last of the year's small olives are still active enough to tempt fish to rise. Then it is once again time to use those winter bugs and nymphs, and for trying once more to locate the shoals of grayling, before the large dark olives of March once more herald another year in the annual invertebrate cycle.

The whole spectrum of riverine environment can be found in my area of the Welsh Borderlands from, on the one hand, a big brute of a river like the middle Wye with its broad reaches and, very often, little bankside cover, to Lilliputian streams tumbling over rocks, stones and slabs, cloaked with trees, and designed to test the skill, patience (and temper!) of even the most expert caster with a six or seven foot rod.

The Reverend Francis Kilvert, a Victorian cleric whose diaries give such a wonderful insight into the country life of his times, was a prodigious walker and the region he described (centred on Hay-on-Wye), is aptly known as 'Kilvert Country'. According to his diary entry of 28 September 1870, William Wordsworth considered that the Wye above Hay was the finest piece of scenery in southern Britain – high praise indeed from the much-travelled North Country poet. One hundred and forty years later one has to agree that he really did have a point. Although *Kilvert's Diary* clearly indicates that the author was not a regular angler, he does report having fished occasionally for trout and for perch, usually with his father. He is buried in the churchyard in Bredwardine, where his old rectory still overlooks the middle Wye. I feel sure that he would be pleased to know that the fishing, walking and scenery in Kilvert Country are still absolutely magnificent. If you haven't been yet, this part of the Welsh Borderlands really is well worth a visit.

Tony Bostock, Heythrop, Oxfordshire

The Onny

My dear mother, when a young girl, fell into the River Onny and was fortunate to be saved from drowning by a farm hand who was working hard by the river. So you could say I have an affinity with the River Onny.

The first castle I ever visited, when on a primary school trip, was Stokesay – probably not really a castle but certainly the finest example of a fortified manor house in the Welsh Borderlands if not the whole of Britain. The castle sits close to Stokesay weir – its salmon pass now allows fish to run upstream for the first time in a hundred years. Also adjacent to Stokesay Castle is the pool that spawned the 'Stokesay Legend'. Apparently two giants sat on opposite sides of the valley; when one giant needed money the other threw him the key to the treasure held below, but one day the key fell into the pool, never to be seen again. The story tells us that should anyone find the key they would be rendered blind, their eyes pecked out by ravens. Thankfully the giants are long gone and anyway I'm too busy hunting for the Onny's trout to worry about the unlucky key.

More years ago than I care to remember I experienced one of best mayfly hatches I've ever seen at Cheney Longville on the River Onny. Clouds of the majestic insects filled the air and fish slashed at them from every conceivable nook and cranny. The trout were going crazy and their mission was to simply intercept every single insect attempting to navigate downstream. I will never forget the one and only time I've witnessed a trout rise and take a mayfly between the legs of cow standing in the shallows. I had no mayfly patterns in the box that day – but a large Blue Dun with the hackles trimmed underneath so that it sat flush in the surface film was attacked the instant it alighted.

The Onny mayfly is something of an enigma and many column inches have been penned over the years describing its quirky habits. Yes, the main hatch occurs from mid-May and into early June, but don't think it ends there. July, August, and even September, see good hatches, which have been written about in the angling press for as long as I can remember.

Shropshire's favourite angler-parson, the Rev. Edward Powell, was a regular Onny visitor. His successes with his own patterns, Baby Sun Fly and Orange Otter, were legendary. He used both regularly to great effect on the Corve, and on streams well beyond his parish boundaries.

Conveniently for me, we had relatives just a stone's throw from the Onny at Craven Arms. The nature of this true Border stream is archetypal – with dark pools, gravel runs, undercut banks, long waving strands of ranunculus, sparkling riffles and meandering course, revealing new secrets at every turn. It's all that a Borderland stream should and can be. And the trout in it can be quick, the grayling even quicker, but its dace can be like lightning!

Gateway to the Borderlands, the Onny valley is a magical and special place – to be shared not only with its fish, but wagtails, dippers and all manner of wildlife. It's a place time forgot and where the sun always travels west – the land of the Shropshire Lad enjoying the lofty shade. The same could be said for me.

The Worfe

So valued was the fishing on the River Worfe back in the 1920s that a full-time river keeper was employed. In those far-off days grayling were plentiful and provided good sport in late summer. Coarse fish were also present: chub, dace, perch and pike, and the river was regularly netted to keep their numbers in check.

The local rector was a regular rod, with the Higford beat his preferred destination. At that time, the half-day holiday fell on Thursdays in Bridgnorth and the head keeper's son, a youthful Norman Sharpe, would accompany the rector after the chores of the morning were completed, to act as his gillie. On one occasion, after a quiet afternoon, an early tea at Higford Mill was followed by capital sport in the evening. Feeling rather jaded, the rector suggested that young Norman try for a fish that they had watched for some time, rising under the near bank. Norman obliged and succeeded in netting the best fish of the day weighing one and a half pounds, to be followed by a further two beauties making a very handsome leash. Reward indeed, as even in those days the Worfe was never an easy river to fish.

My association with the Worfe began when the world was very young and short trousers the order of the day. On Sunday afternoons we would persuade my father to take us for a ride in our newly acquired Simca, with a much-favoured destination, any bridge that straddled a river. The Worfe, Ryton, Beckbury and Grindle bridges were approached with an element of stealth and never disappointed. Fat butter-bellied trout were always to be found casually sipping down their selected favourites from the continuous menu being served, all always seemingly within casting distance.

But my first Worfe trout did not succumb to a delicately presented fly, but to the humble worm – cast into a tiny weir pool on the infant river – the small stream which runs hard by Haughton Hall in Shifnal. Only a couple of years later and just out of school, my first fly-caught Worfe trout was taken on a Blue Dun on the lower Davenport Estate water, just above the confluence of the main river and Stratford Brook, which is aptly named 'The Meeting'.

This was before the weir at Apley, above Pendleton Fort Mill, commonly known as Town Mills, collapsed in the early 1970s. This dried-up the millstream completely and lowered the river level appreciably on the Apley and Rindleford beats. There were plans to reconstruct the weir, but it was never rebuilt and although one can never say with certainty that this accelerated the river's decline as a wild trout fishery, it did herald the start of an influx of coarse fish previously not seen, including barbel.

For over thirty years the Worfe was my number one destination on most Friday afternoons during the season. It didn't have a reputation as an 'early' river, but by late April the olives would hatch in good numbers, to be followed in early May by fantastic falls of hawthorn. Then fish would be on the fin at the surface, providing a fresh challenge around every bend. The mayfly also came, some seasons better than others, but nothing to match the immediate post-war years.

Once the annual mayfly carnival was over I would head for Burcote shallows in mid-afternoon where the sparkling waters were always enticing and fish loved to hug the opposite bank beneath the overhanging trees. Casting was never easy but certainly rewarded more times than not. Blue-winged olives kept the trout keen, and my favoured Blue Dun proved to be the downfall of a good many. Late season, when hatches became somewhat sparse, a smaller, darker pattern was usually demanded and a diminutive Red Quill would be called into action.

The Worfe became my home river and it was never far from my thoughts; it was where I saw my first otter, barn owl and kingfisher. Its bright gravels produced trout with nonchalant ease and even when the brownies failed to play ball, bright dace and chub more often than not gave interesting sport.

The river has never failed to inspire me in all its moods. Now looking back over the best part of fifty years, I realise that the little boy who peered over those bridge parapets and was captivated by those wonderful wild brown trout never really grew up.

Oliver Burch, Gloucestershire

Living near the southern end of Offa's Dyke, I am fortunate to have a marvellous range of fishing for wild trout and grayling within an hour or two from home. From the upland reaches of the Wye and Usk to gentler streams such as Herefordshire's Lugg and Arrow, from the Honddu in the Black Mountains to tiny Forest of Dean brooks, from the native black-finned trout of Llyn Bugeilyn high on desolate Cambrian moors to the red-spotted fish which swim beneath the walls of Abbey Dore in the Golden Valley. The rivers, streams and brooks of the southern Welsh Borderlands offer the angler enough enchanting experiences to fill a lifetime. Over the last few years, the Wye and Usk Foundation has ensured that more of this fishing is available to the general public than ever before.

I have always tied my own flies for river and lake and, over time, have amassed quite a collection. With the idea of trying out all the traditional patterns of the area the collection has grown even further, to include such curiosities as Barrett's Bane and Hereford Alder, Harry Powell's Dogsbody and the Abergavenny, Brookes' Fancy and Colonel's Game Pie. I have, however, now rationalised what actually comes fishing with me: something old and something new, quite a lot which is borrowed. It will be easiest to start with the shortest part of the list – flies to be used on the brooks. This is that carefree kind of fishing where a seven-foot rod is quite long enough and a box of small flies and spool of tippet are really all you need in your pocket.

Some small upland brooks are slow to wake, but in the cold days of March, when fish are reluctant to rise, I fish my way upstream with a single Goldhead Hare's Ear Nymph, in size 14 or 16, casting it into all likely spots and watching the leader for takes. When the weather warms and fish are prepared to rise, I fish a dry fly – a little tan or rust-coloured Klinkhamer, usually tied on a size 16 Kamasan B100 hook. These two simple and impressionistic patterns, nymph and dry fly, have a very high chance of being accepted on small streams and between them take hundreds of trout for me in a season. On those rare occasions when a fly with a prominent wing is hatching, a deer's hair emerger in size 14 has proved useful.

The Welsh Borders are full of charming and secret little streams, such as the Hindwell Brook, which flows out of a large spring in Radnor Forest, or the Escley Brook, a tributary of the Monnow beneath the shadow of Hay Bluff and the Black Mountains. Some anglers disdain these streams as containing only small trout, but I value the fishing days spent scrambling up the valleys of brooks more than any others. If I have learned anything, it is not to forget a net, because just now and again a really good trout or even grayling is encountered at close quarters in a small deep pool. Then the little rod will be bent double and your heart will be racing as your prize fish goes lunging for the tree roots.

Of the main rivers, I tend to concentrate on the Usk during the early season. Through the spring and later in the autumn, I like to fish wet flies in the North Country style, and provided fish are prepared to rise, a team of spiders fished just under the surface with a long, light rod can be absolutely deadly on the more open stretches of our freestone Border rivers. I will fish across and down, mending line when the water is high and currents are strong, but turn round to face upstream and fish a shorter line as the level falls.

The Usk used to be famous for its March Brown hatch, but unfortunately this insect has become much rarer in recent times. However on the upper river, especially around

Brecon, there are some almost indistinguishable 'false March Browns' such as the large brook dun, which shows in late April, and in which the trout seem to be equally interested.

I should mention that all through the year on the larger rivers I carry a very useful little nymph around with me – the Tungsten Hare's Ear. It is tied on a size 14 hook with a black tungsten bead and a body of rough dark hare's ear, ribbed with fine gold holographic tinsel. The tail is made of speckled fibres of lemon summer duck or sometimes coq de Leon. The effect is that of a dark baetis nymph and I turn to this little fly whenever I need depth. It can be used on the point to pull down a team of spiders, or it can be fished on its own with a series of line mends in difficult places like weir pools and fast currents, where the fish are lying deep, or it can be used as one of a team of nymphs.

True mayfly hatches are, these days, not particularly significant on the main Wye and Usk, but we have fine mayfly fishing on the Monnow, parts of the Lugg and Arrow, and some other smaller Wye tributaries – even on certain tiny brooks where you can watch the curious spectacle of a six-inch trout attempting to consume a two-inch fly. The beginning of June on the Monnow will see me equipped with Mike Weaver's Hackle Mayfly – a dun imitation in which I have confidence.

High summer is not generally such a good time to fish the main rivers. Spiders or a tiny Pheasant Tail Nymph suspended under a Klinkhamer can be used in the fast water, and the occasional cooler days of rain or cloud may bring on the fish. More usually, in July and August, I tend to be distracted by shaded brooks which stand up better to the heat.

The Usk has no grayling, and in September I turn with relief to the Upper Wye and major tributaries such as the Irfon where these delightful fish begin to show at their best. During the next couple of months, the combination of free-rising fish and a golden autumn landscape make this a glorious time to be on the river. As the days become cooler and the river is refreshed by rain, spiders will work once more. There comes a point, usually somewhere in late October, when natural fly life is absent. Then I put up a cast of wet grayling fancy flies and these I will fish as long as grayling are prepared to rise from the bottom, which could continue through November and even into December, depending on the weather. A favourite grayling cast of mine is Red Tag on the point, Treacle Parkin on the middle dropper, and Roger Woolley's Grayling Steel Blue on the top. The colourful 'flame tails' on the point and middle dropper are true fancy flies, intended to appeal to the grayling's well-known taste for a splash of bright colour. But the Grayling Steel Blue at the top is a way of hedging my bets, because this grey fly with a hint of dull orange is another which imitates a hatching olive, something which can be seen on any autumn or even winter afternoon.

Sadly, there comes a time, usually before November turns to December, when our grayling become reluctant to rise to the surface. Not so long ago Border anglers would then sigh at the thought of another wonderful autumn of grayling fishing over, and hang up their fly rods until the spring. It is possible to fish wet with weighted versions of the fancy flies, or with a sinking leader butt section to pull them down, but in days gone by the later part of the winter was usually considered more suitable for the trotting rod and bait under an Avon-style float. After Guy Fawkes Night was traditionally the time to start. Where it is allowed, I still adore long trotting which is a delicate and charming method.

What has revolutionised our winter fishing in recent years is the arrival from Eastern Europe of heavy nymphing, close under the rod top. Whether or not you enjoy the 'bugging' or Czech-nymph method of fishing weighted flies at arm's length along the bottom, it cannot be denied that it has opened up the possibility to fish with a fly-rod for grayling right through the winter. Rods, leaders and fly hooks have all been redesigned to accommodate it. Even I can now admit to owning a 10-foot, 3-weight designed for winter bugging, which I believe will also be useful also for fishing spiders on summer days of light winds.

After Christmas and through to the end of the season, I have found some wonderful grayling fishing with nymphs on the middle parts of the Herefordshire Lugg and Arrow. For these meandering streams, characterised by a bed of gravel and deep holes overhung with alders, something lighter is required and I generally fish an 8-foot rod with just two nymphs, which can be flicked upstream or under branches more easily.

With the idea of offering a dull and a bright fly together, a size 14 Tungsten Hare's Ear on the point makes a good pair with a Pink Shrimp eighteen inches above it on a dropper. It is very curious, but the grayling on any given day will show a preference either for the pink or the grey fly, for no apparent reason that I can understand.

During the cold frosts of February the Herefordshire streams are often kinder to anglers than the bleak open reaches of the main Wye, and their deep holes do contain some surprisingly large grayling – fish of eighteen and nineteen inches are not uncommon. I cannot think of a finer place to be in early spring than a mile or two off the Knighton road at Lyepole, where the sparkling Lugg winds through sheep pastures under steep woods and where buzzards mew overhead. The sun is beginning to burn off the white frost, there are clusters of snowdrops on the banks and the first good grayling of the day is already in the net. Now the year has turned full circle. We have fished the season round together, a new one is about to begin and no doubt along the way some new patterns will be found along with the old to replenish our fly boxes.

(Oliver Burch is a game-fishing instructor and guide recommended by the Wye and Usk Foundation. For further details visit: www.wyevalleyflyfishing.com).

Louis Noble, Wrexham

If a random sample of people were asked why they prefer to fish in a particular area, I imagine that a variety of reasons would be offered. Perhaps the scenery is the attraction, the fish may run large, a favourite species may be there, plus other factors we could all suggest. Clearly we are all different and have different needs in life. Thank goodness we do, otherwise certain resources would soon be exhausted.

I've been fortunate to fish in most regions of Britain and each has its attraction but I can honestly say that the pinnacle of my pleasure lies within the boundaries covered by this book. Why? That is something I had to carefully consider when starting this piece.

I've had a love affair with the Borderlands for fifty years and in some respects it could be compared with the initial attraction to one's wife or partner. The impact of physical attraction is probably the starting point but unless she happens to own a stretch of the Usk there has to be something deeper if the affair is to last and not be simply a brief encounter. We hope to experience a relationship which grows stronger as the years pass and one which throws up surprises, excitement, passion and a sense of enduring togetherness – all these things I get from fishing the Borderland!

I consider myself fortunate to have fished all the major rivers, but only some some of the tributaries, covered by this book – which illustrates just how many more opportunities exist. It would be a lucky man who could claim to have an intimate knowledge of all of them but it's such a challenge that keeps me probing deeper into the region. A fascination for me is the changing mood of these rivers and streams – you get to the stage of feeling that you have mastered somewhere only to be dumped metaphorically on your backside. To take these waters for granted is a mistake as mood swings are constant – Borderland waters can be tough teachers and frequently it's a matter of 'must try harder' as the school report used to say.

Natural beauty is very important to me, and being a Shropshire lad I can revel in my home county as well as the neighbouring Marches. Can there be anywhere else which offers such contrasting beauty as you move around the region? As I sit by these waters I feel consumed by an overwhelming feeling of tranquillity – something I've never found anywhere else. If escapism is a main reason for flyfishing then this is my escape route.

I've been an avid fly-dresser for over fifty years with a definite 'traditionalist' leaning. It is the patterns and styles associated with the people of the Borderlands which have given me so much pleasure and provide yet another reason for my love of the region.

And finally to the fish. I've had an affair with the 'Lady of the Stream' for many years and where better to court her than the wide array of Borderland waters? I also revel in the beauty of the trout, whether Usk monsters or the more modest inhabitants of Clun or Honddu. Each one a testament to the beauty of the region – long may I be privileged to walk its banks.

Chapter 3

Borderlands trout and grayling patterns

Once I had determined the parameters of the Welsh Borderlands for this book (with a little history thrown in), introduced you to some of my friends and acquaintances who fish or live on the various the river catchments of the Dee, Severn, Wye and Usk, and discussed some basic fishing tactics that are known to work in the area – my next task was to define the criteria needed to determine which wild trout and grayling fly patterns should be included.

From the earliest records we know that wild trout and grayling flies have primarily been developed and used on a local basis and it is only in recent times, with the increased capacity of communication, that we see a spreading and sharing of such information. It has been my intention to produce a comprehensive list of the flies of the Welsh Borderlands and I have used the following criteria for their inclusion:

1. That the originator of the pattern lives/lived within the region.

2. That the fly was designed or developed primarily for use on the rivers of the region.

3. That the fly was made popular on the rivers of the region although its origins may have been elsewhere.

The primary sources of many of the fly patterns are books, especially Moc Morgan's *Fly Patterns for the Rivers and Lakes of Wales* and Michael Leighton's *Trout Flies of Shropshire and the Welsh Borderlands* and I am grateful to both authors for allowing me to use material from these invaluable sources.

This research has also given me the opportunity of meeting many flyfishers and tyers. I am especially grateful to Michael Leighton, Stuart Jarvis, Ron Pomfret, Jean Williams, Ron Gover and Alan Hudson. These meetings have been most informative and entertaining and have often led my enquiries into unexpected new areas, whilst often allowing me the privilege of seeing their creations at first hand.

One of the results of collating this inventory of fly patterns has been the confirmation of my belief that there are specific characteristics of Welsh Borderland flies. Also, I sincerely hope that by producing this inventory, Welsh Borderland fly patterns may reach a wider audience and I trust that some readers may glean from it some useful patterns for inclusion in their own sport.

PLATE 1

Abergavenny, Alder (Acheson), Alder (Rev. E. Powell)

Amorous Shrimp, Black Ant, Red Ant

Austin's Gold, Austin's Silver, Baby Sun-Fly

Bangor Duster (Ormsley), Bangor Duster (unknown), Bangor Duster (var. 1)

The fly patterns are displayed in alphabetical order and for each the following details are given:

The name of the fly pattern (*and the originator}*
The natural fly that it is intended to imitate.
The number of the plate showing a tied example

Details: for dressing the pattern.
Notes on the origin of the fly and its originator.

Abergavenny (*James Evans*)
A rough water fly (Plate 1)

Hook: 10 – 14
Silk: Bright red
Whisks: A very large bunch of red cock hackles
Body: Bronze peacock herl ribbed with tying silk
Hackle: Red cock hackle wound in front of a badger cock hackle

The Abergavenny was adapted from a Yorkshire river fly pattern, the John Storey, and is deliberately heavily hackled in order to float, and thus be easily seen on the rough stickles of the Usk.

Its originator, James Evans, the author of the 'bible' of Borderlands fishing, *Small-river Fly Fishing for Trout and Grayling* (1972), lived in Luston, just north of Leominster. He was president of The Gamefishers Club – a Birmingham based club with fishing on many Welsh Borderland rivers, streams and brooks, and was a great exponent of the reversed-hackle dry fly. Originally inspired by a magazine article depicting a mayfly pattern devised by David Jacques; it was not until he got together with Peter Flint who had taken over Cosmo Barrett's business in Presteigne, that it occurred to him to transfer the reversed-hackle technique to smaller flies.

James Evans perfected the art of nymph fishing and that of upstream wet flyfishing, for which he developed the William Rufus fly complete with its forward-facing hen hackle. He originated eleven fly patterns: the Abergavenny, Amorous Shrimp, Brown Squirrel Nymph, Daddy Long Legs, Hereford Pheasant-tail, Quill Polo Nymph, Small Yellow Sally, Welsh Terrier, Welsh Fusilier and William Rufus.

ALDER

The Alder or Orl Fly has long been recognised as a fly of importance. It is first mentioned by Bowlker (1747) who reported it to be 'a good killer at all hours of the day, especially after the May Fly is gone.' My research has revealed two patterns with their origins within the region. (See: Barrett's Bane, Ellis' Alder, Herefordshire Alder and Roden Fly)

Alder (*Mr Acheson*)
Alder (Plate 1)

Hook: 12 – 14
Body: Copper peacock herl, tinsel rib optional
Hackle: Dark blue – to match wing
Wing: Starling

Mr Acheson was a river keeper on the Usk during the period of the Rebecca Riots (1839-1843) when Welsh tenant farmers and farm workers, with blackened faces and disguised in female dress, rose up against iniquitous road tolls and other grievances – including restrictions on fishing. One response to this uprising was by the Usk Valley landowners who brought down gillies from Scotland to police their estates and waters against the protesters. Mr Acheson may well have been one of them, or he might have been associated with one of the many Scottish farmers drafted into the area when the Great Forest of Brecknock was broken up for settlement in 1820.

He, and other gillies, would have fished the river with flies derived from their homeland and hence the close resemblance of Usk flies to Tweed-style flies. Acheson's Usk patterns are dressed with short bodies (i.e. covering only half the hook shank); slim feather slips for wings and sparse hackles. It is thought that these features enable the fly to sink quickly to resemble a drowned mature fly. He made a name for himself by sending copies of his flies, especially the Usk Iron Blue, to William Senior, the angling editor of *The Field*. We are fortunate to have seven of his patterns – Alder, Blue Ruff, Brown Moth, Grannom, Iron Blue and March Brown (male) and (female).

Alder (*Rev. Edward Powell*)
Alder or Sedge (Plate 1)

Hook: 12 – 14
Body: Rusty-black sheep's wool or liver-coloured spaniel hair
Ribbing: Three or four turns of single-ply orange wool or floss
Hackles: Head hackle – spade-shaped scapular feather from partridge shoulder, black with buff edges/markings; Shoulder hackle – black cock hackle

The Rev. Edward Powell was undoubtedly the most influential Welsh Borderland angler. He was rector at Munslow from 1922 to 1965, and regularly fished the Onny and the Corve. Affectionately referred to as 'Parson Powell,' and as the 'maestro of south Shropshire,' he has been described as 'a past master of Border fishing with a marvellous understanding of the taste of Border fish.' Serious consideration for all who fish the Welsh Borderland should be given to the inclusion of some or all of the flies from the Powell stable – and there are nearly thirty that I have discovered in my research! Initially he was influenced by his father, and by the Eagles family, masters of the wet fly. He later began taking regular holidays in Tregaron, where he started fishing the dry fly under the watchful eye of Dai Lewis. The list of his flies is impressive and contains a few patterns that have become classics: Alder, Baby Sun-fly, Black Beetle, Black Spot, BSI, Blue Winged Olive, Buzz Olive, Dark Spring Olive, Doctor, Double Black Spot, Ermine Moth, Grannom, Gravel-bed, Iron Blue, Landrail and Rabbit, March Brown, Medium Olive, Model 52, Onny Perlid, Orange Otter, Pale Watery, Paragon, Pink Paragon, Soldier Beetle, Split Willow, Squashed Beetle and Willow.

This Alder is one of Parson Powell's lesser-known patterns but nevertheless is described by him as 'a most useful dressing' to imitate the natural fly of the same name which he described as 'a wonderful fly.'

Amorous Shrimp (*James Evans*)
Gammarus freshwater shrimp (Plate 1)

Hook: 16 double
Silk: Fawn
Body: Bright amber-orange wool
Rib: Fawn tying silk
Hackle: Palmered ginger cock

This is an early summer fly from James Evans designed to imitate Gammarus species (freshwater shrimps) in breeding colours. The main benefit of the double hook is to help the fly sink.

ANTS

Ants can often be an invaluable source of food for opportunistic fish. Inevitably when they swarm close to water some will end up on the surface and will become easy prey for fish. Ant patterns are first mentioned by Bowlker (1747) – these two are a little later, from Scotcher (1820).

Black Ant (*George Scotcher*)
Black ant (Plate 1)

Hook: 16
Silk: Black
Body: Black dyed peacock quill with black ostrich herl for butt and thorax
Hackle: Cock starling
Wing: Pale starling

Red Ant (*George Scotcher*)
Red ant (Plate 1)

Hook: 16
Body: Red tying silk built up to form two thicker sections – a thorax and an abdomen with a thin waist between.
Hackle: Ginger cock
Wing: Blue dun hackle tips

Austin's Gold (*Mr G. Austin*)

Hook: 10 –12
Body: Flat gold tinsel
Hackle: Palmered red cock, cut fibres underneath level with hook gape
Wing: Brown mallard flank feather 'rolled' and tied longer than body

Austin's Silver (*Mr G. Austin*)
Sedges (Plate 1)

The pattern is exactly as Austin's Gold but uses flat silver tinsel for the body. Originally both patterns were intended as wet flies but Austin's Gold is remarkably successful when fished in the surface film – perhaps representing a sedge fly. They were devised by Mr G. Austin, a Birmingham-based angler of whom little is known save that he tied his flies for use on Border streams, especially the Teme.

Baby Sun-Fly (*Rev. Edward Powell*)
Black gnat (Plate 1)

Hook: 12 - 16
Silk: Brown
Whisks: Black cock hackle fibres
Body: Dark-coloured rabbit fur ribbed with tying silk
Hackle: Small coch-y-bonddu cock hackle (two on a size 12 hook)

A pattern designed to represent the black gnat adapted by the Rev. Edward Powell from his very successful Paragon pattern, which was itself inspired by Dai Lewis of Tregaron. It is regarded by many to be an excellent general-purpose pattern throughout the season.

Bangor Duster (*Mr Ormsley*)
A fly for the Dee and Ceiriog (Plate 1)

Hook: 10 - 14
Silk: Brown
Tail: Three fibres Plymouth Rock cock hackle
Body: Mixture of hare's fur and rabbit under-fur
Rib: Two or three turns of gold wire
Hackle: Plymouth Rock cock hackle (longer fibre than usual)

This fly was a long-kept secret pattern of the Oswestry stonemason, Mr Ormesley, for use on the Ceiriog and Dee. This particular dressing was derived from a 'lost' fly retrieved from a tree beside the Ceiriog by another angler. It was then given to Ted Jones, a fly-tyer from Bangor-on-Dee who made faithful copies of it. An alternative dressing, claiming to be the original adopted by several Ceiriog anglers is:

Bangor Duster (*unknown*)
A fly for the Dee and Ceiriog (Plate 1)

Hook: 12 – 16
Whisks: Three fibres of bronze mallard
Body: Hare's ear fur
Hackle: Plymouth Rock cock hackle

Bangor Duster (variant 1) (*unknown*)
For use on the Tanat (Plate 1)

Hook: 12 – 16
Silk: Brown
Whisks: Four pheasant or partridge tail fibres
Body: Hare's ear fur
Hackle: Plymouth Rock cock hackle

This variant, bearing the same name, was devised for use on the Tanat.

Bangor Duster (variant 2) *(Wilf Roberts)*
For use on the Ceiriog (Plate 2)

Hook: 12 – 16
Silk: Brown
Whisks: Three fibres of well-marked bronze mallard feather
Body: Rabbit's fur – outer hairs only
Hackle: Plymouth Rock cock hackle

This variant was tied by Wilf Roberts who had a hand in obtaining the original pattern.

Barrett's Bane *(Cosmo Barrett)*
Alder fly (Plate 2)

Hook: 12 – 16
Body: Cock pheasant tail feather herl
Rib: Gold wire (optional)
Hackle: Blue Dun cock wound on the bend of the hook

This fly is one of Cosmo Barrett's ingenious and highly successful patterns which are ideally suited to the rougher waters of the rain-fed Welsh Borderland rivers and streams; it is really a reverse-hackled Herefordshire Alder. This and the fly that follows were developed by Cosmo Barrett and his brother Bruce in the back of their shop in Presteigne.

Cosmo was an upholsterer who moved, for reasons of health, from Crewe to Presteigne in Radnorshire in 1928, where he set up business in partnership with his brother, who was a cabinetmaker. At the back of their property – the black-and-white timbered Radnor Building in the centre of Presteigne, now beautifully restored, the brothers built split

PLATE 2

Bangor Duster (Var. 2), Barrett's Bane, Barrett's Professor
Bastard Adams, Black Beetle, Black Gnat (Henderson)
Black Gnat (Hughes-Parry), Black Gnat (Gallichan/Hudson), Black Gnat (Leighton)
Black Gnat (Leighton 2), Black Gnat (Thomas), Black Spot

cane fly rods and tied flies.

The Barrett brothers were largely responsible for the development of reversed-hackle dry fly patterns. A number of these patterns, purchased directly from the Barrett brothers' shop were taken to Norway where some were remarkably successful in catching fish. This success caught the attention of Hardy Brothers of Alnwick, where copies were made of some of the patterns and advertised in the 1938 *Hardy's Anglers' Guide*. The first thing that the Barrett brothers knew of this was when they received a copy of the guide and saw their flies illustrated. An exchange of letters between the brothers, their solicitor and Hardy Brothers occurred over the next year and the dispute was amicably resolved in time for the publication of the 1939 Hardy's Anglers' Guide which advertised nine trout patterns, three sea-trout patterns and two mayfly patterns under the title *The Hardy-Barrett Special Improved Dry Flies*.

Of the nine trout flies listed, the Barrett's Bane is the only one surviving and I expect that the Barrett's Professor either came into being a little later or is listed under an earlier name. In correspondence with Hardy Brothers the Barretts state the following about their reverse-hackled flies: 'We claim for our flies, and the method of dressing, many distinct advantages … Firstly, the fly floats better even on the roughest water. Secondly, the hook is well hidden, resulting in a greater number of fish deceived into rising. Thirdly, the fish take these flies more boldly, and few that 'take' fail to miss being hooked.'

They also recommend to their customers the use of a small toothbrush to dress the fly after drying and oiling, holding the fly upwards by the eye and brushing the hackle downwards.

Cosmo Barrett regularly fished the Borderland waters – especially the Kinsham beat of the Lugg, up until his death in 1963 when he was in his sixties. James Evans speaks of

Peter Flint, who succeeded the Barretts in the business, as having absorbed much of Cosmo's 'near-supernatural fishing mystique.'

Barrett's Professor (*Cosmo Barrett*)
A general-purpose pattern (Plate 2)

Hook: 12 – 16
Body: Pale fawn sheep's wool
Rib: Fine gold wire
Hackles: White cock (nearest the bend) and red game cock. This fly carries plenty of hackle!

In essence this fly is a reverse-hackled and modified Dogsbody. It is a heavily hackled high floating dry fly which is relatively easy to see even in the roughest of stickles.

Bastard Adams (*Stuart Jarvis*)
Spring dark olive (Plate 2)

Hook: 14 – 16
Tail: Dark blue dun
Body: Slate grey underfur of rabbit/muskrat
Hackle: Dark blue dun, four or five turns
Wing: Bunch of brown partridge back feathers

This pattern was designed as an imitation of the spring dark olive on the Usk.

Stuart Jarvis has been a gillie on the Usk for nearly half a century, primarily looking after the needs of clients on the Glanusk Estate waters. He has an unfathomable depth of knowledge of the history of fishing on the Usk in the Brecon area. He is also a highly inventive fly-dresser, as testified by his early season Bastard Adams and Grouse-and-Gold patterns.

BEETLES (*Coleoptera*)

According to Courtney-Williams, the importance of beetles to flyfishers is not fully appreciated. There are hundreds of aquatic species taken by trout and grayling, to say nothing of the thousands of terrestrial ones that drift onto the water's surface. Coleoptera are a major food source for fish and it is not surprising to find a number of patterns. The following ten patterns originate in the Welsh Borderland region: Black Beetle, Coch-y-Bonddu, Claret Coch-y-Bonddu, Doctor, Green Insect, Henderson's Dark and Light Beetles, Marlow Buzz, Orange Otter and Soldier Beetle.

Black Beetle (*Rev. Edward Powell*)
Soldier Beetle (Plate 2)

Hook: 12 – 14
Whisks: Four fibres of black cock
Tag: Pale orange wool or orange-scarlet dyed goose or swan primary
Body: Black rabbit fur
Hackles: Two black cock hackles

Designed by the Rev. Edward Powell for use on Shropshire streams when soldier beetles are in evidence from the end of June to start of August.

BLACK GNAT (*Bibio johannes*)

The Black Gnat is an important fly within the region and so it is not surprising to find a number of dressings in existence. It is described by Bowlker in 1747 as a good killer, especially in low water and on cold stormy days. It also is featured by Scotcher.

I have 'uncovered' the following eight patterns:

Black Gnat (*John Henderson*)
Black Gnat (Plate 2)

Hook: 14 – 16
Body: Black ostrich or three fibres from a magpie's tail
Rib: Fine gold wire
Body hackle: Black cock, palmered and then trimmed
Hackle: Black cock

John Henderson (1882 – 1981) moved to Ashford House, Talybont near Brecon, in the 1930s after the death of his father, having lived previously in Ireland and Derbyshire. He owned the Ashford House fishing on the Usk from Talybont Bridge downstream to the top of the Buckland water. His fishing companion and near neighbour was Mr P. Naylor who lived at Worcester Cottage, Llangynidr, and who was responsible for Gordon Price's tying of the Usk Naylor Fly.

Henderson kept numerous wild and exotic birds as well as breeding Old English Game Fowl, feathers of which were used for many of the flies he used on the Usk. He wrote numerous articles for the *Flyfishers' Club Journal* and the *Salmon and Trout Association* magazine. Like so many Usk fishermen, he used a favourite selection of flies through the season, mostly of his own invention. There are 21 of his patterns in this chapter.

He was a very influential man in the area, and the benefactor of the Talybont Village Hall, now called the Henderson Hall. His ashes are scattered in the Garden of Remembrance at Llandetty Church, where there is also a small plaque.

Black Gnat (*J. Hughes-Parry*)
Black Gnat (Plate 2)

Hook: 14 – 16
Body: Grey floss silk
Hackle: Black hen for wet fly and black cock for dry fly

Jack Hughes-Parry of Llangollen was author of *Fishing Fantasy: a Salmon-fisherman's Notebook (1949)* and a well-known angler on the River Dee and its tributaries. His Feather Duster pattern was designed to imitate stoneflies and his Black Gnat is a simple pattern to imitate the natural.

Black Gnat (*Walter M. Gallichan & Alan Hudson*)
Black Gnat (Plate 2)

Hook: 16
Whisks: Two bronze mallard fibres
Body: Stripped peacock herl – undyed
Hackle: Black cock

Walter M. Gallichan was a prolific author of angling books. Of particular interest to us, are *Fishing in Wales* (1903), *The Trout Waters of England* (1908) and *Fishing in mid-Wales* (1939). Gallichan was actively fishing Border streams in the late 1800s and early 1900s, and lived for many years in Llandrindod Wells. He has left us a legacy in the form of the famous Borderer fly and five other patterns: Black Gnat, Grizzle Dun, Olive Quill Gnat, Orange Dun Hackle, and Whirling Dun. He was very secretive about his patterns and it is largely as a result of Alan Hudson's investigative work in the 1980s (*Man of Mystery* in *Flydresser* magazine) that we have details of these flies.

Gallichan refers in his books to using a Black Gnat pattern but unfortunately he fails to give the dressing. This tying is the result of research by Alan Hudson and is thought to be close to Gallichan's pattern.

Black Gnat (*Michael Leighton*)
Black Gnat (Plate 2)

Hook: 16
Body: Palmered black cock hackle, clipped short
Hackle: Black cock
Wing: Tip of a white cock hackle

Michael Leighton is the author of the region's great flyfishing detective work, *Trout Flies of Shropshire and the Welsh Borderlands*, which gives an abundance of historical information regarding fly-tying, flyfishing, and the people of the region. Michael, who lives close to the River Roden, is the creator of the well known Grizzly Bourne (with its unique method of hackling), as well as eight other effective flies: two Black Gnats, Golden Duck, Green Devil, Mayfly, Red Grizzly, Roden Fly, and White Grizzly.

He came across this dressing when he first started fishing Shropshire streams and it used to be his main standby to move fish when all else failed. Another pattern he found successful is:

Black Gnat (*Michael Leighton*)
Black Gnat (Plate 2)

Hook: 14 – 16
Whisks: Very dark blue dun cock hackle fibres
Body: Dark brown polypropylene yarn
Hackle: Very dark blue dun cock

Black Gnat (*Thomas Thomas*)
Black Gnat (Plate 2)

Hook: 14 – 16
Body: Black ostrich herl
Hackle: Black hen
Wing: Starling or snipe

This pattern was devised by Thomas Thomas, known locally as Tom Tom, who lived for a while in Llangurig. It was used widely on the upper reaches of the Wye and neighbouring rivers.

Black Spot (*Rev. Edward Powell*)
Black Gnat (Plate 2)

Hook: 16
Body: 3/4 shank bare plus a pinch of black rabbit
Hackle: Small dark blue cock

This is the original pattern for the Rev. Edward Powell's black gnat imitation; also known as Tregaron Black Gnat.

BSI (*Rev. Edward Powell*)
Black Gnat (Plate 3)

Hook: 16 long shank
Body: Long black cock hackle wound two thirds or half down shank and clipped very short
Hackle: Long white cock dyed a neutral grey-green – the colour of grass when seen edgeways

This is the Rev. Edward Powell's refinement to his original Black Spot which he called Black Spot Improved, hence BSI. According to the parson the function of the grey-green head hackle 'is to lift the black speck of the body slightly above the

PLATE 3

BSI, Black Midge, Bloody Mary
Blue-Arsed Fly, Blue Ruff, Blue Upright (Peters)
Blue Upright (Sweet), Blue Variant, Blue-Winged Olive (Var. 1)
Blue-Winged Olive (Var. 2), Orange Quill Variant, Blue-Winged Olive (Law)

water, in order to make clear focussing difficult for the trout.'

Black Midge (*John Henderson*)
Midges (Plate 3)

Hook: 14
Tail: Point of black hackle that is used for the body ribbing
Body: Two black turkey tail fibres
Body ribbing: Remainder of hackle wound on and trimmed
Rib: Fine gold wire
Hackle: Black cock wound in front of wings
Wings: Two light grey cock hackle points

A pattern designed by John Henderson for use on Talybont Reservoir.

Bloody Mary (*unknown*)
An attractor fly (Plate 3)

Hook: 10 – 12
Tag/Tail: Red wool or ibis
Body: Peacock herl with gold at tail
Hackle: Grizzle hackle dyed scarlet

A variation on the Coch-y-bonddu for use as an attractor fly on the Elan Valley Reservoirs in the 1940s.

Blue-Arsed Fly (*trad. Abergavenny fly*)
March Brown (Plate 3)

Hook: 10 –12
Whisks: Brown partridge
Body: Purple seal's fur
Beard hackle: Brown partridge
Wings: Hen pheasant wing

A most successful and popular wet fly pattern for the Usk in the Abergavenny and Crickhowell area; the pattern is thought to have been developed by a local jeweller.

Blue Ruff (*Mr Acheson*)
Olives (Plate 3)

Hook: 14 – 16
Body: Heron fibre or green wool
Hackle: Pale to dark blue dun hen or pale to dark olive hen hackle

This is an early season Usk pattern that was sent to William Senior by Mr Acheson. It is usually fished on the dropper just within the surface film.

Blue Upright (*Leslie Peters*)
Dark olive/iron blue/willow fly (Plate 3)

Hook: 12 – 14
Tail: Light blue dun hackle fibres
Body: Grey/blue rabbit fur
Hackle: Light blue dun cock

Leslie Peters was one of Brecon's most notable fishermen for a period of fifty years. He apparently tied his flies without a vice, holding the hook in his left hand. Such was his reputation that that the initials 'L.P.' were appended to variants of flies that he had produced. He has left us with three of his original flies: Blue Upright, Leslie Peter's Special and Yellow Cob, each one with a tremendous local reputation.

Blue Upright (*Molly Sweet)*
Dark olive/iron blue/Willow fly (Plate 3)

Hook: 12 – 14
Tail: Blue dun (dark) hackle fibres
Body: Natural stripped peacock quill
Hackle: Blue dun cock
Wings: Moorhen (optional)

Molly Sweet was one of the best-known commercial fly-tyers of the Borderlands region. She worked for Harry Powell (see No. 72 Dogsbody) in his tackle shop and fly-tying business in Porthycarne Street, Usk and inherited Harry's business on his death in 1944. She married Lionel Sweet (see no. 87 Grannom) two years later. Molly has left us two fine patterns, the Blue Upright and Brown Owl.

Having its origins in the West Country, this pattern (and the next by Ted Coombs) are highly successful variations designed for the Usk.

Blue Variant (*Ted Coombes)*
Small/medium olives (Plate 3)

Hook: 14 – 16
Silk: Pale yellow
Whisks: Olive cock hackle fibres
Body: Blue rabbit under-fur
Rib: Pale yellow tying silk
Hackle: Olive cock hackle

This simple fly has few equals when small and medium olives are hatching and also very effective when small stoneflies are in evidence.

In 1922 Ted Coombes moved to 22 Cross Street, Tenbury Wells, where he set himself up as a master bootmaker and fishing tackle dealer. Apparently his upper room was an Aladdin's cave filled with fishing tackle and fly-tying materials. The flies he tied were of an imitative nature and he is reported to have tied an imitation of a bluebottle which regulars in the Royal Oak found hard to distinguish from the natural fly when placed alongside one in a glass! His Blue Variant gained tremendous popularity and spread to the USA, and his hackled March Brown proved to be a popular and most effective wet fly pattern.

BLUE-WINGED OLIVE (*Serratella ignita*).

The Blue-Winged Olive is perhaps better known as a chalkstream fly but is nevertheless an important fly in this region, especially the Usk valley from where all these patterns originate. It is recognised as a difficult fly to imitate.
(See also: Pink Paragon).

Blue-Winged Olive (Var. 1) *(John Henderson)*
Blue-winged olive (Plate 3)

Hook: 14
Whisk: Medium-light blue dun fibres
Body: Blue rabbit followed by green/yellow heron herl
Rib: Fine gold wire
Hackles: Golden dun and green olive cock hackles

Blue-Winged Olive (Var. 2) *(John Henderson)*
Blue-winged olive (Plate 3)

Hook: 14
Whisk: Tips of herl used in body
Body: Yellow seal's fur ribbed with green/yellow olive heron herl
Tag: Flat gold tinsel
Hackles: Greenish olive and blue dun cock

Orange Quill Variant (*John Henderson*)
Blue-winged olive (Plate 3)

Hook: 14
Whisk: Blue dun cock hackle tips
Body: Blue rabbit followed by hot orange goose quill
Rib: Fine gold wire
Hackles: Two medium light blue dun hackles

These three variations come from John Henderson for use on the Usk.

Blue-Winged Olive (*William Law*)
Blue-winged olive (Plate 3)

Hook: 12 – 14
Whisks: Greenish-blue hen hackle fibres
Body: Green wool
Rib: Gold wire
Hackle: Greenish-blue hen

William Law (1880 – 1947) was originally from Kintore in Aberdeenshire where he fished the River Don as a young man before moving to Wales to become river keeper for the Buckland Estate on the Usk. His influence over matters fishing in the Usk valley was significant, though he left us but one fly pattern, a Blue-Winged Olive. He and his wife are buried in Llandetty Churchyard on the banks of his beloved River Usk.

Blue-Winged Olive (*Rev. Edward Powell*)
Blue-winged olive (Plate 4)

Hook: 14 – 16
Silk: Primrose
Whisks: Honey dun

PLATE 4

Blue-Winged Olive (Rev. E. Powell), Blue-Winged Olive Nymph, Borderer
Brooke's Fancy, Brown Moth, Brown Owl
Brown Silverhorn, Brown Squirrel Nymph, Buzz Olive
Caddis, Caenis Nymph, Fisherman's Curse

Body: Dunne's artificial silk Nos. 287 and 298a. Two strands of the first and one of the second, twisted and wound over shank covered with white enamel
Rib: Primrose tying silk
Hackle: Honey dun or pale olive
Wings: Tips of two dark blue Andalusian hen breast feathers

This pattern, devised by the Rev. Edward Powell, did not feature that prominently in his repertoire but was mentioned in articles on grayling fishing.

Blue-Winged Olive Nymph (*John Henderson*)
Blue-winged olive nymph (Plate 4)

Hook: 14
Whisks: Short fibres of dark blue hen hackle
Body: Deep red cow hair
Shoulder: Deep red cock hackle trimmed to 1/10th inch
Hackle: Two turns dark blue dun

Another pattern from the Henderson stable for use on the Usk.

Borderer (*W. M. Gallichan*)
A fly for all seasons (Plate 4)

Hook: 12 – 16
Silk: Red
Whisks: Rusty blue-dun cock hackle fibres
Body: Blue rabbit under fur, with a red silk tip
Hackle: Rusty blue-dun cock hackle

A small fly with a big reputation and probably the best known of Walter Gallichan's six patterns. This fly must rank as one of the most outstanding and deadly patterns of the region.

Brookes' Fancy *(Mr Brookes)*
A general-purpose wet fly (Plate 4)

Hook: 12 – 14
Silk: Purple
Body: Purple silk
Rib: Peacock herl
Hackle: White or off-white hen

Mr Brookes was a postman in Ludlow who fished the Teme thereabouts and devised the fly that bears his name – Brookes' Fancy. It is a most effective general-purpose wet fly for trout and grayling and is especially useful when fished semi-dry in October for grayling. He was listed in the weekly reports of the *Fishing Gazette* not only for the Teme but also the Onny, Corve, Ledwych, Rea Arrow and Lugg. He also contributed a column to that magazine under the pseudonym 'S. (Sam) Ludlow.'

Brown Moth *(Mr Acheson)*
Moths (Plate 4)

Hook: 12 long shank
Body: Dark green olive wool
Rib: Silver tinsel (optional)
Hackle: Ginger hen
Wing: Hen pheasant secondary – narrow

Brown Owl *(Molly Sweet)*
Evening moths (Plate 4)

Hook: 12
Body: Camel-coloured fur
Rib: Gold wire
Hackle: Red cock
Wing: Barn owl primary wing feather

A pattern devised by Molly Sweet in Usk town to imitate the summer evening moths on that river.

Brown Silverhorn (*John Henderson*)
Silverhorns (Plate 4)

Hook: 14
Body: Dark green seal's fur mixed with hare's ear to give a brownish-green shade
Rib: Yellow silk
Body hackle: Woodcock neck feather ribbed and trimmed to taper from thorax to abdomen
Neck hackle: Woodcock neck feather

Silverhorns are day-flying sedges that swarm over the water surface, especially on lakes. This pattern was developed by John Henderson for use on Talybont Reservoir.

Brown Squirrel Nymph (*James Evans*)
Ephemerid nymph (Plate 4)

Hook: 14
Tail and wing case: Twelve hairs of Canadian pine squirrel tail, doubled & re-doubled
Abdomen: Bronze raffene over a silver Lurex underbody, counter ribbed with fine gold wire
Thorax: Fur from back of Canadian pine squirrel

A hard-wearing pattern using unusual material, Canadian pine squirrel fur, whose brown/black/fawn barring forms an attractive tail and thorax.

Buzz Olive (*Rev. Edward Powell*)
Olives (Plate 4)

Hook: 16 long shank
Whisks: Olive cock
Body: Yellow seal's fur mixed with a little green mole, or heron dyed in picric acid
Rib: Gold twist
Hackles: Head, dark blue cock; shoulder, yellow-olive cock, about half the size of the head hackle – three or four turns of each

Designed to imitate early season olives. The use of the word 'Buzz' in the title means hackled.

Caddis (*Eric Taverner*)
Sedge (Plate 4)

Hook: 14
Silk: Dull green
Body: Brown hare's fur – dubbed thickly
Hackle: Blue hen medium hackle

This pattern was designed by Eric Taverner for use on the Dee and tributaries in May and June when greenish-bodied sedge are in evidence.

CAENIS

Caenis species flies are the smallest of the Ephemeroptera which hatch in large clouds at dawn and dusk in the summer months. Despite their abundance my research has only revealed two patterns, one for the nymph stage of the life cycle and the other for the adult which rejoices under the nickname, the Fisherman's Curse.

Caenis Nymph (*John Henderson*)
Caenis nymph (Plate 4)

Hook: 16
Silk: Light brown
Tail: Four or five short fibres of white cock hackle
Rib: Fine gold wire
Body: Stone-coloured herl
Thorax: Several turns of bronze peacock herl

Fisherman's Curse (*Peter Flint*)
Caenis (Plate 4)

Hook: 16
Silk: Pink
Whisks: Three white cock hackle fibres – splayed out
Body: White silk
Rib: Pink silk
Wing: Two layers of polythene with air trapped between them,
stuck to hook shank with Evostick and tied in
Hackle: Small white cock hackle

This ingenious and at one time highly sought-after Fisherman's Curse, with its air-sac wing for buoyancy, was designed after Peter Flint after being challenged by Cosmo Barrett to produce a successful imitation.

Flint, a jeweller from Birmingham, took over Cosmo Barrett's business premises in Presteigne in 1962, where he restored antiques, sold fishing tackle and continued tying the Barrett style of fly patterns as well as his own. He was responsible for developing the Polo Nymph and four other patterns: Fisherman's Curse, Grizzly Mayfly, Peter Flint's Pheasant Tail, and Peter's Peril.

PLATE 5

Cambrian Dun, Capel Celyn, Ceiriog Spinner
Brecon Cob, Olive Cob, Orange Cob
Yellow Cob, Cochen-las, Coch-y-bonddu
Claret Coch-y-bonddu, Coch-yn-las, Colonel's Game-Pie Nymph

Cambrian Dun (*Ken Glover*)
Olives (Plate 5)

Hook: 14 – 16 (16 most effective)
Silk: Brown
Whisks: Ginger cock hackle fibres
Body: Blue mole's fur or rabbit under-fur
Rib: Fine silver wire
Hackle: Ginger cock hackle

This simple pattern was designed by Ken Glover when he lived in Newtown for use on the upper Severn. He now lives beside the river in Caerhowel near Montgomery. It is reputed to be effective when a wide variety of natural flies, especially olives, are hatching.

Capel Celyn (*traditional*)
(Plate 5)

Hook: 12
Tail: Two strands of mallard fibres
Body: Peacock quill
Rib: Copper wire
Hackle: Black hen
Wing: Jay or blue dun

This fly was originally designed in the 1920s for use on the Afon Tryweryn, which now, along with the village of Capel Celyn, lies drowned under the waters of Llyn Celyn, the reservoir which was constructed in the 1950s. It was traditionally fished as a point fly on a three-fly wet cast and has proved quite effective on the tributaries of the Wye and Usk.

Ceiriog Spinner (*Alan Hudson*)
Light olive spinners (Plate 5)

Hook: 16
Silk: Primrose
Whisks: Longer than normal Plymouth Rock cock hackle fibres
Body: Yellow Labrador hair
Rib: Fine gold wire
Hackle: Plymouth Rock cock hackle

This pattern was tied by Alan Hudson of Chirk for use the Ceiriog – a tributary of the Dee – which flows over a steep, rocky, riverbed. It is especially effective when light olive spinners are on the water.

Alan, a former editor of *Flydresser* magazine, is a fine and inventive fly-tyer. His particularly effective dressings include stonefly imitations especially suited to the Welsh Dee catchment. In total he has eight patterns to his name: Badger May, Black Gnat, Ceiriog Spinner, Dark Stone, Early Olive, Hare's Ear Duster, Large Stonefly and Medium Olive.

COB

Cob is a name given to the March Brown by local anglers in the Brecon area and it is not surprising to find a number of patterns in existence, principally differing in body colour. The Brecon, Orange and Yellow Cob patterns were used extensively by Leslie Peters, the doyen of Usk fishing in the Brecon area for over fifty years.

Brecon Cob (*traditional pattern*)
March Brown (Plate 5)

Hook: 12
Body: Dark red silk or seal's fur
Rib: Gold wire
Hackle: Dark partridge neck
Wing: Hen pheasant wing

Olive Cob (*Haydn Havard*)
March Brown (Plate 5)

Hook: 14
Silk: Olive
Body: Olive brown/orange seal's fur mix
Rib: Flat gold
Hackle: Blue dun hen

This pattern was developed by Brecon-based Haydn Havard for use on the Usk.

Orange Cob (*Leslie Peters*)
March Brown (Plate 5)

Hook: 12
Silk: Orange
Body: Orange floss
Rib: Gold wire
Hackle: Dark brown partridge
Wing: Hen pheasant

Yellow Cob (*Leslie Peters*)
March Brown (Plate 5)

Hook: 12
Silk: Yellow
Body: Yellow seal's fur
Rib: Gold wire
Hackle: Dark partridge neck
Wing: Hen pheasant wing

Leslie Peters has great faith in these two Cob patterns for early season work on the Usk close to Brecon.

Cochen-las (*Ned Hughes*)
Any dark natural fly (Plate 5)

Hook: 12 – 14
Body: Black floss
Hackle: Coch-y-bonddu
Wing: Dark dun or coot feather

Credit for this fly is given to Ned Hughes, a well-respected Rhayader angler who tied it for the Elan Valley lakes. Its literal translation into English is 'red-blue one.'

Coch-y-bonddu (*Welsh traditional pattern*)
Phylloperthera sp. (Plate 5)

Hook: 12 – 14
Silk: Crimson
Body: Two strands of bronze peacock herl tied full
Hackle: Coch-y-bonddu hen (wet fly), cock (dry fly)

The Coch-y-bonddu is a famous old Welsh fly pattern. Long used as a generic beetle representation, it is recognised in

Mid-Wales as a specific representation of the natural beetle, *Phyllopertha horticicola*, which appears on the bracken-clad hillsides in June and July. Although traditionally it was fished as a wet fly, these days it is most often used on stillwaters (such as Llyn Clywedog and the Elan Valley lakes) as a dry fly, fished on the surface.

It is used throughout Britain, and indeed all over the world, as a general beetle representation. Indirect reference to this fly is made by Scotcher (1820) in the form of the Drop Fly.

Claret Coch-y-bonddu (*Gordon Forrest*)
Beetles (Plate 5)

Hook: 12 – 14
Body: Two or three strands of copper-coloured peacock herl
Tag: Flat gold tinsel
Hackle: Claret-coloured hen hackle

This claret variation of the original fly was designed by Shrewsbury-based tackle dealer, Gordon Forrest, for use on Lake Vyrnwy before the Second World War. He referred to it as the Claret Bumble but it was renamed by Michael Leighton to avoid confusion with the Derbyshire Bumble.

Coch-yn-las (*Pryce-Tannatt*)
An early (and late) season fly (Plate 5)

Hook: 14
Body: Strands from brown turkey tail dyed purple
Hackle: Dark rusty dun cock
Wings: Water hen secondary quill

This fly is reputedly a good trout and grayling pattern for use early in the trout season and again in September for grayling. It was at one time used extensively on the Ithon and

Ceiriog. In name it is not to be confused with the Cochen-las fly – coch-yn-las literally means 'red-in-blue' resulting in a purple colouration.

Colonel's Game-Pie Nymph (*Col. George Ellis*)
Freshwater shrimp or cased caddis (Plate 5)

Hook: 12 Capt Hamilton International
Silk: Brown
Tail: Bronze mallard fibres
Body: Dark hare's ear fur
Rib: Fine gold wire
Wing cases: Cock pheasant tail feather fibres
Thorax: Rabbit under-fur and guard hairs well mixed – (can be weighted)
Legs: Brown partridge fibres, tied beard fashion

Colonel George Ellis of Preston Gubbals, Shropshire, was a keen fishing and shooting man – hence his Game-Pie Nymph, which was concocted from materials obtained in the field. Depending upon the depth at which it is fished, it can be taken for a shrimp, cased caddis, hatching sedge or merely a generic creepy-crawly.

The Colonel's other pattern, Ellis's Alder, makes full use of home dyeing, a skill at which he was most adept.

Coltman's Duster (*F. H. Coltman*)
An all season fly (Plate 6)

Hook: 14 – 16
Silk: Brown
Body: Condor herl (natural) or heron
Hackle: Badger cock hackle – tied at the bend

From 1945 onwards, F.H. Coltman was advertising his trout

PLATE 6

Coltman's Duster, Cound Shrimp, Cowdung Fly
Cow's Arse, Crawshay's Olive, Crickhowell Killer
Cul-de-Canon, Daddy Long Legs, Dark Spring Olive
Dark Stone, Doctor

and grayling flies in *Angling* magazine from an address in West Kirby, Wirral. He ran a series of advertisements, sometimes with the headline 'Flies by Coltman of Llay' sometimes with 'Try my deadly Silver March Browns and Black Gnats.' Later his regular ad read, 'To kill fish you must use Featherdusters.' From the Jan-Feb 1949 issue his address changed to Boar's Head Yard, Oswestry. He stopped advertising in 1950, but in a letter to *Angling* in October of that year he mentions advertising in the local Labour Exchange for skilled fly-tyers (which the Labour Exchange staff misread as fly-catchers!) He devised this reversed-hackle fly, and was also recognised throughout the area as the best tyer of the Grey Duster.

Coltman is remembered as dry fly purist who fished the River Ceiriog, never taking more than one fish from each pool, for his motorbike and sidecar, and for the accuracy of his fly-tying.

Cound Shrimp (*Tim Williams*)
Shrimp (Plate 6)

Hook: 10 –12 wide gape
Silk: Orange
Body: Orange and yellow seal's fur. Lead under-body
Back: Polythene – stretched tight
Hackle: Palmered honey or ginger cock hackle

Tim Williams, the originator of this pattern sums up the philosophy of Welsh Borderlands flyfishing when he says of this fly 'it is quickly and easily tied, and is simply a variation on a host of general shrimp patterns. I think it is important for a brook pattern to be easily tied so you don't mind losing a few, which you have to risk doing to get your fly among the better fish in the more awkward lies.'

Cowdung Fly (*Richard Bowlker)*
Cowdung fly (Plate 6)

Hook: 12 – 14
Body: Dirty yellow wool, with a pinch of brown
Hackle: Pale ginger
Wing: Woodcock

Richard Bowlker lived in Ludlow and fished the Teme in the seventeen hundreds. He published his *Art of Angling* in 1746.

This old fly pattern, which is referred to in his book, is an imitation of one of the commonest insects found near rivers and is particularly useful on the upper reaches where fly life is sparse and terrestrial flies are an important food source. The wing is often omitted in the dry fly version and replaced with a starling hackle.

Cow's Arse (*Mike Judge)*
General Olive (Plate 6)

Hook: 12 – 14 up-eyed
Body: Two or three pheasant tail fibres
Rib (optional): Fine gold wire
Hackles: Red cock and pale ginger wound through each other, tied at the bend

In the 1950s Mike Judge used to stay at the Severn Arms Hotel at Penybont on the River Ithon, where he tied this reverse-hackled pattern under the watchful eye of Jack Hamer the local keeper. It was for some time the only dry fly in his box.

Crawshay's Olive (*traditional Usk pattern*)
Olive dun (Plate 6)

Hook: 12
Tail: Honey dun fibres
Body: Mole fur
Rib: Yellow silk (prominent)
Hackle: Honey dun
Wing: Coot or starling

This delicate pattern was developed for use on the Glanusk and Crawshay estate waters of the Usk as an effective evening pattern when fished just under the water surface.

Crickhowell Killer (*Tom Probert*)
Usk (cold clear water) (Plate 6)

Hook: 12
Tail: Three strands of cock pheasant tail
Abdomen: Hare's ear
Rib: Gold wire
Thorax: White baby wool

A fly with a considerable local reputation which was given to Stuart Jarvis, keeper of the Glanusk estate water on the Usk, in the early 1970s by Tom Probert. It is reported to be especially useful in cold clear water.

Cul-de-Canon (*Gwilym Hughes*)
Olive emergers (Plate 6)

Hook: 16
Body: Waxed yellow tying silk – using dark cobbler's wax
Under-wing: A few strands of deer hair tips, splayed out
Over-wing: Four natural coloured cul-de-canard feathers

Dee fishing guide, Gwilym Hughes started fishing at the age of twelve on the River Dwyfor on the Lleyn Peninsula, under the watchful eye of his father who was a local water bailiff. He has been captain of the Welsh flyfishing team and in 1998 became International Rivers Champion. In 1994, after a career in the police force, he turned to professional game angling and is now a STANIC and APGAI instructor.

Gwilym devised the Cul-de-Canon whilst he was competing in the 1998 International on the River Tweed in Scotland. It is a clever modification of the traditional Greenwell's Glory in the style of an F-fly, which results in a fly that sits well in the water film. Gwilym also reports its success as a dry 'sight fly' with two additional bright orange CdC feathers for use in the New Zealand method with a lightweight nymph tied into the hook bend.

Daddy Long Legs (*James Evans*)
Crane fly (Plate 6)

Hook: 10 – 12 Mayfly hook
Legs: Six pairs of 'knotted' cock pheasant tail fibres
Body: Condor herl, dyed browny-grey
Wings: Long-fibred brown/olive cock hackle bunched by figure of eight winding

This is one of two crane fly patterns originating in the region (the other being Palmer's Big Daddy) and was the handiwork of James Evans. It is important, first of all, to set the legs in pairs, the front pair inclined slightly forward, the second pair square to the hook shank and the rear pair facing slightly backwards. Then wind in hackle for the wings which is divided by 'figure-of-eighting'; finally close-wind the condor herl along hook shank and in between the legs.

Dark Spring Olive (*Rev. Edward Powell*)
Large dark olive (Plate 6)

Hook: 14
Whisks: Olive cock hackle fibres
Body: Blue rabbit under-fur mixed with a pinch of green mole fur
Hackles: Two blue dun hen (dark)

This fly bears the old name given to the large dark olive, a common early season and autumn showing fly. This pattern is one of Parson Powell's less well-known flies but is reputedly very effective when fish are feeding on the natural. The green mole fur was obtained by soaking the natural in picric acid overnight.

Dark Stone (*Alan Hudson*)
Stonefly (Plate 6)

Hook: 14 – 16
Silk: Black
Body: Hare's ear
Rib: Medium gold or silver tinsel
Hackles: Badger cock hackle in front and black cock hackle behind

Another fly tied for the tumbling waters of the Ceiriog by Alan Hudson to imitate the early brown, a medium sized stonefly.

Doctor (*Rev. Edward Powell*)
General beetle pattern (Plate 6)

Hook: 12 – 14
Silk: Brown
Whisks: Coch-y-bonddu cock hackle fibres
Body: Rear quarter rabbit fur dyed yellow in picric acid, front

three-quarters, black rabbit fur. The body is tied 'fat'
Hackle: Ten or eleven turns of coch-y-bonddu cock hackle

This fly is not really a new pattern but a dry fly variation of the wet Devonshire Doctor. It is deliberately heavily hackled so that it remains buoyant at all times. It represents numerous beetles and is effective throughout the season especially on the smaller streams.

Dogsbody (*Harry Powell*)
General-purpose dry fly (Plate 7)

Hook: 12 – 16
Silk: Brown
Whisks: Three strands of cock pheasant tail feather
Body: Camel-coloured dog hair ribbed with oval gold tinsel
Hackles: In front, red cock; behind, Plymouth Rock/grizzle

The Dogsbody is a most effective general-purpose dry fly pattern which is a cross between a Gold-ribbed Hare's Ear and a Rough Olive. The story of its creation in 1924 is legendary – Harry Powell, a hairdresser in Usk town, and his assistant Mr Hickey, were struggling to find suitable body material to copy a fly they had been given by a client from North Wales, when into the salon came a farmer with the answer to their problem – his foxy-looking mongrel dog. Not only was the farmer shorn but his dog too!

Being a keen flyfisherman, Powell tied his own flies while waiting for his next client, and sold them from a corner of his shop. One day Ted Rudge, who ran a tackle manufacturing business in Redditch, called in for a haircut and convinced him to stock a range of fishing tackle to complement his fly sales. In 1927 he sold the hairdressing business to his assistant, Mr Hickey, and moved around the corner to a little shop in Porthcarne Street where he set up a fishing tackle and fly-

PLATE 7

Dogsbody, Double Black Spot, Droitwich
Early Brown, Early Olive, Eaton Dun
Edmondson's Welsh Fly, Ellis' Alder, Ermine Moth
Feather Duster, February Red, Francis's Fly

tying business, employing Molly Salter (later Sweet) as a fly-tyer. Today the Dogsbody is faithfully tied in its traditional manner by Jean Williams who now owns Sweet's Tackle Shop, the fishing tackle business started by Harry Powell in 1927.

The Dogsbody was a 'sheet-anchor' fly for James Evans, who found that as a size 16 it was suitable for grayling while at size 12 or 14 it was very effective for trout.

Besides his famous Dogsbody fly, Harry Powell's Iron Blue is one of the most popular Border patterns and a third creation, Whiskers, a useful attractor fly for use on sunny summer days.

Double Black Spot (*Rev. Edward Powell*)
Black gnat (Plate 7)

Hook: 14 long shank
Body: Two pinches of black rabbit separated by the hackle
Hackle: Very short grizzled Andalusian cock or badger cock wound in a central position on shank of hook

This is the third 'relation' in the Rev. Powell's 'Black Spot family' representing black gnats – see entries for Black Spot and BSI for the others. This one is useful all year round, especially for smutting trout and grayling.

Droitwich (*Cyril Hancock*)
A grayling pattern (Plate 7)

Hook: 12 – 16
Tag: Orange wool
Body: Rear half – narrow oval silver tinsel
Front half – green peacock herl, ribbed with narrow oval tinsel
Hackle: Badger

Cyril V. Hancock was the angling correspondent of the *Birmingham Post* for 35 years and author of an angling book,

Rod in Hand (1958), and of a beautiful chapter *The Land of Teme and Gleam* in Maurice Wiggin's *The Angler's Bedside Book*. He was an avid stream fisherman and a collector of rivers, especially Welsh Borderland streams. He developed his highly prized and well-known March Brown pattern and has five other Border fly patterns to his credit: Fore-and-Aft Mayfly, Midget Mayfly, PET, Stokesay and Droitwich.

Hancock devised the Droitwich as his own variation of the Grayling Witch. Its name is truly tongue-in-cheek since, on giving the dressing to a lady professional fly-tyer, he told her he'd named it the Droitwich. When she asked why, he replied 'I've found the right Witch and when I go grayling fishing now, my motto is *Dieu et mon Droitwich!*' He and others claim to have had success with it as a tail fly fished at depth.

Early Brown (*Pryce-Tannatt collection*)
Stoneflies (Plate 7)

Hook: 12 – 14
Body: Hare's ear dubbed thinly on hot orange tying silk
Hackle: Under covert feather from a woodcock wing

A wet fly imitation of the early brown stonefly, best fished as the middle fly of a three-fly cast on fine days early in the season.

Early Olive (*Alan Hudson*)
Early olives (Plate 7)

Hook: 14
Silk: Black
Whisks: Plymouth Rock cock hackle fibres
Body: Hare's ear fur
Hackles: Plymouth Rock and red/brown cock hackles wound together

Another gem of a dry fly from the vice of Alan Hudson of Chirk for use on rougher waters typified by his local river, the Ceiriog.

Eaton Dun (*Michael Meddings*)
Pale watery duns (Plate 7)

Hook: 16
Silk: Black
Whisks: Brassy cock hackle fibres
Body: Yellow-olive condor herl
Rib: Oval gold tinsel
Hackles: Yellow-olive cock hackle and a blue dun cock hackle in front

Michael Meddings was a south Shropshire fisherman, an active member of the Salopian Fly Fishers who predominantly fished the Onny. He also fished the tiny and under-rated River Worfe near Bridgnorth, which gave rise to the name of his other pattern, the Worfield Amber Beauty.

Both patterns were designed to represent pale wateries when they appear towards the end of June.

Edmondson's Welsh Fly (*John Edmondson*)
Sedge (Plate 7)

Hook: 10
Silk: Brown
Body: Dirty yellow mohair
Tag: Gold tinsel
Hackle: Furnace hen hackle
Wing: Woodcock wing feather

This pattern, over 150 years old and once considered first class on Welsh lakes whilst also being useful on the rivers and streams towards the end of the season, was the handiwork of Liverpool tackle dealer John Edmondson.

Ellis' Alder (*Col. George Ellis*)
Alder (Plate 7)

Hook: 12 – 14
Silk: Red
Body: Swan herl dyed dark claret
Rib: One strand of bronze peacock herl (four turns on size 12 hook)
Hackle: Black henny-cock with a long fibre tied in front of the wing as a collar
Wing: Brown turkey

Despite its name this fly was originally designed to imitate small sedges. It has become known as a general-purpose wet fly.

Ermine Moth (*Rev. Edward Powell*)
White moths (Plate 7)

Hook: 12 – 14
Tag: A loop of orange-yellow wool tied in flat, then trimmed to form a forked tail
Body: White rabbit fur
Rib: Coarse black thread
Hackle: Two grey partridge breast feathers

This splendid fly from the Rev. Edward Powell, originally tied to imitate light-coloured moths, is most effective from June to the end of the season. Of it Powell said 'It is a marvellous fly all day and its colour gives one an extra half-hour's fishing at nightfall when other patterns would be invisible.' He also notes that for some unknown reason the pattern is very successful when black gnats are in evidence.

Feather Duster (*Jack Hughes-Parry*)
Stonefly (Plate 7)

Hook: 12 – 16
Silk: Maroon
Body: Grey fur with a slim underbody of cork (optional)
Hackle: Blue dun

First mention of this fly appears to be in Jack Hughes-Parry's *Fishing Fantasy*, but it could well be the work of H. Moore, a well-known Liverpool-based tackle dealer.

February Red (*trad. Dee and Ceiriog*)
Stonefly/February Red (Plate 7)

Hook: 14
Silk: Claret
Body: Orange mohair
Hackle: Blue dun hen hackle

A wet fly with a long history first mentioned by Dame Juliana Berners in 1496. The natural is an early-season fly that is common on the slower flowing stretches of many streams of the region.

Francis's Fly (*Francis Francis*)
Caterpillars (Plate 7)

Hook: 10 – 12
Body: Copper-coloured peacock herl
Rib: Copper-red silk
Hackle: Medium blue dun
Wings: Two hackle points – grizzly blue dun cock set upright

A fly with a widespread reputation, first developed by

Francis Francis in 1858 or thereabouts, and used on Welsh rivers where it was a rival to the Coch-y-bonddu, apparently out-fishing that fly three to one!

Golden Duck (*Michael Leighton*)
Attractor wet fly (Plate 8)

Hook: 12 round-bend hook
Tail: Red wool tag
Body: Gold embossed flat tinsel
Hackle: Blue dun cock hackle fibres, tied beard fashion
Wing: White duck

Originally Michael Leighton developed this fly for use on Lake Vyrnwy but it has also been successful on streams in the region. It is a fly for early season when the water still has a bit of colour in it.

GRANNOM

The grannom (*Brachycentrus subnubilis*), commonly known as the greentail, is a day-flying small sedge that makes brief, but intense, appearances early in the season. If you are fishing at the time of a grannom hatch you will be overwhelmed by the sheer quantity of fly life but you may also be frustrated by the lack of success in catching fish since it is a hard fly to imitate. The Rev. Edward Powell commented in *The Country Sportsman* on this phenomenon 'speed is everything … you must know what to do and do it at once.' My research has found the following patterns from the region: three older patterns imitating the adult fly and four, relatively modern creations, for the pupal/emerger stages.

PLATE 8

Golden Duck, Grannom (Acheson), Grannom (Rev. E. Powell)
Grannom (H. Powell/L. Sweet), Shuttlecock Suspender
Parachute Emerger, Cul de Grannom, Partridge & Green Spider
Grant's Murderer, Grasshopper, Gravel Bed

Grannom (*Mr Acheson*)
Grannom adult (Plate 8)

Hook: 14
Body: Front half dark greenish-olive wool, rear half green wool
Hackle: Blue dun hen
Wing: Freckled partridge tail

Grannom (*Rev. Edward Powell*)
Grannom adult (Plate 8)

Hook: 14
Silk: Green
Body: Mole fur dyed in picric acid
Hackles: Two partridge hackles from mid-neck region of the bird

This pattern was developed by the Rev. Powell under the watchful eye of Dai Lewis of Tregaron, where Rev. Powell spent his summer holidays fishing the River Teifi.

Grannom (*Harry Powell/Lionel Sweet*)
Grannom adult (Plate 8)

Hook: 14
Butt: Green silk
Body: Rabbit and mole fur
Hackle: Medium red cock
Wing: Hen pheasant wing

Jointly developed by Harry Powell and Lionel Sweet for use on the Usk and still dressed today by Jean Williams in Sweet's Tackle Shop. The Grannom is a particularly difficult fly to imitate so we are remarkably fortunate to have this dressing.

Lionel Sweet, an Usk builder, was a champion fly-caster

and an avid fisherman. It must have been a very pleasant for him to meet his childhood sweetheart, Molly Salter, each time he visited Harry Powell's fishing tackle shop where she was employed as a fly tyer. During Harry's final illness in 1944 he asked Lionel to 'look after' Molly when he was gone, and that's precisely what he did since in 1946 they were married.

Shuttlecock Suspender (*Dave Collins*)
Grannom pupa/emerger (Plate 8)

Hook: 14
Thread: Tan 8/0
Rib: Uni Big Fly, black
Abdomen: Masterclass 14 Gammarus watery olive
Thorax: Superfine Amber
Thorax back: Black raffene
Wing buds: Natural grey CDC tips pre-treated with well-thinned varnish or Foo-Gloo (allowed to dry) to stop it floating
Legs: Black rabbit fur, Antron or similar – picked out
Wing: Natural grey CDC (four plumes at least)

Parachute Emerger (*Dave Collins*)
Grannom pupa/emerger (Plate 8)

Hook: 14
Thread: Tan 8/0
Abdomen: Masterclass watery olive
Rib: Uni Big Fly, black
Thorax: Superfine amber
Hackle: Black cock, two turns
Wing post: Grey Aero or similar floating yarn

Cul de Grannom (*Dave Collins*)
Grannom pupa/emerger (Plate 8)

Hook: 14
Thread: Tan 8/0
Rib: Uni Big Fly, black
Abdomen: Masterclass 14 Gammarus watery olive
Thorax: Superfine amber
Legs: Black rabbit fur, Antron or similar – picked out
Wing: Natural grey CDC, three plumes at least with deer hair underneath

Dave Collins lives at Moccas in Herefordshire and regularly fishes the middle and upper Wye and the Usk. Being a methodical sort of person (a retired scientist who worked in research and development in the agricultural chemicals industry), he has carefully studied the stomach contents of many fish and has produced some remarkably faithful imitations of grannom pupae which, according to articles in both *Trout & Salmon* and *Fly-fishing and Fly-tying* magazines, are quite deadly.

The three previous emerger patterns are variations on a common theme devised by Dave when he was trying to find a solution to Moc Morgan's question 'if anyone had succeeded in getting a dry fly pattern that worked effectively during a big Grannom hatch?' Dave studied autopsies of many fish before setting-to at the vice. All three are reportedly most effective.

Partridge & Green spider (*Louis Noble*)
Grannom pupa/emerger (Plate 8)

Hook: 14
Thread: Pearsall's Highland green 18, or similar
Tag: Danville's signal-green floss, or wool, 2mm maximum

Body: Tying silk, touching turns
Rib: Pearsall's brown silk, or similar (note close spacing)
Hackle: Grey/brown partridge, two or three turns

Louis Noble, Shropshire-born and now living in Wrexham, is a fully qualified APGAI instructor and a former joint editor of the Flydressers Guild magazine – *Flydresser*. He was responsible for producing the Llyn Du, a wet fly for use on the hill lakes above Newtown. His Partridge-and-Green Spider is another wet fly which is reported to be a very effective grannom pupa pattern.

Grant's Murderer (*Herbert Grant*)
Dry fly for May and June (Plate 8)

Hook: 12 – 14
Whisks: Pale blue dun cock hackle fibres
Body: Gold tinsel
Wings: Starling, rolled and tied sloping forward over the eye of the hook
Hackle: Long-fibred pale blue dun cock hackle

This fly is the handiwork of Herbert Grant, a tackle dealer once based in Ludlow, and originates from around 1933 for use on the Teme, Onny and Ledwych. It started life under the name 'Indispensible' and may have been listed as such by Hardy's. However the fly's name was later changed to Grant's Murderer, and apparently it lives up to its name! It is most effective for trout in May and June but is also good for grayling in the autumn.

Grasshopper (*Francis Francis*)
Grubs/caterpillars (Plate 8)

Hook: 6
Body: Green wool with copper wire underbody tapered thin at tail
Rib: Thin yellow wool

This fly is steeped in the history of the Leintwardine Club on the River Teme near Ludlow. Francis Francis stated that this fly 'in nowise resembles a grasshopper.' It is really not far removed from nymph patterns in common use today and on reading the original description of the method of fishing it, you might be forgiven for thinking that you were reading about modern day Czech nymphing.

Gravel Bed (*Rev. Edward Powell*)
Gravel bed insect (Plate 8)

Hook: 14
Whisks: Long dark brown partridge or mallard feather fibre
Body: Blue rabbit or fox under-fur
Hackles: Light Rhode Island Red hen wound on first with a blue dun hen hackle wound through it and an extra turn at the eye.

The Gravel Bed is found in abundance in the stony beds of the fast streams of the Welsh Borderlands. The Rev. Powell used this dressing to imitate the natural, having pride in it above all his many patterns.

Green Devil (*Michael Leighton*)
Blue-winged olives or aphids (Plate 9)

Hook: 14 – 16
Silk: Hot orange
Whisks: Honey cock hackle fibres

PLATE 9

Green Devil, Green Insect, Grey Duster
Grizzly Bourne, Grizzle Dun, Grizzly Palmer
Grouse & Gold, Hare's Ear Duster, Hare's Ear Parachute Emerger
Hawthorn Fly, Henderson's Dark Beetle, Henderson's Light Beetle

Body: Sheep's wool, dyed pale medium olive, dubbed on very lightly so that the silk shows through when wet
Hackles: Light ginger cock hackle wound through a grizzle cock hackle

A pattern that Michael Leighton finds useful when the blue-winged olives are on the water, but can also be used to imitate aphids when tied on size 18 or smaller hook.

Green Insect (*unknown*)
Small beetle/caterpillar (Plate 9)

Hook: 14
Body: Green peacock herl
Hackle: Pale grey hen hackle – palmered over the length of the body

A traditional grayling fly which, although popular on Welsh Borderland rivers, may well have its origins in Yorkshire. It was highly thought of on the rivers Lugg and Teme and was a reputed killer on the River Vyrnwy. It has the hallmarks of the Grayling Witch family of flies which were developed by H. A. Rolt.

Grey Duster (*collected by A. Courtney-Williams*)
Small perlidae (Plate 9)

Hook: 10 – 20
Silk: Brown
Body: Rabbit's blue under-fur and the guard hairs
Hackle: Badger cock, well marked

Alfred Courtney-Williams, author of the classic book, *A Dictionary of Trout Flies*, is reported to have had some of his most enjoyable days fishing on streams such as the Alwen, Ceiriog, Monnow and Irfon. He created two remarkable flies;

Simple Simon (a spider version of the classic Coachman) was developed on the banks of the Lugg, and his Welsh Partridge. He was also responsible for bringing to public notice the Grey Duster.

The Grey Duster is one of the most famous general-purpose dry fly patterns in existence. It was first described by Courtney-Williams, who suggested that it has its origins on the River Alwen, a Dee tributary, where the locals reckoned it was the only fly you ever needed. It was popularised by professional fly-tyer, F. H. Coltman of Boar's Head Yard in Oswestry. For grayling Coltman added a tag of bright yellow wool, and he tied another reverse-hackled variation which is listed separately under Coltman's Duster. Another variation of this pattern is Alan Hudson's Hare's Ear Duster.

Grizzly Bourne (*Michael Leighton*)
General-purpose fly (Plate 9)

Hook: 12 – 18 (Capt. Hamilton – featherweight)
Silk: Orange (pre-waxed)
Whisks: Honey cock hackle fibres
Body: Rabbit's blue under-fur
Rib: Pearsall's golden yellow floss
Hackles: Light red/brown cock hackle wound through a grizzle cock hackle

Michael Leighton originally developed this pattern for use on the Bourne, a southern chalkstream. However he has subsequently used it extensively on Welsh Borderland brooks and streams with great success. It is tied as a general-purpose dry fly pattern, well hackled and is a good floating fly since it has a hackle which is palmered over a third of the body.

Grizzle Dun (*Walter Gallichan*)
Small Stoneflies (Plate 9)

Hook: 14 – 16
Whisks: Grizzle cock hackle fibres
Body: Well waxed yellow silk
Hackle: Badger cock hackle

This is one of Walter Gallichan's six patterns in this inventory. He developed this one for use on Welsh and Shropshire streams to imitate small stoneflies such as the willow and needle flies. However it is also successful as a general-purpose pattern which can be fished either wet or dry.

Grizzly Palmer (*Mike Green*)
Grayling fly (Plate 9)

Hook: 14 – 16
Tag: Red wool
Body: Black silk
Rib: Silver wire
Hackle: Grizzle cock – palmered

This grayling fly has its origins in the Corwen district on the River Dee and is the handiwork of Mike Green, a local fly-dresser of exceptional ability.

Grouse & Gold (*Stuart Jarvis*)
Early season Usk fly (Plate 9)

Hook: 10 – 12
Silk: Brown
Tail: Three strands of cock pheasant tail
Body: Flat gold tinsel
Hackle: Back feather from a Welsh grouse

Created by Stuart Jarvis on Christmas Day 1973, the gold tinsel for the body came off a Christmas tree decoration! It is a very effective fly in coloured water.

Hare's Ear Duster (*Alan Hudson)*
Stonefly (Plate 9)

Hook: 12 – 20
Silk: Black
Body: Hare's ear fur – tied rough
Hackle: Badger cock hackle

A variation of the Grey Duster by Alan Hudson of Chirk for use as a stonefly imitation on Border streams – it is also a good general-purpose fly, as is the original Grey Duster.

Hare's Ear Parachute Emerger (*Dave Collins)*
Emerging insects (Plate 9)

Hook: 14 – 20 Oliver Edwards Nymph Emerger K14ST
Thread: Uni 8/0 tan
Body: Dark or light hare's ear
Thorax: Peacock herl or similar dubbing
Wing post: Floating yarn or Dry Aero – dun or white
Hackle: Red game

A generic pattern from Dave Collins with the potential to tempt surface-feeding fish all year round – a great prospecting fly, either on its own or in conjunction with a small nymph on the point fished 'duo' style. The fly was developed on the banks of the Wye very close to Moccas where he lives.

Hawthorn Fly (*North Shropshire origin*)
Hawthorn fly (Plate 9)

Hook: 12
Silk: Black
Body: Black floss silk – rear half tied thin, front half built up
Hackle: Black hen – two turns of long-fibred feather

The importance of the natural insect, *Bibio marci*, has been known to anglers for centuries – there is a clear reference to it in the *Treatyse of Fysshynge with an Angle* (1496) by Dame Juliana Berners. According to Michael Leighton this 'large, juicy fly appears in May and is eagerly taken by trout.' It is therefore surprising to find that this is the only local dressing. This one comes from north Shropshire where the streams are slower flowing, giving the fish more time to view their food.

Henderson's Dark Beetle (*John Henderson*)
Dark beetles (Plate 9)

Hook: 12 – 14
Silk: Grey
Body: Peacock herl or ostrich herl or fibres from a magpie tail
Body hackle: Palmered black cock – trimmed close to body
Hackle: Black cock

Henderson's Light Beetle (*John Henderson*)
Light beetles (Plate 9)

Hook: 12 – 14
Silk: Grey
Body: Natural condor herl
Body hackle: Palmered medium dun cock – trimmed close to body
Hackle: Medium dun cock

Two beetle patterns from John Henderson of Ashford House near Talybont-on-Usk, for use on Talybont Reservoir. The trimmed, palmered, body hackle is a hallmark of this most prolific fly-dresser.

Herefordshire Alder (*wet*) (*Canon C. F. Eagles*)
Alder (Plate 10)

Hook: 10 – 14
Silk: Purple silk
Body: Pheasant tail herl wound in open turns over an underbody of tying silk
Hackle: Brown dun hen hackle

Canon Charles Frederick Eagles was a member of a large and very active Border fishing family that was based at the foot of the Black Mountains, in the catchment of the River Monnow. His father was at Oxford with the Rev. Edward Powell's father and was vicar of Clodock, near Longtown, where it is said that he was able to cast a fly from the pulpit into the River Monnow. After his ordination Canon Eagles served as curate at Powick, near Worcester, where he fished the Leigh Brook. Later he was a curate in Redditch before moving to the Rectory at Coughton, Warwickshire, from where he fished the Herefordshire and South Shropshire streams for the remainder of his life. He perfected the art (acquired from his father) of accurately casting a team of wet flies upstream, three for trout and four for grayling! He was a mentor to the Rev. Edward Powell and was therefore influential in the development of flyfishing in the region. He developed a series of flies but only the highly successful patterns, Hereford Alder and Willow, have survived. He died in 1931.

This is the Canon's most famous Borderland pattern. He always fished it wet and caught a prodigious number of fish with it.

PLATE 10

Herefordshire Alder (wet), Herefordshire Alder (dry), Hereford Pheasant Tail
Iron Blue (Acheson), Iron Blue (Rev. E. Powell), Glas Cwta
Iron Blue (H. Powell), Iron Blue (Henderson), Iron Blue Nymph
Knotted Midge, Landrail & Rabbit, Large Dark Olive

Herefordshire Alder (*dry*) (*var. Canon Eagles wet fly*)
Alder (Plate 10)

Hook: 10 –14
Silk: Scarlet
Body: Tying silk under-body
Rib: Peacock herl
Hackle: Coch-y-bonddu cock hackle

Nowadays the Herefordshire Alder is fished as a dry fly and over the years this dressing has evolved for use on Borderlands waters.

Hereford Pheasant Tail (*James Evans*)
Alder (Plate 10)

Hook: 12 – 16
Whisks: Honey cock hackle
Body: Cock pheasant tail feather herl
Rib: Fine gold wire
Hackles: Honey-dun cock and blue-dun cock wound on together

Whilst preparing to dress some Barrett's Bane and Herefordshire Alder flies James Evans came up with the idea of a composite fly bearing the same body but having a hackle from each of the original flies. The result, he reckoned, proved to be better than either of the original flies.

THE IRON BLUE

The iron blue (*Baetis spp.*) is a relatively small member of the Ephemeridae whose importance to fishing is significant and has been documented since Bowlker's time. It has been given a number of names in different localities and on the Usk it is known as the Little Purple. Iron blues hatch until late afternoon and are usually taken in an extraordinarily violent manner by fish. My research has uncovered five Borderland patterns to represent the dun fly, one for the spinner and one for the nymph.

Iron Blue (*Mr Acheson*)
Iron blue dun (Plate 10)

Hook: 12 – 14
Silk: Yellow
Body: Blue fur
Rib: Yellow tying silk (optional)
Hackle: Blue dun hen

Old Usk flies were dressed very lightly in a style similar to that of the Clyde flies in Scotland, and Acheson's were no exception to this rule. This fly, like many other Acheson flies, has a short body using only half the shank perhaps to aid quick sinking and so representing a hatching or drowned dun.

Iron Blue (*Rev. Edward Powell*)
Iron blue dun (Plate 10)

Hook: 16 – 18
Whisks: Olive-green cock hackle fibres
Body: Mole fur – lightly dubbed
Hackle: Olive-green cock hackle
Wings: Tips of tom-tit feathers with spine left in and shaped

This was the only fly that the Rev. Powell found necessary to be precise with in colour and size. He described the natural as 'a little fiend in fly's shape' and is perhaps his only fly with a wing.

Glas Cwta (*Dee pattern*)
Iron blue dun (Plate 10)

Hook: 14
Silk: Claret
Body: Claret quill
Hackle: Almost black with brown tips

This fly has its origins in the Harlech area but is a popular iron blue imitation on rivers in the Dee valley.

Iron Blue (*Harry Powell*)
Iron blue dun (Plate 10)

Hook: 14 – 16
Silk: Crimson
Whisks: Iron-blue cock hackle fibres
Body: Dubbed mole fur – tying silk to form red tip at tail
Hackle: Iron blue cock hackle

A remarkably effective fly: one of the most popular fly patterns of the Welsh Borderlands.

Iron Blue (*John Henderson*)
Iron blue dun (Plate 10)

Hook: 14
Silk: Purple or claret
Whisks: Light dun cock hackle fibres
Body: Fibres from cock pheasant tail dyed dark blue
Rib: Fine gold wire or claret silk
Hackles: Medium dun cock with two turns of hen hackle dyed dark blue

Iron Blue nymph (*John Henderson*)
Iron blue nymph (Plate 10)

Hook: 14
Silk: Purple or claret
Whisks: Three short fibres of medium dun hen hackle
Body: Fibres from cock pheasant tail dyed dark blue
Rib: Claret tying silk
Hackle: Two turns of small feather from jackdaw's throat

These two patterns were created by John Henderson for use on the Ashford House beat of the Usk in mid-April to the end of May. The nymph pattern is most effective, especially during a big hatch of iron blues.

Knotted Midge (*unknown*)
'Pairing' black gnats (Plate 10)

Hook: 14 – 20
Thread: Black
Body: Black thread
Hackles: Two small black cock hackles, one at either end of body

This is a most effective fly designed to represent a pair of black gnats locked in their tail-to-tail copulating position. Cyril Hancock advocated that one should always carry copies of this fly for what he delightfully called 'the frequent summer days of persistent Black Gnatitude.'

Landrail & Rabbit (*Rev. Edward Powell*)
General-purpose nymph (Plate 10)

Hook: 14
Body: Buff rabbit neck
Hackle: Landrail

One of his lesser-known flies; probably a general-purpose nymph pattern.

Large Dark Olive (*John Henderson*)
Large dark olive (Plate 10)

Hook: 12 – 14
Silk: Olive
Whisks: Three fibres from medium rusty dun cock hackle feather
Body: Heron herl or mouse fur
Rib: Olive silk or fine gold wire
Hackle: Rusty dun cock

Large Dark Olive nymph (*John Henderson*)
Large dark olive nymph (Plate 11)

Hook: 12 – 14
Silk: Olive
Whisks/Body: Three fibres from blue gamecock tail feather, the points forming the tail and the remainder wound up the body to the shoulder to form the abdomen
Rib: Olive silk
Thorax: Mouse fur
Hackle: Small dun hen hackle – two turns

Flyfishing for trout on the Usk starts in March and the fly for early season forays is the Large Dark Olive. These patterns come from John Henderson.

Large Whirling Dun (*Lascelles*)
An early season fly (Plate 11)

Hook: 12
Silk: Yellow
Body: Blue squirrel fur mixed with yellow marten

PLATE 11

Large Dark Olive Nymph, Large Whirling Dun, Leslie Peters' Special
Llyn Du, March Brown (Bowlker), March Brown (male)
March Brown (female), March Brown (Coombs), Edmond's March Brown
March Brown (Evans), March Brown (Hancock), March Brown (Rev. E. Powell)

Hackle: Brown partridge
Wing: Starling

An old fly pattern from the Usk that has, over time, become a firm favourite with anglers above Brecon. It is a fly for the opening months of the season and is usually the middle fly on a three-fly cast.

Leslie Peters' Special (*Leslie Peters*)
Duns or pupae (Plate 11)

Hook: 12 – 14
Silk: Yellow
Whisks: Honey dun
Body: Orange and natural wool mixed with tying silk visible through body
Hackle: Honey dun tied parachute style

A remarkably modern style of fly from the doyen of Brecon flyfishers, Leslie Peters – this is reputed to be a marvellous fly for the Usk glides where parachute style flies work supremely well.

Llyn Du (*Louis Noble*)
An attractor pattern (Plate 11)

Hook: 12 – 16
Silk: Black
Tail: Lady Amherst pheasant tippets
Body: Rear half – flat silver tinsel, front half – black seal's fur with silver wire rib
Hackle: White henny-cock – tied beard style and full
Wing: Well marked guinea fowl or teal

Originally tied by Louis Noble in the 1970s for lake fishing in the hills above Newtown, the Llyn Du is an attractor wet fly pattern, which in smaller sizes passes for a buzzer.

MARCH BROWN

The March Brown (*Rhithogena germanica*) is one of the most famous flies known to anglers and is one of the oldest artificial patterns. Dressings date back to Bowlker (1747) and have changed very little since that time. The natural used to hatch in vast numbers in March and April on Welsh Borderland rivers, but in recent years numbers have declined significantly. I have discovered the following regional patterns for the dun and nymphal stages.

March Brown (*Richard Bowlker*)
March Brown (Plate 11)

Hook: 12
Body: Hare's fur
Rib: Yellow silk
Wing: Partridge or pheasant

March Brown (*male*) (*Mr Acheson*)
March Brown (Plate 11)

Hook: 12
Body: Dirty orange wool
Rib: Gold wire (optional)
Hackle: Brown partridge
Wing: Freckled partridge tail

March Brown (*female) (Mr Acheson*)
March Brown (Plate 11)

Hook: 12
Body: Dark olive wool
Rib: Gold wire (optional)
Hackle: Brown partridge
Wing: Hen pheasant

March Brown (*Ted Coombes*)
March Brown (Plate 11)

Hook: 12 – 14
Whisks: Partridge hackle fibres
Body: Rabbit fur
Rib: Oval gold tinsel
Hackle: Brown partridge hackle

According to Michael Leighton, Ted Coombes of Tenbury Wells produced a popular wet March Brown pattern whose correct dressing, sadly, has proved hard to find. James Evans suggests the pattern above might be typical of Coombes' style.

Edmond's March Brown (*Edmonds*)
March Brown (Plate 11)

Hook: 12
Body: Orange silk dubbed with rabbit neck fur lightly tinged with red
Hackle: Mottled brown feather from snipe rump

This fly has a local following on the tributaries of the Severn and Wye.

March Brown (*Major J. D. D. Evans*)
March Brown nymph (Plate 11)

Hook: 12
Tail: White gallina (cock hackle fibres dyed dark sepia or reddish-brown)
Rib: Fine gold wire
Body: Dub half hook length with a mixture of black rabbit and seal fur, claret seal fur and a small amount of fiery-brown fur
Wing cases: Six dark fibres (e.g. turkey) varnished when tied in
Thorax: Large 'hump' of body dubbing mixture

Major J. D. D. Evans lived at Ffrwdgrech near Brecon in the 1930s and was described by Courtney-Williams as the foremost amateur trout entomologist of his time, and who apparently described the Rev. Edward Powell's flies as 'fuzzy wuzzie.' He bred game fowl and was a contemporary of John Henderson at Ashford House.

The major invented this dressing for the nymph which is most effective in the early months of the season.

March Brown (*Cyril Hancock*)
March Brown (Plate 11)

Hook: 10 – 12
Whisks: Brown partridge
Body: Yellow seal's fur
Rib: Round gold tinsel
Hackle: Brown partridge hackle

Cyril Hancock originally tied this wet fly version for use on the Dee and its tributaries during April. However it is a most useful pattern throughout the region.

March Brown (*Rev. Edward Powell*)
March Brown (Plate 11)

Hook: 12 – 14
Whisks: Brown cock hackle fibres
Body: Dark/reddish rabbit flank fur
Hackles: Head – snipe rump feather; shoulder – pale ginger cock dyed brown or two large brown partridge hackles

The Rev. Powell produced this fly for when trout were feeding on the natural and wouldn't take one of his general-purpose patterns.

March Brown (*John Henderson*)
March Brown (Plate 12)

Hook: 12
Silk: Brown
Whisks: Tips of four fibres of cock pheasant tail
Body: The remainder of the tail fibres wound up to near eye of hook
Rib: Fairly thick buff-coloured silk
Hackles: Head – brown partridge back feather. Shoulder – rusty dun cock

Silver March Brown (*Leslie Peters*)
March Brown (Plate 12)

Hook: 12 – 14
Whisks: Pheasant tail fibres
Body: Flat silver tinsel
Thorax: Red seal's fur
Hackles: Grey partridge neck hackle

This is Leslie Peters' variation of this well-known fly,

PLATE 12

March Brown (Henderson), Silver March Brown, March Brown Nymph (Henderson)
March Brown Nymph 1, March Brown Nymph 2,
Mayfly, Badger May
Fore-and-Aft Mayfly, Border Mayfly

developed for use on the River Usk on those early season days when the river is running clear and cold.

March Brown Nymph (*John Henderson)*
March Brown nymph (Plate 12)

Hook: 12
Silk: Brown
Whisks: Tips of four fibres of cock pheasant tail
Body: The remainder of the tail fibres wound up to shoulder
Rib: Fine gold wire
Thorax: Mixture in thirds of – dark hare's ear, red cow hair, dark olive seal's fur dubbing
Hackles: Head – brown partridge back feather; Shoulder – rusty dun cock

Living beside the Usk at Ashford House John Henderson had time to study the elusive March Brown and these imitations of the dun and nymph are the result.

March Brown Nymph 1 (*unknown*)
March Brown nymph (Plate 12)

Hook: 12
Silk: Claret
Tail: Honey dun whisks
Body: Claret seal's fur
Rib: Gold wire
Legs: Dark honey dun
Wing case: Pheasant tail herl, tied over

March Brown Nymph 2 (*unknown*)
March Brown nymph (Plate 12)

Hook: 12
Silk: Yellow
Tail: Two strands pheasant tail
Body: Orange silk
Rib: Gold wire
Thorax: Yellow seal's fur
Legs: Partridge hackle
Wing case: Pheasant tail herl, tied over

Two patterns for one of the better-known nymphs that used to be common on many rivers in the region. The nymph is a stone clinger and so prefers rivers with stony or gravelly beds. In early season there is little doubt that the fish prefer the nymph to the dun.

MAYFLY

Mayflies (*Ephemera danica*) appear on most Welsh Borderland rivers and brooks towards the end of May for about three weeks. For a variety of reasons today's numbers are nothing like those of the past but even so the mayfly is a significant food source for fish and it would be a foolish flyfisher who failed to carry one or two imitations. My research uncovered the following patterns with roots in the region; they all represent either the dun or spinner stages.

Mayfly (*Michael Leighton*)
Mayfly (Plate 12)

Hook: 10 long shank
Silk: Orange

Whisks: Honey cock hackle fibres
Body: White ostrich herl
Rib: Brown sewing thread
*Hackles: Hot orange cock hackle wound in open turns with honey
cock hackle wound through it and olive cock hackle in front*

A pattern developed by Michael Leighton for the River
Roden. Sadly, this river is a mere shadow of its former glory
because of pollution.

Badger May (*Alan Hudson)*
Mayfly (Plate 12)

Hook: 10
Silk: Black
Whisks: Plymouth Rock cock hackle fibres
Body: Yellow labrador fur
Rib: Black silk
Hackles: Large badger cock and red cock wound together

This is one of Alan Hudson's patterns which he devised to
imitate the Mayfly for use on the enchanting River Clun.

Fore-and-Aft Mayfly (David Jacques)
Mayfly (Plate 12)

Hook: 12 long shank
Silk: Brown
Body: Pale raffia
*Hackles: Short olive cock at the eye and a long-fibred olive cock
hackle at the bend of the hook.*

David Jacques was a well-known angling entomologist and
author of numerous articles in the angling press. It is likely
that it was he who first popularised reversed-hackle flies

with his rudimentary but very effective Fore-and-Aft Mayfly.

This pattern was 'rediscovered' by James Evans in a fishing magazine whilst he was weather-bound in a fishing lodge, and provided him with the inspiration to develop his own Border Mayfly.

Border Mayfly (*James Evans*)
Mayfly (Plate 12)

Hook: 12 long shank
Silk: Brown
Body: Natural condor herl
Hackle: Large olive and orange at the bend, small ones in the same colours at the eye

This fly illustrates James Evans' firm conviction in the efficacy of multiple hackling.

Dulas Brook Mayfly (*Ron Pomfret*)
Mayfly (Plate 13)

Hook: 10
Whisks: A bunch of blue/olive dun hackle fibres, as long as the shaft of hook
Body: Sisal, dyed green-yellow in 10% picric acid
Hackles: Two long blue/olive dun hackles, tied in at the bend of the hook

This substantial reverse-hackled and tailed fly, described by its originator as 'a back-to-front affair,' was first tied for use on the Dulas Brook, a delightful small tributary of the River Dore, close to Ewyas Harold.

Ron Pomfret has been a life-long flyfisher, a member and one-time Secretary of the Piscatorial Society. When living in Herefordshire he fished the Lugg, Arrow, Dore and Dulas Brook.

PLATE 13

Dulus Brook Mayfly, Grizzly Mayfly
Midget Mayfly
Medium Olive (Henderson), Medium Olive (Hudson)
Medium Olive (Rev. E. Powell), Medium Olive Nymph, Model 52

Coincidentally Ron's family owned the property in Usk used by Harry Powell as a barber's shop. He moved to Llandetty Hall, near Talybont-on-Usk in the 1950s where he was a near neighbour of John Henderson at Ashford House, whose beat he fished. Another of his life-long interests is breeding Old English Game Fowl, some of which were kept for him by Gordon Price who lived close by at Worcester Cottage. He has provided a wealth of information for this book especially with regard to John Henderson and his flies. Ron lives in Abergavenny and still breeds Old English Game.

Grizzly Mayfly (*Peter Flint*)
Mayfly (Plate 13)

Hook: 10 – 12
Silk: Brown
Hackles: Palmered Cree cock hackle – long fibred feather, the stiffer the better

This remarkably simple yet effective fly was tied by Peter Flint after he had experienced an unsuccessful morning with Cosmo Barrett's Professor during a Mayfly hatch. (Note the comment about stiffness of hackle.)

Midget Mayfly (*Cyril Hancock*)
Mayfly (Plate 13)

Hook: 12
Silk: Brown
Body: Raffia
Rib: Silver twist
Hackles: White cock and olive cock wound together

This is one of C.V. Hancock's patterns developed for use on the Lugg and Teme.

MEDIUM OLIVE

The medium olive (*Baetis rhodani*) is without doubt one of the most important flies for fish and flyfishers alike. It is found on the water every month of the year and is common throughout the Welsh Borderlands.

Medium Olive (*John Henderson*)
Medium olive dun (Plate 13)

Hook: 14
Silk: Light olive
Whisks: Five or six fibres of honey dun cock hackle
Body: Heron or goose quill dyed olive
Rib: Fine gold wire
Hackle: Medium dun cock hackle

Medium Olive (*Alan Hudson*)
Medium olive dun (Plate 13)

Hook: 14 – 16
Silk: Black
Whisks: Plymouth Rock cock hackle fibres
Body: Rabbit's fur – mix of under-fur and guard hairs
Hackle: Plymouth Rock cock hackle

Medium Olive (*Rev. Edward Powell*)
Medium olive dun (Plate 13)

Hook: 14
Body: Light rabbit flank fur with a pinch of jade green mole fur
Hackle: Two medium blue dun hen hackles

Medium Olive Nymph (*John Henderson*)
Medium olive nymph (Plate 13)

Hook: 14
Silk: Pale olive
Whisks: Three fibres tips of blue game cock tail feathers dyed light yellow
Body: The remainder of the tail fibres wound up to the shoulder
Rib: Fine gold wire or waxed olive silk
Thorax: Mouse fur
Hackle: Two turns of small dun hen

Model 52 (*Rev. Edward Powell*)
Black gnat (Plate 13)

Hook: 16
Body: Black sewing cotton
Hackle: Black cock cut short, above and below the wing
Wing: Very small thrush primary tied flat

Devised by the parson and first used on the Onny on 21st July 1952, originally on a Model Perfect size 16 hook – hence its name.

Morfa Dun (*Tony Bostock*)
General spinner pattern (Plate 14)

Hook: 14
Silk: Black
Whisks: Rhode Island Red hen hackle fibres
Body: Sheep's wool
Rib: Black silk
Hackle: Rhode Island Red hen hackle (cock hackle for dry-fly)

Tony Bostock assembled this fly from the pickings of a

PLATE 14

Morfa Dun, Natural Dun,
Blue Needle, Ginger Needle, Olive Emerger
Olive Quill Gnat, Onny Perlid, Orange Dun Hackle
Orange Otter

barbed-wire fence and a henhouse during a wet interlude in a caravan holiday in West Wales, and named it for the farm where he gathered the ingredients. It is possible to replace the hen hackle with cock – making a dry fly variant. He admits the similarity of this fly to a wingless Coachman.

Tony is currently the Trust Director of The Severn Rivers' Trust which has been set up to improve the management of the rivers, streams, water courses and impoundments of the Severn and Teme catchments for the benefit of the public generally as well as the conservation of the natural heritage.

Natural Dun (*William Law*)
Yellow upright spinner (Plate 14)

Hook: 12 – 14
Whisks: Blue dun hackle
Body: Rabbit
Rib: Oval silver
Hackle: Blue dun

William Law was keeper on the Buckland Estate water on the Usk.

NEEDLE FLY

Blue Needle (*Len Hewittson*)
Needle fly (Plate 14)

Hook: 16 – 20
Silk: Orange
Body: Orange tying silk
Hackle: Blue dun cock hackle

Ginger Needle (*Len Hewittson*)
Needle fly (Plate 14)

As above but using a ginger cock hackle.

These two needle fly patterns are the handiwork of Len Hewittson for use on the upper reaches of the Ceiriog. They are both very effective when the fish are feeding on natural needle flies – small dark stoneflies found on swift flowing rocky rivers in summer and autumn.

Olive Emerger (*Mark Roberts*)
Generic Olive (Plate 14)

Hook: Oliver Edwards emerger hook K14ST size 16
Thread: White sheer 14/0
Tail: 4 or 5 Antron fibres, cut short and dyed moss green with dye pen
Rib: Body material dyed olive brown with dye pen
Body: Clear translucent body (Tyers' Mate) dyed moss green, over white tying silk. Similar to body quills from Hends Products
Hackle: Good quality red game saddle or cock, tied parachute style

This modern-day fly is the handiwork of Mark Roberts who designed it for use on the Usk. It can be tied in any size and coloured with dye pen to match the hatch. The tail gives the impression of a shuck and the body, when viewed from below, is translucent. Inspired by J. W. Dunne's book *Sunshine and the Dry Fly*.

Olive Quill Gnat (*Walter Gallichan*)
Olive dun (Plate 14)

Hook: 14 – 16
Whisks: Dyed medium or dark olive cock hackle

Body: Peacock quill – dyed olive
Hackle: Medium or dark olive cock hackle
Wings: Medium or dark starling's wing feather

Another fly from Walter Gallichan, who seldom divulged the dressings of his creations in print. This one imitates the natural olive dun and care must be taken to ensure the wing colour is on the darker side.

Onny Perlid (*Rev. Edward Powell*)
Willow fly (Plate 14)

Hook: 14
Body: Nearly black rusty sheep's wool tied with a distinct thorax and short thinner abdomen
Hackles: Shoulder hackle (behind thorax) – light brown hen; Head hackle (in front of thorax) – light blue hen

After much experimentation Rev. Powell settled for this dressing for his imitation of an early season willow fly that he had observed on the Onny.

Orange Dun Hackle (*Walter Gallichan*)
Orange dun (Plate 14)

Hook: 14
Silk: Hot orange
Whisks: Deep red cock hackle fibre
Body: Hot orange tying silk
Hackle: Deep red cock hackle
Wing: Starling

The details of this pattern are the result of Alan Hudson's research into Walter Gallichan's flies. This fly, one of

Gallichan's favourites, was originally an old late season Yorkshire pattern

In *Fishing in Wales* Gallichan gives the following dressing, which may have been intended to imitate the same natural fly.

Body: Dull orange silk
Hackle: Sooty cock hackle

Orange Otter (*Rev. Edward Powell*)
Soldier beetle (Plate 14)

Hook: 14 - 16 (long shank)
Silk: Orange or hot orange
Whisks: Red cock
Hackle: Placed centrally, about ten turns of a long feather with short-fibred wild red jungle cock
Body: Soft under-pelt of otter dyed orange in picric acid and red ink – tied full and blobby especially at the tail

This famous pattern from Rev. Powell was developed to imitate the soldier beetle. The 1934 prototype had orange wool for body parts and no whisks. However, over the next ten years the parson evolved (in his words) this 'phenomenal' or 'devastating' pattern. He declared that it was the only hackled dry fly he used successfully for grayling whilst also being the only fly that would bring grayling up from the bottom when they are not on the feed. He even went as far as saying that 'it is so deadly that I am sometimes sorry I ever invented it.' The pattern has stood the test of time and is still a very successful fly, which over the years has accounted for countless fish.

PLATE 15

Pale Olive (Henderson), Pale Olive (Pomfret), Pale Watery or Caenis
Palmer's Big Daddy
Paragon, Parry's Stonefly, Pet
Peter's Peril, Pheasant Tail (Flint), Pheasant Tail (Henderson)

Pale Olive (*John Henderson*)
Pale watery dun (Plate 15)

Hook: 16
Whisks: Tips of light blue dun feather fibres from body
Body: Light blue dun cock tail feather fibres
Rib: Silver wire or tinsel
Hackle: Medium blue dun cock

This Henderson pattern imitates the grey pale-bodied flies that hatch on the Usk in mid-summer.

Pale Olive (*Ron Pomfret*)
Pale watery dun (Plate 15)

Hook: 16 – shank painted with white enamel and covered with white plastic from a supermarket bag
Whisks: Medium cock hackle fibres
Body: Light rabbit fur from side of wild rabbit
Rib: Silver wire or tinsel
Hackle: Lightish medium dun cock

Ron Pomfret tied this fly for the River Arrow, adapted from John Henderson's pattern for the same natural. The purpose of the white hook shank is to prevent the body from becoming too dark when wet.

Pale Watery or Caenis (*Rev. Edward Powell*)
Pale watery dun (Plate 15)

Hook: 14-16 – shank painted with white enamel after being brazed by boiling in soda
Silk: White
Whisks: Pale olive or cream
Body: One strand palest biscuit coloured artificial silk wound

over the painted hook shank
Rib: Primrose tying silk
Hackle: Palest olive cock, clipped to size
Wings: Two tips of breast feathers of a very pale silvery-blue hen,
shaped with scissors and tied in back to back

A relatively complicated pattern devised by Parson Powell after he had had some frustrating times trying to imitate these small yet important naturals.

Palmer's Big Daddy (*David Palmer*)
Crane fly (Plate 15)

Hook: 10 Partridge Flashpoint SUD
Tail: Coq de Leon saddle, light pardo, dyed ginger
Hackle: Coq de Leon saddle, light pardo, dyed ginger
Body: Fiery brown cock pheasant tail
Legs: Three sets of centipede legs from Veniard or Orvis (see note below)
Wing post: Natural snowshoe rabbit foot

In designing this fly David Palmer was mindful of three things – his desire to fish a dry fly, the lack of *Ephemeroptera* countrywide, and his failing eyesight. The product of his labours is a highly successful lifelike fly that draws fish up from the depths of a wide variety of waters. He also suggests the importance of using a substantial leader (7lb or more) in order to reduce the spin and kinking of the leader which may occur with such a large fly.

(Note for tying in legs: The front set of legs tied in close to the wing post is made from half a hank of centipede legs and the rear two sets are made from a quarter of a hank.)

Paragon (*Rev. Edward Powell*)
Sedge fly (Plate 15)

Hook: 12 –16
Whisks: 3 or 4 dark red cock fibres
Body: Rabbit face fur, very full. Equal quantities of brown and black mixed together
Hackles: Two Rhode Island Red hen hackles – purple chocolate approx. 10 turns

Originally designed as a dark sedge imitation, the Rev. Powell used this fly as a general pattern throughout the season. Undoubtedly it is a modification of a Dai Lewis original. The natural sedge does not have tails, but the addition of the whisks does make the fly float better. It was top of the parson's fly league, taking one thousand, nine hundred and eighteen fish over a six year period!

Parry's Stonefly (*unknown*)
February Red (Plate 15)

Hook: 14
Body: Claret quill
Hackle: Dark rusty dun cock

A very effective yet straightforward pattern for use on the River Dee.

Pet (*C.V. Hancock*)
Peter Ross variant (Plate 15)

Hook: 8 – 15
Body: Rear half – narrow oval silver tinsel; Front half – scarlet seal's fur ribbed with silver tinsel
Hackle: Black henny-cock hackle with a good 'spring' about it

This Peter Ross variant has proved to be most effective for trout and grayling when fished wet as a bob fly in smaller sizes. When dressed on a size 8 hook it has even accounted for salmon on the Dee.

Peter's Peril (*Peter Flint*)
Caterpillar or similar (Plate 15)

Hook: 12 long shank
Silk: Brown
Body: A strip of un-vulcanised white rubber about 3/8" wide and the length of the shank plus 1/4" long, tied into the bend of hook with 1/4" as tail, then big open turns of silk to produce a segmented body.
Hackle: Grey partridge

A peculiar pattern designed by Peter Flint of Presteigne to imitate those caterpillars that plop into the water from overhanging branches in high summer. Ethafoam makes a useful alternative for body but needs a little added weight in the form of copper or lead wire to allow it to ride in the water's surface.

PHEASANT TAIL

The Pheasant Tail is one of the oldest patterns for all-round fishing and possibly the most useful all-purpose fly in existence – it can be fished either wet or dry. It is thought to have its origins in Devon but it is not surprising to find a number of Welsh Borderland patterns. (See also entries for the Herefordshire Pheasant Tail, Shropshire Pheasant Tail.)

Pheasant Tail (*Flint*) (*Peter Flint*)
Ephemera spinner (Plate 15)

Hook: 14
Silk: Red
Whisks: Three fibres from golden pheasant red spear hackle
Body: Medium claret seal's fur or wool
Rib: Red tying silk
Hackles: Blue dun cock hackle at the bend and then a red/brown cock hackle

Rather different from the norm, this pattern from Peter Flint of Presteigne is a reverse-hackled fly.

Pheasant Tail (*Henderson*) (*John Henderson*)
Ephemera spinner (Plate 15)

Hook: 12 – 14
Silk: Orange
Whisks: Five or six fibres brassy dun cock hackle
Body: Three cock pheasant tail fibres twisted together and wound up the shank
Rib: Fine gold wire
Hackle: Brassy dun cock hackle

Pheasant Tail (*Jones*) (*Ted Jones*)
Ephemera spinner (Plate 16)

Hook: 14 – 16
Tail: Three pheasant tail fibres – splayed out well
Body: Coarse black cotton
Hackle: Rhode Island Red cock hackle

This is a pattern from the vice of Ted Jones of Bangor-on-Dee (of Bangor Duster fame) for use on the rivers Ceiriog

PLATE 16

Pheasant Tail (Jones), Pheasant Tail Nymph, Pheasant Tail Nymph (Henderson)
Pink Paragon, Polo Nymph, Price's Pride
Quill Polo Nymph
Rabbit Nymph, Red Ass, Red Grizzly

and Dee. This is a straightforward but yet effective pattern: a 'sure-fire' trout catcher.

Pheasant Tail Nymph (*unknown*)
Ephemera nymph (Plate 16)

Hook: 10 – 12
Silk: Hot orange
Body and tail: Rusty pheasant tail fires
Rib: Gold wire
Thorax: Hare's ear fur

A pattern developed for up-river presentation on a floating line on those cold early-season days on the Usk.

Pheasant Tail Nymph (*John Henderson*)
Ephemera nymph (Plate 16)

Hook: 12 – 14
Silk: Light brown
Whisks: Three fibre tips of cock pheasant tail
Body: The remainder of the tail fibres wound up to the shoulder
Rib: Fine gold wire
Thorax: Dark fiery brown seal's fur
Hackle: Two turns of dark dun hen

Another early-season John Henderson pattern for the Usk.

Pink Paragon (*Rev. Edward Powell*)
Blue-winged olive (Plate 16)

Hook: 14 – 16
Whisks: Three or four fibres dark red cock feather
Body: Well mixed fur from rabbit's face
Hackles: Blue Andalusian cock hackle with Rhode Island Red hen hackle wound in front of it

This is a modified version of the Paragon and RB Sedge which the Rev. Powell used to imitate the fiendishly difficult blue-winged olives.

Polo Nymph (*Peter Flint*)
Ephemera nymph (Plate 16)

Hook: 14
Silk: Fawn
Tail plus wing cases: Six strands of cock pheasant tail feather
Abdomen: Lead under golden yellow Pearsall's Floss silk ribbed with tying silk
Thorax: Browny-green (greengage-coloured) wool

Peter Flint's best-known fly came into existence by pure accident. An old polo neck sweater happened to be hanging by his fly-tying bench and its browny-green colouring with a little yellow and a pinch of bright red provided the material for the thorax. This colour is probably impossible to reproduce!

Price's Pride (*Gordon Price*)
Beetle (Plate 16)

Hook: 12
Body: Peacock herl

Hackle: Saddle badger with black centre

Gordon Price, gillie on the Worcester Cottage beat, lived beside the River Usk at Llangynidr, where he kept some of Ron Pomfret's Old English Game Fowl. In his late fifties he became interested in fly-tying, and for a number of years he tied flies for the guests at Gliffaes Hotel. He has two patterns of his own creation; Price's Pride and Troubleoff's Fancy, and is believed to have been the first person to tie the Usk Naylor, a fly invented by Mr P. Naylor (owner of Worcester Cottage) in the 1950s

Quill Polo Nymph (*James Evans*)
Nymph (Plate 16)

Hook: 14
Tail plus wing: Four strands cock pheasant centre tail – doubled and re-doubled for wing cases
Abdomen: Stripped peacock quill over a silver Lurex under-body, the turns of the former only just touching so that a glimmer of silver can be seen to sparkle between them
Thorax: Browny-green seal's fur, with a pinch of black

Based on Peter Flint's Polo Nymph, James Evans named this pattern, saying of it, 'This is a nymph pattern whose effectiveness is such that it would be a disservice to my readers were I to fail to include it.' Flat silver tinsel is a suitable substitute for the Lurex mentioned in the original pattern.

Rabbit Nymph (*David Palmer*)
Nymph (Plate 16)

Hook: 10 Partridge Czech nymph
Tail: Rabbit guard hairs

Tag: Fluorescent red (or yellow) floss
Underbody: Medium lead wire
Body: Rabbit fur
Hackle: Rabbit guard hairs tied in a loop

This is another modern pattern developed by David Palmer for use the Ceiriog, Teme, Onny and Clun. It accounts for many fish throughout the season.

Red Ass (*unknown*)
Heather fly (Plate 16)

Hook: 14 – 16
'Ass': Red ibis
Body: Peacock herl
Hackle: Grizzle cock hackle

This once-popular pattern on the Dee and Ceiriog may have been a variation on the Red-tailed Green Insect, designed to imitate the heather fly.

Red Grizzly (*Michael Leighton*)
Variant of Grizzly Bourne (Plate 16)

Hook: 10 – 18
Silk: Palest primrose
Whisks: Honey cock hackle fibres
Body: Red, or orange floss silk – tapered
Rib: Tying silk
Hackles: Red/brown cock hackle wound through a grizzle cock hackle

Michael Leighton states that this variation on his Grizzly Bourne works throughout the season whatever fly happens to be on the water, and would be his 'one-and-only pattern' if he had to have one. It can be fished either as a dry fly or awash in the surface film and is equally effective for trout and in the smaller sizes, grayling.

Red Tag (*Thomas Flynn)*
Willow fly (Plate 17)

Hook: 14 – 18
Tag: Bright red wool
Body: Green peacock herl
Hackle: Red/brown cock hackle

This famous fly originated in Worcestershire on the banks of the River Teme and was probably the invention of Thomas Flynn in about 1850 when it was called the Worcestershire Gem. Around 1878 it made its way to Yorkshire, acquired an orange tag and changed its name to Orange Tag and then to Treacle Parkin before returning to Worcestershire where it was re-named the Worcestershire Wonder.

Originally a wet grayling fancy pattern, it is nowadays usually fished either as a wet or dry fly for trout or grayling. It is reputed to be a fly for which fish either go mad or totally ignore!

(See Chapter 6 for the poem *The Song of the Red Tag*.)

Red-tailed Green Insect (*unknown)*
Grayling fly (Plate 17)

Hook: 14 – 16
Tail: Red ibis substitute
Body: Peacock herl
Hackle: White cock hackle

This fly was popular on streams of Clwyd in the late 1940s and bears a close resemblance to the Red Ass as well as to the Grayling Witch.

PLATE 17

Red Tag, Red-tailed Green Insect, Ridgeback Nymph
Roden Fly, Sander's Special, Severn Ke
Shropshire Pheasant Tail, Silver Twist, Simple Simon
Small Yellow Sally, Smokey Blue, Snowshoe Emerger

Ridgeback Nymph (*Alan Hudson*)
Nymph (Plate 17)

Hook: 12 – 14 long shank
Thread: Black or brown
Head: Gold or copper tungsten bead
Tail: Well-barred olive wood duck
Abdomen: Pale red fox squirrel with a pinch of fluorescent pink SLF
Rib: Fine gold wire
Thorax: 40% dark red fox squirrel, 40% hare's ear, 20% brown SLF

This relatively modern dressing from Alan Hudson of Chirk derives its name from having Rhodesian Ridgeback fur in earlier versions; the resulting fly is said to be most devastating. The gold head is used for coloured water and the copper head for clear water.

Roden Fly (*Michael Leighton*)
Alder fly (Plate 17)

Hook: 12 – 14
Silk: Orange
Whisks: Four golden pheasant tippets, sticking out half length of body
Body: Green peacock herl
Hackle: Light fawn henny-cock – long fibred
Wing: Hen pheasant secondary wing feather no longer than the body

Originally tied by Michael Leighton for use on the Roden when the Alder flies begin to appear. He reports that it is best fished in the surface film and is effective even when other flies are hatching.

Sanders' Special (*Walter Sanders*)
Trout and grayling fly (Plate 17)

Hook: 14
Body: White floss silk
Rib: Oval gold tinsel
Wings: Starling
Hackle: Cinnamon henny-cock hackle

This fly is a favourite old Teme pattern.

Severn Ke (*unknown*)
Grayling fly (Plate 17)

Hook: 16 – 18
Tail: Red fluorescent wool on top of golden pheasant tippets
Body: Peacock herl
Hackle: White cock

This fly, used by grayling anglers on the upper Severn around Llanidloes, is a variant of the Ke-he, a popular Orkney trout fly. Tied on a size 12 hook and with two hackles it can cope with swift flowing water, whilst for slacker water a lightly dressed version is better. The white hackle is certainly a great help in the poor light conditions which are so often the norm when grayling fishing.

Shropshire Pheasant Tail (*unknown*)
Back-end fly (Plate 17)

Hook: 14 – 16
Silk: Brown
Whisks: Four white cock hackle fibres, well splayed out
Body: Single strand of pheasant tail fibre
Hackle: Furnace cock hackle

Referred to as a 'back-end fly' by the gentleman that introduced it to Michael Leighton, this pattern is meant to be especially effective in low water conditions.

Silver Twist (*unknown*)
Blue dun (Plate 17)

Hook: 12 – 14
Body: Rabbit's blue under-fur
Rib: Silver twist
Hackle: Blue dun cock hackle, palmered from bend to eye

This old Teme grayling pattern was used by the Rev. Powell in his early days, before he came under the influence of Dai Lewis. It is especially useful for grayling and is usually fished as the top dropper but can also be effective on the point with a little weight under the body and fished as a nymph.

Simple Simon (*A. Courtney-Williams*)
June bug (Plate 17)

Hook: 10 – 14
Body: Peacock herl tipped with a turn of gold tinsel
Hackles: Red cock hackle with a sparse short white hackle behind it

This Courtney-Williams pattern is a hybrid of a Coch-y-bonddu and a Coachman which came into being on the banks of the River Lugg.

Small Yellow Sally (*James Evans*)
Small yellow Sally (Plate 17)

Hook: 14 – 16
Body: Yellow un-stripped condor herl
Hackles: Yellow cock and cream badger cock hackles – twisted together and wound on

A conventionally dressed fly from James Evans representing the small yellow stonefly which is to be found throughout the region, particularly on the upland streams.

Smokey Blue (*Pryce-Tannatt*)
Iron blue/dark olives (Plate 17)

Hook: 14 – 16
Body: Mole fur
Hackle: Covert feather from water hen wing

This is a useful Pryce-Tannatt wet fly, tied for the upper Severn area for use as an early season fly as well as a grayling pattern in the autumn.

Snowshoe Emerger (*Mark Roberts*)
Dark olive (Plate 17)

Hook: 14 – 16 Varivas T-2000 terrestrial
Thread: White sheer 14/0 (later dyed moss green with dye pen)
Rib: Three turns of fine dual 'Peacock and Copper' mylar tinsel
Thorax: Rabbit face fur dubbed as a split thread dubbing loop
Wing: Snowshoe rabbit foot tied as a post and cut short
Hackle: Good quality red game saddle or cock tied parachute style

This modern pattern from Mark Roberts uses new materials

and techniques. It was developed on the Usk to take fish that were feeding on emerging dark olives, and has been found to work throughout the season when olives are hatching. It must be fished with a drag-free drift.

Soldier Beetle (*Rev. Edward Powell*)
Soldier beetle (Plate 18)

Hook: 12 – 14
Body: A white plumelet from the outer edge of a goose primary feather dyed orange with picric acid and red ink – wound on as a quill, or alternatively, orange otter fur
Hackles: Two light furnace or coch-y-bonddu hackles

During the years spent developing the Orange Otter the Rev. Powell made a separate pattern to represent the soldier beetle – hence the similarities.

Southam's Silver Twist (*Mrs Southam*)
Floating attractor fly (Plate 18)

Hook: 14 – 16
Whisks: Badger cock hackle fibres
Body: Oval silver tinsel
Wing: Dark starling or pale starling wing
Hackle: Badger cock hackle

Members of the Southam family fished the River Tanat for many years and devised two fly patterns for use on it, which were dressed by Morrisons of Wrexham. The two patterns are essentially the same except for the colour of the starling wing. Apparently grayling would not take the pale fly whereas the dark fly was successful with both trout and grayling.

PLATE 18

Soldier Beetle, Southam's Silver Twist, Split Willow
Squashed Beetle, Stokesay, Stonefly
Large Stonefly
Tanat Dun, Terry's Fly, Troubleoff's Fancy

Split Willow (*Rev. Edward Powell*)
Trout and grayling fly (Plate 18)

Hook: 16
Whisks: A few fibres of dark olive cock hackle
Body: Peacock quill, dyed in picric acid
Hackle: Dark olive cock – very small
Wings: A bunch of thrush primary (the part of the web above the yellow) rolled and then split to lie horizontally, tied in by a figure-of-eight lashing

Courtney-Williams calls this 'a thoroughly sensible dry fly' designed by the Rev. Powell to suggest small Perlidae, and particularly valuable for grayling during October and November. The willow fly is a member of the *Perlidae*, abundant on Border streams and affectionately named Old Besom. As an alternative to the whisks, a minute scrap of pale primrose wool may be used as a tag to suggest an egg sac.

Squashed Beetle (*Rev. Edward Powell*)
Beetle (Plate 18)

Hook: 14 – 16
Tag: Loose longish wisp of yellowish-orange wool to suggest the protruding viscera
Body: Peacock herl, dark and iridescent
Hackle: Three or four turns of green-black starling neck to represent legs and outer wing cases

This is yet another Rev. Edward Powell creation, which he devised, then abandoned after a few years, and then re-instated following particular success with it at Leintwardine on the Teme. This most effective fly was inspired by his childhood memories of examining black beetles and discovering that their innards were pale orange.

Stokesay (*C. V. Hancock*)
Ephemeridae (Plate 18)

Hook: 12 – 14
Whisks: Three strands from cock pheasant tail
Body: Dark claret cock hackle – palmered and clipped
Rib: Fine gold wire
Hackle: Rusty red cock hackle

A Welsh Borderland pattern that stands on its own merits and is Cyril Hancock's most famous fly. It derives its name from the stretch of the River Onny on which the fly had its first success. It is especially useful at mayfly time.

STONEFLIES (*Perlidae*)

Stoneflies are a major group in the insect life of the region. They are found in abundance on any of the swift flowing, stony, rain-fed rivers of the Borderlands. The nymphal stage, sometimes called a creeper, takes two or three years to develop, moulting as many as twenty times prior to crawling to the underside of stones lining the river and moulting into the imago (adult). The earliest reference to these flies in the region is in Scotcher's *The Fly Fisher's Legacy*. Research has revealed many stonefly patterns with their roots in the Borderland region.

Stonefly (*Scotcher*)
Stonefly (Plate 18)

Hook: 10
Body: Black sheep's wool mixed with 'strong yellow' wool
Rib: Waxed yellow silk
Hackle: Dark red cock

The earliest stonefly imitation from the region and made from simple materials.

Large Stonefly (*Alan Hudson*)
Stonefly (Plate 18)

Hook: 10 – 12 long shank
Silk: Black
Body: Mixture of hare's ear fur and yellow seal's fur
Rib: Gold wire
Body hackle: Palmered grizzle cock hackle
Hackles: Two grizzle cock hackles and a red cock hackle behind – twisted and wound together
Wings: Four grizzle hackle-points tied flat – extending beyond bend

This pattern was developed by Alan Hudson who copied it from a photograph in John Goddard's book *Trout Fly Recognition*. Whilst not turning out quite as he expected, it is a most successful fly nevertheless.

Tanat Dun (*Ted Painter*)
Olive dun (Plate 18)

Hook: 14 – 16
Whisks: Honey dun cock hackle fibres
Body: Condor herl, dyed medium olive
Hackles: Honey dun cock hackle with cree cock hackle wound through it

This general-purpose olive imitation was devised by Ted Painter, of Myddle near Shrewsbury, after a visit he had made to a zoo when he managed to 'procure' with the aid of a stick, a condor feather from an aviary cage floor. He dyed it with a medium olive dye to produce a rich golden/

honey tint. He then tied this fly for use on the River Tanat and found it successful throughout the trout season as well as when grayling are rising.

Terry's Fly (*Terry Carrington*)
Medium olive (Plate 18)

Hook: 14
Silk: Brown
Whisks: Honey cock hackle fibres
Body: Anchor stranded cotton no. 965 – vivid orange
Hackle: Honey cock hackle

Terry Carrington is an enthusiastic River Tanat angler who, on running out of fly-tying silk of the colour he needed, turned to the contents of a box of embroidery silks. The resulting fly is good early in the season, and has been successful on many Border streams.

Troubleoff's Fancy (*Gordon Price*)
Early season Usk fly (Plate 18)

Hook: 12 – 16
Silk: Purple
Tail: Three grizzle fibres
Body: Purple silk (very thin)
Hackles: Bright blue Andalusian cock in front of blue Andalusian hen
Head: Purple silk

This Gordon Price pattern for the Usk used to be particularly popular with residents of Gliffaes Hotel early in the season.

Ugly Alder (*A. H. York)*
Alder (Plate 19)

Hook: 12 –16
Body: Peacock herl
Hackles: Black cock hackle with grouse hackle wound in front of it

Michael Leighton's researches into the origins of this pattern involved an article in *The Shropshire Magazine* by Thurlow Craig, a glass-cased fish in The Horseshoe Inn at Llanyblodwel on the Tanat, a chimney sweep in Oswestry, and finally the factory of A. H. York in Redditch.

Usk Dark Blue (*traditional Usk pattern)*
Early/dark olives (Plate 19)

Hook: 12 – 14
Body: Mole fur
Hackle: Dark blue hen, nearly black if possible
Wing: Moorhen

This is an early season wet fly to imitate the early and dark olives that hatch on the Usk in March and April.

Usk Light Blue (*Leslie Peters)*
Olives (Plate 19)

Hook: 12 – 14
Body: Yellow wool
Hackle: Pale Andalusian hen
Wing: Starling wing

A good early season Usk pattern from Leslie Peters of Brecon. The source of the yellow wool of the original can be traced

PLATE 19

Ugly Alder, Usk Dark Blue, Usk Light Blue
Usk March Brown, Usk Naylor, Usk Purple
Wasp-Grub
Water Rat, Welsh Fusilier, Welsh Partridge

to the colour of the body material of the little toy chicks sold with Easter eggs. Their presence in the shops happily coincides with the emergence of the early olive.

Usk March Brown (*Major J. D. D. Evans*)
March Brown (Plate 19)

Hook: 10 – 12
Tail: Three fibres of white gallina (guineafowl), dyed dark sepia
Abdomen: Dub half the hook shank with a mix of black rabbit, black seal's fur and a little fiery brown fur
Thorax cover: Six fibres of any large dark feather tied over thorax dubbing – varnished after tying in and trimming
Thorax: Dub a large amount of abdomen fur mixture

A rather complex pattern from Major J. D. D. Evans, formerly one of our foremost fly-tying entomologists, who lived close by the Usk.

Usk Naylor (*Mr P. Naylor*)
Early season fly (Plate 19)

Hook: 12
Silk: Purple
Tail: Four strands bronze mallard
Butt: Purple silk
Body: Bronze mallard
Rib: Embossed gold
Hackle: Dark Andalusian

Invented by Mr P. Naylor who, in the 1950s, was tenant of the Worcester Cottage beat at Llangynidr on the Usk. It was tied by Gordon Price, the gillie on the beat, and has a great reputation as an early season Usk fly.

Usk Purple (*traditional Usk pattern*)
Iron blue nymph (Plate 19)

Hook: 12 – 14
Body: Purple floss
Hackle: Dark blue dun
Wing: Snipe wing (blue dun)

This very old Usk pattern includes the magic colour purple for which the Usk is renowned. It has the reputation of being a particular favourite early in the season, and is normally fished as a middle fly on a cast of three. (5)

Wasp-Grub (*Francis Francis*)
Wasp or other grub (Plate 19)

Hook: 6
Head: Green peacock herl
Body: Dirty white wool – copper wire underbody, tapered at both ends!

This is another fly which is important in the history of the Leintwardine Club on the River Teme. Francis Francis stated that this fly 'is almost equally killing for grayling and trout as the Grasshopper.' It closely resembles Frank Sawyer's Killer Bug and is fished in a similar fashion.

Water Rat (*Mr G. Austin*)
Iron Blue (Plate 19)

Hook: 12 – 14
Silk: Yellow
Whisks: Blue Andalusian cock hackle fibres
Body: Water rat's fur – dubbed lightly
Hackle: Blue Andalusian cock

This is a useful all-round hackled dry or wet pattern from Mr G. Austin of Birmingham, which, on smaller hook sizes, could perhaps pass for an Iron Blue. The body is dubbed very thinly to allow the yellow silk to show through.

Welsh Fusilier (*James Evans*)
Soldier beetle (Plate 19)

Hook: 12
Body: Hot orange hackle – palmered and clipped
Hackles: Hot orange, furnace and blue dun hackles

James Evans developed this fly as an imitation of the soldier beetle which appears in large numbers on streams in the region. It is an extremely good floating fly which may be useful when fish are not co-operating, particularly in sunny conditions.

Welsh Partridge (*A. Courtney-Williams*)
Sedge/Alder (Plate 19)

Hook: 12 – 14
Body: Claret seal's fur
Rib: Fine gold tinsel
Hackle: Claret cock hackle with snipe rump or partridge back-feather wound in front
Whisks: Two strands from partridge tail

A fly for the rivers of mid-Wales, designed by the father of A. Courtney-Williams, and popularised through Courtney-Williams' well-known *Dictionary of Trout Flies* with the comment that it 'will kill on any river except the chalk streams.' Quite what fish take it for is hard to establish but it is most effective when fished in the surface film and when sedge and alder are on the water.

PLATE 20

Welsh Terrier, Whirling Dun, Whiskers
White Grizzly, William Rufus, Willow Fly (Eagles)
Willow Fly (Rev. E. Powell), Wiper, Worfield Amber Beauty
Y Diawl Bach, Yellow Dun

Welsh Terrier (*James Evans*)
Reverse-hackled Dogsbody (Plate 20)

Hook: 12 – 14
Body: Fawn condor herl
Head hackle: Cream badger
Shoulder hackle: Two red cock hackles

James Evans, the creator of this most effective pattern, states that he does 'not regard this as a substitute for the standard Dogsbody but as an improved alternative on rougher water.' In essence it is a reverse-hackled Dogsbody, but James Evans felt it was so far removed from the original with condor herl and reverse hackle that it deserved a name of its own.

Whirling Dun (*Walter Gallichan*)
Blue-winged Olive (Plate 20)

Hook: 14
Body: Brown floss silk
Rib: Grey silk
Wing: Starling
Hackle: Red/brown cock hackle
Whisks: Red/brown cock hackle fibres

Another of Gallichan's patterns which has been unearthed by Alan Hudson. There is no natural fly of this name but this artificial is most effective and was thought by Major J. D. D. Evans, the entomologist, to be taken for the blue-winged olive.

Whiskers (*Harry Powell*)
An attractor fly (Plate 20)

Hook: 12 – 14
Body: Red floss

Hackle: Red game cock
Wing: Starling
Tag: Peacock herl

This pattern is always fished as a floater and is reported to be effective on the Usk and Teme especially in the mid-summer months.

White Grizzly (*Michael Leighton*)
Pale wateries (Plate 20)

Hook: 14 – 16 Capt. Hamilton featherweight
Silk: Orange
Whisks: Honey cock hackle fibres
Body: Pale honey-coloured (dyed) white rabbit fur
Rib: Close turns of Pearsall's golden-yellow floss
Hackles: Grizzle cock wound in open turns with pale badger wound behind, through, and in front of it

Another variation on Michael Leighton's Grizzly Bourne (see also Red Grizzly).

William Rufus (*James Evans*)
Variant of William's Favourite (Plate 20)

Hook: 14 – 16
Body: Crow herl, lead under-body
Hackle: Black hen hackle, tied in with the concave face forward so that the fibres have plenty of 'kick'
Tag: Fluorescent red wool

James Evans's modification of the William's Favourite tied especially for the grayling on the Lugg. It is designed to be fished as an upstream wet fly and having the hackle fibres facing forwards give it extra 'kick'.

WILLOW FLIES (*Perlidae*)

The willow fly is a species of stonefly which is abundant on some streams and rivers in the Welsh Borderlands. In flight it flutters in an ungainly manner and appears to be larger than it really is. It forms a substantial part of the fish's diet on the turbulent waters of the upland rivers and streams of the region.

Willow Fly (*Canon C. F. Eagles*)
Dark olives and iron blues (Plate 20)

Hook: 10 – 12
Body: Peacock quill
Rib: Fine silver wire
Hackle: Grizzle blue-dun hen hackle – wound from half-way down the body

This wet fly pattern used to have a tremendous reputation on the Herefordshire and South Shropshire streams and rivers. It has accounted for numerous fish over the years and has invariably been fished wet.

Willow Fly (*Rev. Edward Powell*)
Small Perlidae (Plate 20)

Hook: 16
Body: House mouse fur with some turns of yellow tying silk showing at the tail
Hackle: Light yellowish dun cock hackle wound half-way down the hook shank

This last fly from the Rev. Edward Powell has been referred to variously as Buzz Willow, Grey Willow, Sandy Willow and Yellow Willow. It was used with resounding success on the River Banwy and the other variants were intermediates in the evolution of the Onny Perlid. It is fitting that this is Parson Powell's final offering to this inventory since he wrote many articles for the *Fishing Gazette* and *Game & Gun* under the pseudonym 'Willow.'

Wiper (*via Stuart Jarvis*)
Ephemera (Plate 20)

Hook: 12 – 14
Silk: Yellow
Tail: Bunch of red cock hackle fibres
Body: Blue rabbit
Rib: Fine yellow silk
Hackle: Medium blue dun – wound full

This dry fly hackle pattern probably has its origins in the West Country, but has recently been 'imported' into the Welsh Borderlands by Stuart Jarvis of the Glanusk Estate on the Usk. He reports that it is a remarkably effective dry fly for the summer months.

Worfield Amber Beauty (*Michael Meddings*)
Pale watery olives (Plate 20)

Hook: 16
Silk: Light orange
Whisks: Honey dun cock hackle fibres
Body: 50/50 mix of yellow and orange seal's fur
Hackle: Honey cock hackle

Michael Meddings used to fish the Salopian Fly Fishers water on the underrated River Worfe near Bridgnorth. He tied this fly especially for that stream, to cover the emergence of pale wateries in mid summer.

Y Diawl Bach (*Dewi Lewis*)
General nymph (Plate 20)

Hook: 14 – 16
Tail: Ginger brown hen hackle fibres
Body: Green peacock
Hackle: Ginger brown hen

This wet fly, whose name translated means Little Devil, was originally the handiwork of Dewi Lewis of Bala for use on the River Dee. It has evolved into one of the best-known buzzer imitations for stillwater fishing throughout Britain and beyond.

Yellow Dun (*Richard Williams*)
Yellow May dun (Plate 20)

Hook: 12
Whisks: Guinea fowl dyed a yellow dun colour
Body: Mixture of yellow wool and a little orange seal's fur
Rib: Fine gold tinsel
Hackle: Pale blue dun cock hackle with pale honey points

This pattern was devised by Mr Richard Williams of Kingsland, Herefordshire, for use on the Lugg. It may be difficult to obtain the correct shade of hackle (a honey hackle dyed with a pale blue dun dye will give almost the correct shade), but it is worth persevering since it is remarkably effective.

PLATE 21

Yellow May Shuttlecock Emerger
Yellow Sally, Yellow Upright, York's Favourite
York's Hare's Ear, York's Special

Yellow May Shuttlecock Emerger (*Dave Collins*)
Yellow May emerger (Plate 21)

Hook: 12 Oliver Edwards nymph emerger K14ST
Thread: Uni 8/0 light Cahill
Rib: Uni 8/0 tan
Tail: Two yellow microfibetts
Body: Flyrite 38 pale watery yellow
Thorax: Masterclass 24 amber caddis
Wing: CDC – natural grey, or yellow for better visibility
Legs: Mallard flank feathers dyed with yellow marker pen
Wing buds: After dubbing the body, tie in two lengths of black Super Stretch Floss (halfway along each length), halfway up the fly. Then after dubbing thorax, ribbing and tying in the legs, fold both ends of each length of floss forwards in tight 'V's and tie them both in about 2mm behind the head. Trim off the ends, lightly dub and wind forwards to tie off. Alternatively use fine black goose biots.

This pattern has been used with great success since 2005 after observing fish feeding on the middle Wye during Yellow May emergence, but when they were clearly not taking floating duns. Following autopsies and to the exclusion of just about anything else, large numbers of Yellow May emergers were recovered from stomach contents, and the pattern is based on some of these. From observations by Oliver Edwards and Stuart Crofts, it is known that *Heptaginea sulphurea* nymphs behave rather atypically in that they not only shed the nymphal shuck as the dun emerges at the surface (in common with other up-winged flies), but also shed the nymphal shuck whilst still attached to rocks and stones, before swimming, as a true emerger, up to the surface.

On the way to the surface, this emerger, neither nymph nor dun, can also begin to expand its wings; stomach contents reflect this, containing emergers with small as well as with partially expanded wings. Another Heptaginid, *H. lateralis*, is also known to behave in this way. The contrast of the striking black wings buds and orange/amber thorax with the yellow body is probably a powerful trigger in the artificial. The pattern has proved highly successful, luring many fine trout, grayling and chub on the Wye and Usk. Fish frequently create big bow-waves when attacking the emerger from distance, just as when they are aggressively feeding on the naturals, whilst others have offered barely-perceptible sips whilst partaking of more leisurely meals! A pattern with more expanded wings works too.

Yellow Sally (*unknown*)
Yellow Sally (Plate 21)

Hook: 14
Body: Light canary quill or pale canary-coloured wool
Hackles: Two small pale ginger cock hackles

This straightforward pattern, popular on the Usk and Monnow, represents the easily recognised stonefly of the same name, which is present throughout the region.

Yellow Upright (*Barry Lloyd*)
Yellow upright (Plate 21)

Hook: 16
Whisk: Honey dun
Body: Yellow floss silk
Rib: Fine gold
Hackle: Honey grizzle

The natural yellow upright is very common on the Usk, Wye and several other Welsh Borderland streams and hatches in profusion in late May and June. This particular pattern, devised by Barry Lloyd, became a favourite with a number of Usk fishermen in the 1960s.

York's Favourite (*A. H. York*)
Heather fly (Plate 21)

Hook: 14
Tail: Red swan or red ibis
Body: Black wool or floss silk
Hackle: Coch-y-bonddu cock hackle

This pattern is thought to represent a heather fly. A.H. York (Yorkie) had tackle business based in Redditch and travelled throughout the Welsh borderlands in his old motor car (in which he slept at night) selling flies that he and his 'ladies' had tied. He was a keen angler on the lakes and rivers of Wales and created four patterns for this purpose: Ugly Alder, York's Favourite, York's Hare's Ear and York's Special.

York's Hare's Ear (*A. H. York*)
General pattern dry fly (Plate 21)

Hook: 12 – 14
Whisks: Ginger cock hackle fibres
Body: Hare's ear fur
Rib: Fine gold wire
Hackle: Pale to medium blue dun cock

Michael Leighton rates this as Yorkie's best fly saying that it is a tremendous dry fly that is effective throughout the season and is easy to dress. It is best tied with a short-fibred hackle feather. Some people might view this fly as a variation on the Gold-ribbed Hare's Ear.

York's Special (*A. H. York*)
Heather fly (Plate 21)

Hook: 8 – 12
Body: Black wool tied to form a tapered body
Rib: Oval silver tinsel
Hackle: Red hen hackle, tied thick

The final fly of this inventory was sold to anglers for use on the streams and lakes in the Oswestry area. It was used extensively and successfully as a bob fly on Lake Vyrnwy, especially in the larger sizes, whilst being effective on the rivers in the smaller sizes.

Chapter 4

Regional adaptations of fly patterns

'The uncomplicated patterns are the best on Border streams'
James Evans (*Small River Fly Fishing for Trout and Grayling*)

If you make a study of the variations in fly patterns that
have been traditionally used around the country you'll
find some surprising examples. Local patterns such as
'spiders' of Yorkshire and 'bumbles' of Derbyshire spring to
mind as obvious examples. It is not until you look closely
at the regional patterns of the Welsh Borderland that you'll
discover there are also some distinct adaptations appropriate
to this region, some of which could be unique. There appear
to be two significant adaptations to wet flies and dry flies
that warrant further attention.

Wet flies

1) Usk-style patterns

These flies are likely to based, as previously recorded in this book, on the flies introduced by the Scots who arrived in the area in the 1800s. They are dressed with short bodies (covering only half the hook shank), slim feather slips for wings and sparse beard hackles. These flies are well suited to the Tweed/Usk styles of fishing with quick repeated casting of flies across and slightly upstream enabling them to sink quickly. There are a number of examples of this style of fly, most of them coming from Mr Acheson; his Alder, Blue Ruff, Iron Blue and March Brown are the most obvious ones.

2) Forward-facing hackled flies

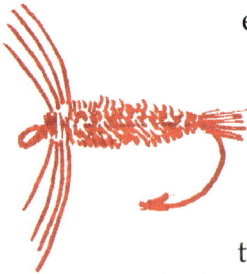

James Evans was a great exponent of experimentation with the flies he used on the Borderland streams. His adaptations of traditional hackled wet flies such as the Red Tag were simple, yet effective. He was used to fishing his team of wet flies in the conventional upstream method, which was de rigueur on the Herefordshire streams near Luston where he lived. There were two simple adjustments that he made to all his conventionally hackled wet flies. Firstly, in order to inject more life into the fly, he tied the hackle in with its fibres facing forwards, in similar fashion to what one might do for a dry fly. And secondly, he wound in an under-body of either copper wire or fine lead. The effect of these two modifications is quite striking, and apparently catch rates increased significantly as a result. Probably the finest example of these modifications is shown in one of James Evans's patterns, the William Rufus.

Dry flies

It is interesting to see how different fly-dressers have tried to overcome the problems associated with the turbulent water that is so common to Welsh Borderland rivers and streams. Maintaining the floatation of the dry fly is a major factor in the development of a successful pattern and fly-dressers in the region have used the following four strategies to overcome this problem:

1) Heavy hackled, long or bushy-tailed dry flies

These flies are characterised by extensive hackling – either many turns (up to ten in some cases) of a single hackle, or two hackles tied in one behind the other or one wound through the other. The tail whisks are numerous, making it bushy, and they often exceed the body length of the fly. The effect of these two measures is to create a fly the sits on the surface film of the water, often holding the hook out of the water. These flies also make a 'footprint' in the surface film which fish find irresistible. There are approximately thirty flies designed in this manner from the region and the Rev. Edward Powell's Baby Sun Fly and Paragon and Harry Powell's Dogsbody are the best-known examples.

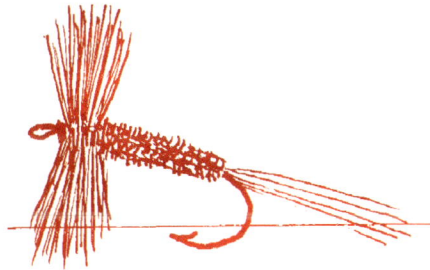

2) Head-and-shoulder hackled flies

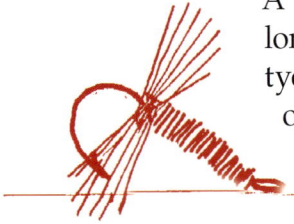

A modification of the heavy-hackled, long or bushy-tailed dry flies that some tyers have used. Two distinct hackles, one at the head of the fly, and the other with slightly shorter feather fibres at the shoulder, are tied in close turns, extending about a third of the way down the hook shank.

There are six Welsh Borderland patterns showing this modification: Rev. Edward Powell's Alder, Buzz Olive and March Brown and John Henderson's Brown Silverhorn, March Brown and March Brown Nymph.

3) Reverse-hackled flies

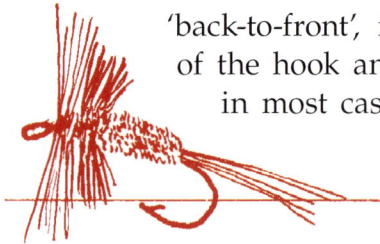

A reverse-hackled dry fly is one that is dressed 'back-to-front', i.e. with its head at the bend of the hook and the tail at the eye. However in most cases there is no tail, or wing, in evidence. The hackle is tied in just short of the bend of the hook so that the hook point is entangled with the hackle fibres. This means that no part of the hook is visible to the fish since it is above the water at all times. The eye end of the hook sits on the water, held there by surface tension. The effect of this is made greater if up-eyed hooks are used since the natural 'lie' of the hook will be flush with the water surface. The tippet material will naturally be submerged when the fly is sitting on the water surface and will not be so visible to the fish.

The principal exponents of this method of dressing flies in the region were, as previously mentioned, the Barrett brothers, Cosmo and Bruce, with their famous Barrett's Bane and Barrett's Professor.

Another advocate of this method of dry fly dressing was James Evans, who accidentally stumbled upon the idea while reading an article by David Jacques about the 'fore-and-aft mayfly' pattern. He experimented extensively with the concept and his fly box apparently contained a very high percentage of 'tail-less back-to-front' variations of regular dry flies as well as some of his own creations. His Border Mayfly and Welsh Fusilier are two of the most effective flies for use on any river.

Two other flies of this construction were created independently of the aforementioned mentioned tyers – the Coltman's Duster, developed for use on the River Ceirog by F. H. Coltman. The second was the Dulas Brook Mayfly which was developed by Ron Pomfret.

4) Centrally-hackled flies

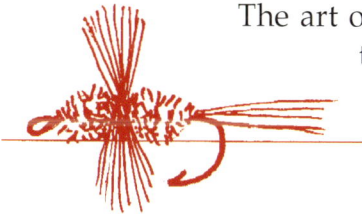

The art of invention was never lacking in the vicarage at Munslow in Shropshire. The Rev. Powell's conversion to dry-fly fishing by Dai Lewis was followed by a multitude of creations to represent winged insects. Perhaps his most innovative patterns were those he created with a central hackle. There are no natural flies with this sort of body construction but from a purely practical point of view this type of pattern is remarkably buoyant and rides the rough stickles of the Borderland streams exceptionally well.

In essence, these flies, (of which he constructed only two, the Orange Otter and the Double Spot), have a body divided fore and aft on the hook by a prominent central hackle, with tail whisks to give extra floatation.

Chapter 5

Borderlands flyfishing literature

From *A Treatyse of Fysshinge with an Angle* (1496)
to *Fishing in Time* (2011) with selected extracts

An advantage in my research into the history of the wild trout and grayling fishing of the Welsh Borderlands was the discovery that the number of books on the topic was relatively small and finite, thus making a literary review a manageable task. The books included in this review are by authors who lived, or are living, within the region, or the contents of the book relate to locations within it.

Naturally my research started with Dame Juliana Berners' *A Treatyse of Fysshynge with an Angle*, first published in 1496. Since then there have been a number of other significant local contributions to piscatorial literature. Early titles include Scotcher's *The Fly Fisher's Legacy* (1820), which was the first attempt by anyone to produce a definitive entomology for flyfishers, and Sir Humphry Davy's masterpiece *Salmonia* (1828).

Over a century later the enigmatic character Walter M. Gallichan not only fished extensively within the region but also wrote three books with strong ties to the Welsh Borderlands: *Fishing in Wales* (1903), *The Trout Waters of England* (1908) and *Fishing in Mid-Wales* (1939). Rather later Cyril V. Hancock crafted the delightful book *Rod in Hand* (1958) as well as the short article entitled *The Land of Teme and Gleam* that featured in Maurice Wiggin's *The Angler's Bedside Book* (1965). Some twenty years later two books of special interest to the fly-tyer were produced: Moc Morgan's *Fly Patterns for the Rivers and Lakes of Wales* (1984) and Michael Leighton's *Trout Flies of Shropshire and the Welsh Borderlands* (1987). Last, but by no means least, Christopher Knowles' very thorough account of the life of the Rev. Edward Powell is portrayed in his book *Orange Otter* (2006).

A total of forty-one books have been included in this review, including Housman's *A Shropshire Lad* (1896) which, although having no direct references to fishing, has specific reference to many Shropshire rivers.

A TREATYSE OF FYSSHYNGE WITH AN ANGLE
Dame Juliana Berners (1496)

The book that surely has to be the starting point for any research into the history of flyfishing anywhere in Great Britain is *A Treatyse of Fysshynge with an Angle*, presumed to be written or compiled by prioress Dame Juliana Berners in 1496. Some authorities believe that it may have been written some fifty years earlier than that date. For its time it is a remarkably comprehensive (albeit short) book

covering the subject of fishing in its many branches.

The book advocates twelve fly patterns for trout and grayling and gives the time of year to fish them – from March to August. These twelve patterns form the starting point of the evolution of trout and grayling flies in the whole of British fly-tying. Angling historian Jack Heddon of the Honey Dun Press believed that these flies could well have had their origins in the Welsh Borderlands areas of Shropshire, or possibly Derbyshire. So the birth of fly-tying, or at least its infancy, could well have been right here.

MARCH

The Dun Fly (1)

Body of dun wool, wings of partridge.
(May imitate the natural March Brown or February Red.)

The Dun Fly (2)

Body of black wool, wings of the blackest drake, jay under wings and tail.
(Could be a large dark olive or an early black gnat of the Bibio species.)

APRIL

The Stonefly

Body of black wool with yellow under the wings and tail, wings of a drake.
(As its name implies this is probably a stonefly imitation.)

The Roddyd Fly

A reddish wool body, with a black silk rib, wings of a drake and red capon hackle.
(May imitate the red spinner.)

MAY

The Yellow Fly

Body of yellow wool, wings of red cock hackle and of the drake.
(Imitating Ephemera danica, little yellow May dun or the Yellow Sally stonefly?)

The Black Louper

Body of black wool, peacock herl from an eye feather, and wings of red capon with a blue head.
Imitates a looper caterpillar (could this be the original palmered fly?)

JUNE

The Dun Cut

Body of black wool with yellow either side; wings of buzzard bound with hemp.
(Imitates a caddis fly or yellow dun?)

The Maure Fly

Body of dark wool and the wings of the darkest wild drake.
(Imitates an alder fly or green drake?)

The Tandy Fly

Tan wool body, wings from the speckled feathers of the wild drake.
(Imitates the cowdung fly, oak fly or grey drake?)

JULY

The Wasp Fly

Body of black wool ribbed with yellow silk, wings of buzzard.
(Imitates a wasp, hover fly or crane fly.)

Shell fly

Body – green wool with peacock herl, wings – buzzard.
(Another sedge or grannom pattern.)

AUGUST

The Drake Fly

Body of black wool ribbed with black silk, wings of speckled feather of the black drake with the black head.
(Imitation uncertain, perhaps the alder?)

Note: The suggested imitations (given in brackets) of the twelve fly patterns described in the *Treatyse* are derived from John Waller Hills and G.E.M. Skues as outlined in W. H. Lawrie's book *English and Welsh Trout Flies.*

THE ART OF ANGLING
Thomas Barker (1651)

We have to wait a century and a half after the publication of *A Treatyse of Fysshynge with an Angle* before we find the first book with specific reference and relevance to the Borderland region. *The Art of Angling* written by Thomas Barker, a native of the village of Meole Brace (now a suburb of Shrewsbury), is a slender volume that attempts to cover many facets of fishing including flyfishing for trout and grayling.

The book opens with some very practical advice regarding suitable conditions for fishing: 'a man that goeth to the River for his pleasure … the first thing he must do is to observe the Sun and the Wind for day … to set forth his tackles and accordingly to go for his pleasure and some profit.'

There follows quite an elaborate section on fishing for trout

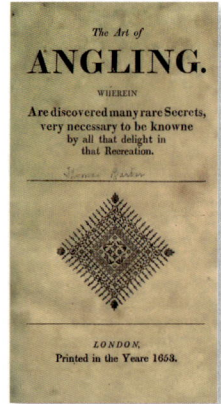

including choice of rod and selection of line, 'with tender hasel top ... he that angles with a line made of one haired link, shall kill five to other's one' (i.e. using a single strand of horsehair). And as for tactics, 'you must angle always with the point of the rod down the stream' and be sure to 'observe the seasonable times ... if it prove cloudy, you may angle with baits all day long; but if it prove bright and clear, you must take evening or morning.'

A short interlude on baits, the culturing of worms and fishing with the minnow precedes the section on fishing with the fly which is introduced thus: 'I will shew you the way to angle with the flye, which is a delightful sport ... be sure you be casting always down the stream with the wind behind you, and the Sun before you.'

In detailing suitable flies for the month of March, Barker advocates 'severall kinds of Palmers that are good for that time.' He then gives the patterns for five palmered flies which he claims will 'serve all the year long morning and evening, windy or cloudy.'

Various patterns for the 'May flye' are then considered, followed by the 'Oak-flye', a brownish fly that is good 'from the beginning of May to the end of August.' Next is the 'Flesh-flye, which is very good in a bright day' and finally the 'Grasse-hopper, which is green.'

Fly colour choice is then explained with the adage: 'note the lightest of your flies for cloudy and dark, and the darkest of your flyes for the brightest dayes.' A short section on dapping as we know it today is explained under the heading 'dopping'.

Following sections on cooking your catch (complete with some elaborate recipes), and fishing for eight different species of fish, our interest is alerted once again in the final piece on grayling fishing in Shropshire. 'The manner of angling for him is with good long rod with casting ... the bait must be either a small artificiall or a nature flye ... the way to angle with the Cod bait* … you must have a little float of cork … when the fish taketh the bait you shall see the cork flee after the fish, then strike.'

This all sounds remarkably similar to today's fishing with a strike indicator!

* Caddis grub.

BARKER'S DELIGHT
Thomas Barker (1659)

In 1659 Barker produced a 'much enlarged' second edition of *The Art of Angling*, retitled *Barker's Delight,* in which we find the first reference to the Hawthorn Fly as well as amendments to the original text following the publication in 1653 of Isaac Walton's famous and ever popular *Compleat Angler.* There are a number of witty, light-hearted poems of appreciation of the first edition by some of Barker's friends and relatives, who even had fun with how they signed themselves. 'Nagrom Notpoh' (Morgan Hopton) is one such.

> *Angling doth bodyes exercise,*
> *And maketh soules holy and wise:*
> *By blessed thoughts and meditation:*
> *This, this is Anglers recreation!*
> *Health, profit, pleasure, mixt together,*
> *All sport's to this not worth a feather.*

Nagrom Notpoh *Armiger*

THE ART OF ANGLING
Richard Bowlker (c. 1746)

Bowlker's *Art of Angling*, first published in Ludlow around 1746, is the next book of interest to us with its specific reference to grayling on the River Teme. (The author was a member of a Ludlow family.) The book, of which subsequent editions were enhanced and expanded by Bowlker's son, Charles, proved to be a popular and long running angling bible. Within the text there are graphic descriptions of 26 species of fish including trout and grayling, 30 fly patterns, details of life-cycles of flies and the first references to upstream flyfishing. Details of fishing with worm, maggot, wasp grub, 'cod-bait' and grasshopper are included in the text.

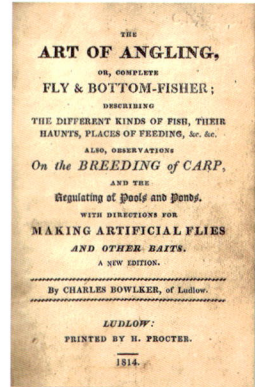

Of the trout there are descriptions of its natural history, typical locations and some interesting angling strategies including: 'in March angle with worm, or troll with minnow in the morning; towards 12 o'clock Blue Dun and March Brown flies make their appearance – commence fly-fishing until 3pm when they disappear; in the evening again use the worm. As the season advances the flies daily appear earlier and continue later.'

He informs readers that grayling 'abound in rivers of Derbyshire and Yorkshire, in the Teme near Ludlow and in the Lugg and other streams near Leominster.' And that the largest fish were reputed to be 'above half-a-yard in length and weighed four and a half pounds' and that its 'ancient name is umbra or umber and the fishing season is September, October and November.'

Methods of fishing to be adopted include: 'trolling for deeper fish using baits suspended from quill floats; grub (natural and artificial) fishing adopting a sink and draw method.' (Like modern-day Czech nymphing perhaps?)

A number of chapters of this book contain delightful stanzas or poems and details of some of these may be found in Chapter 6.

Later editions of the book contain added material including: *The Principal Rivers of England; Trolling for Trout; Flyfishing* (from Col. Peter Hawker's Instructions to Young Sportsmen) and *Fishing Stations in North Wales Including the Dee, Alyn and Ceiriog, the Severn and its Tributaries.*

The book concludes with an extract from *Songs of the Chase.*

The Angler envies no man's joys
But his who gains the greatest sport;
With peace he dwells far from the noise
And bustling grandeur of a court.

ANGLING IN ALL ITS BRANCHES
Samuel Taylor (1800)

In 1800, Samuel Taylor, who started his fishing career in Shropshire, wrote *Angling in all its Branches*. It is a book in three distinct parts: *Fishing Locations* (in which he had fished – by county), secondly, *Different Kinds of Fish*, and then *Flyfishing*.

A significant number of Borderland rivers feature in the first part: the Severn (with a reference to catching a five pound grayling), and tributaries Teme (with reference to grayling within three miles from Worcester and *excellent* trout in its upper reaches), and the

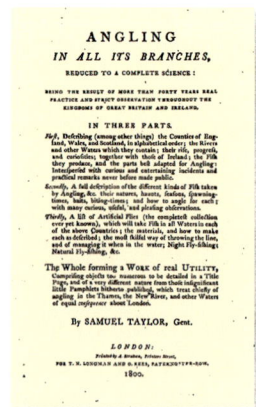

Roden and Tanat. The Wye and tributaries Trothy, Lug [sic], Monnow, Irvon [sic], Ithon (also *excellent* for trout and grayling) and Somergil. The Usk (especially for trout near Brecon) and the Gavenny

Trout and grayling feature amongst many other fish in the second part. Trout are referred to as 'fish of prey' owing to their voracious feeding habit and are noted to move higher up rivers in February, where they 'generally choose rocky, stony and gravely bottoms' on which to spawn.

Reference is once again made to the daily tactical sequence of fishing first the worm, then a minnow and then fly. The fly is also recommended as the rivers clear. A 14ft rod with base section of ash and mid/top sections of yew or hickory is advocated.

The section on grayling opens with a wonderfully accurate description of the fish's physiology: 'back is of a dusky green inclining blue … sides are gray hence its name … top of back fin reddish lower part blueish-purple … seldom exceeds eighteen or twenty inches in length.' The chief season is advertised as September to January and spawning occurs in April/May.

Tactics, under the heading *How to Angle for them; their Baits and Biting-times* are, 'When water clears – fly, otherwise cadbait, gentle, maggot or worm.'

Grayling are 'very sportive at the fly during spring and summer … best time 8am – 12 noon and 4pm – sunset in spring/summer and in September – January middle of the day.'

In the third section he states of fishing with the fly: 'this ingenious and delightful part of angling is, in every respect, superior to all the rest put together.'

Of flies for trout, grayling and other fish he introduces a selection of eight flies to 'set down as standards: the Black Hackle, the Wren's Tail, the Grouse Hackle, the Smoky Dun Hackle, the Brown Rail, the Hare's Ear, Winged Hare's Ear and the Red Hackle.' To these eight are added a further twenty-four to complete the collection and there are detailed fly dressing instructions for all thirty-two flies.

The book concludes with reference to tactics and techniques.

THE MODERN ANGLER, IN A SERIES OF LETTERS
Robert Salter (1800)

The Modern Angler, in a Series of Letters, written by Robert Salter and printed by J. Salter in Oswestry, is a series of sixteen 'letters' written to a friend of the author, the Rev. Morgan Pryse. Unfortunately we do not know where the reverend gentleman lived but we do know from the first letter that they were intended to be 'imparting to you the knowledge I have obtained in the course of more than twenty years' practice in the art of angling' during which time the author picked up information from other anglers which in turn 'induced me to commit their hints to writing' in order to 'enable you to become a complete and a fair angler.'

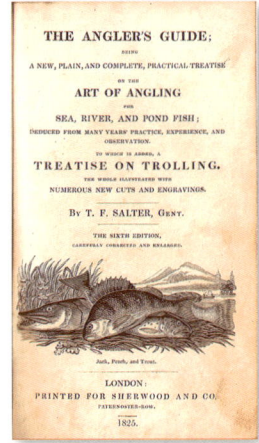

The second letter gives brief descriptions of various fish including grayling and trout.

Of grayling he says, 'it resembles dace but with a much finer nose … rarely found above four pounds weight, spawns in April, and is in the greatest perfection in October … his large scales are bright in summer and darken as winter approaches … delights in the same streams as trout and … the same flies too but in September retires to the lower end of still pools where he will eagerly take a fly at the top or if you angle for him below the surface it should be as near the bottom as possible.'

Of trout he comments that it is 'well known in almost every river in Great Britain … its flesh colour varies with locations from white to salmon red but that its sides are … yellow and beautifully decorated with red spots.' Also that the trout 'tries to find the source of the river in order to spawn (usually in November) after which it will remain solitary as the monarch of the brook through the winter months only to be reinvigorated in the following spring.'

The third letter opens by describing 'the most pleasant methods of tempting each of them' and includes details of rod length and construction for fishing with flies; the nature of material used for line, including Indian weed (hemp) and silkworm gut; fly numbers and tactics. The final section of this letter is concerned with fly-tying materials: hackles; other feathers; body materials; silks and wax.

In the next five letters (the fourth to eighth), are descriptions of 27 flies taken in sequence through the season from early March to the end of October.

The ninth letter mentions other flies and methods that must not be overlooked but do not fit into the season's sequence.

The tenth to fourteenth letters describe methods of fishing for salmon and pike while the final (fifteenth) letter congratulates the reverend gentleman in person for the 'laudable exertions' of the Severn Society and hopes that other similar societies will flourish in the 'vales of Vyrnvyy (*sic*) and Tanat' to 'stimulate our countrymen to compel a general observance of those laws that were wisely enacted by our forefathers, to prevent the premature destruction of so delicate a luxury of life.'

All of which suggests that environmental awareness is nothing new.

A SERIES OF LETTERS
ON ANGLING, SHOOTING & COURSING
Robert Lascelles (1815)

These sporting letters are written to an unknown recipient referred to as 'G'. The first nine letters are on the topic of Angling, and are signed by Piscator.

The first letter is by way of introduction to the topic and sets the scene admirably by stating that, 'Fishing, like most other pursuits, originated in necessity; and is indebted for any improvements, which the art has since acquired, to the genius which has accompanied the different gradations of society.'

The second letter, written from Gloucester whilst en route for South Wales, introduces the rivers Severn, Wye and Usk and develops the theme of salmon fishing by suggesting that the salmon of the Severn are considered to be 'nearly as good as those of the Thames.' This letter concludes with details of the patterns of seven favourite salmon flies.

The third letter was written in March 1811 from the banks of the Usk at Crickhowell. In the first part he recounts fishing the river hereabouts as well as describing the flies present on the water and describe suitable patterns for artificial flies to imitate them in the following way: 'The fly on the water, when I began fishing, was a sort of red dun, and is the first of the season; I caught one with my landing-net, and found him exactly similar to some I had brought with me, and which are made thus: the body is of copper coloured hog's fur from near the tail, and the wings either of a dark mottled red feather of a mallard, and the same coloured hackle for legs, or a dark grizzle cock's hackle, simply over the whole, on a hook, (No. 6) … the next fly that appeared

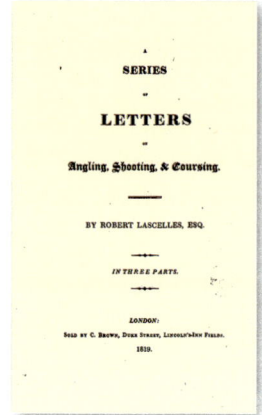

was the March-brown, or, what is generally termed in Wales, the cob-fly: he is much bigger than the last, and one of the best of the season … I should recommend every one before he attempts the artificial fly to catch a natural one, as their bodies vary so much in colour … and made thus: his wings, which stand nearly upright, are from the feather of a hen-pheasant's wing, a good deal dappled, with a partridge's hackle wrapped twice round close under the but for legs; his body, which is pretty large, is made of a mixture of yellow camlet and the light brown fur of an hare's ear, about equal quantities of each, on a hook, (No. 6).'

The latter part of this letter recalls: 'I have been chiefly employed to-day in making flies, for it blew a cold east wind in the morning, and some of the hills were likewise covered with snow, so that I did not care to venture out.'

In the fourth letter, written on 30 March he describes how his 'sport has been tolerably good' during the month and a new fly has appeared on the scene, namely a Blue Dun. 'The wings of this fly are from the feather of a starling's wing; the body of light blue fur, mixed with a little yellow mohair, a fine blue hen's hackle over it for legs, and forked with two fibres of the same – the hook 7 or 8.'

The fifth letter opens by extolling the virtues of the Usk as a great river for trout fishing and then continues with the most elaborate description of making flies using the right hand as the vice! This letter concludes with a charming little stanza from Thomson which will be found in Chapter 6.

In the sixth letter he gives 'an account of the best (flies) I am acquainted with' by describing them under five separate classes: Blues, Browns, Reds, Yellows and Palmered flies. For each of the classes he gives descriptions of patterns to be followed to make appropriate artificial flies.

Under the Blues: Blue Dun, Spider or Gravel fly, Black Gnat, Larger Whirling Dun, Iron Blue fly, Black Caterpillar, Sky-coloured Blue, Violet Fly, Blue Gnat and Little Pale Blue.

Under Browns: March Brown, Cow-dung Fly, Stone Fly, Granam (*sic*), Fern Fly and Latter Stone Fly.

Under Reds: Red Fly, Shorn Fly, Orl Fly, (Welshman's) Button Fly and two Red Spinners.

Under Yellows: Sally Fly, Green Drake, Grey Drake.

Under Palmers: Black Palmer, Brown Palmer, Golden Palmer and Red Palmer.

This letter concludes with a comprehensive listing of twenty-six flies to be used in sequence from March to September:

Bed Fly	– from the middle of February to the end of March.
March Blue	– from the first week in March to the end of April.
March Brown	– from the first week in March to the end of April.
Cow-dung Fly	– from the third week in March to the end of April.
Stone Fly	– from the middle of April to the end of May.
Granam Fly, or Green Tail	– from the second to the last week in April.
Spider or Gravel Fly	– from the last week in April to the second in May.
The Black Gnat	– from the last week in April to the end of May.
Larger Whirling Dun	– from the last week in April to the end of May.
Iron Blue Fly	– from the last week in April to the middle of June.
Black Caterpillar	– from the first to the third week in May.
The Shorn Fly	– from the second week in May to the second in June.

Yellow Sally Fly	– from the first to the third week in May.
The Green Drake	– from the third week in May to the first in June.
The Grey Drake	– from the third week in May to the third in June.
The Orl Fly	– from the last week in May to the end of June.
Sky-coloured Blue	– from the last week in May to the middle of July.
Violet Fly	– from the last week in May to the second week in June.
Fern Fly	– from the middle of June to the middle of July.
Welshman's Button	– from the middle of June to the end of June.
Red spinners (two)	– from the middle of June to the middle of August.
Blue Gnat	– from the latter end of June to the second week in August.
Ant Flies	– from the middle of June to the middle of July.
Lesser Whirling Dun	– from the end of June to the end of August.
Latter Stone Fly	– from the middle of July to the second week in August.
Little Pale Blue	– from the middle of August to the end of September.

The seventh letter is devoted to fishing with minnows and worms and also contains a reference to grayling fishing, which was consided to be best on the Wye and Irvon (*sic*) but notably missing from the Usk.

The eighth letter gives a graphic account of the qualities required of cock birds used for making flies and concludes with descriptions of cock fighting.

The ninth letter takes a closer look at birds and their plumage as well as the times of the year when they are most suited to making flies and concludes with similar treatment being given to animal furs and the quality of natural gut and silk used in casts.

THE FLY FISHER'S LEGACY (1820)
George Scotcher

In 1820 George Scotcher of Chepstow made a valiant attempt to produce an entomological account of the species of flies found beside rivers, thereby filling a gap he felt existed in angling literature. The result of his labours *The Fly Fisher's Legacy* (printed and sold by M. Willett of Chepstow) is a notable book giving the natural and artificial details of 25 flies, with seven of the artificials of his own design. The flies are described in order of appearance on the rivers and the naturals were beautifully illustrated and hand-painted in the frontispiece. This is perhaps the first book giving definite evidence of flyfishing in Wales, and of historic note in this context is the pattern of his 'Drop Fly' for use on the River Usk which is believed to be the forerunner of the Coch-y-bonddu.

In the section *Preliminary Remarks* there is a most perceptive fishing almanac that takes you through the months of the season, a reference to ideal weather conditions and some enlightening advice on striking too soon, playing fish, rod types as well as leader and fly drill.

The life cycles of some flies are to be found in *Some Account of Aquatic Insects* in which there is a graphic description of

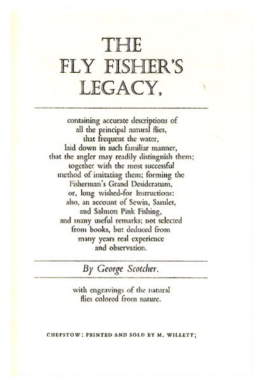

the caddis larva hatching.

The succinct section entitled *General Flies* gives the reader a wonderful account on the lines of matching the hatch.

Here is an extract from the chapter *Preliminary Remarks, Warranted by Experience*:

'Although some few fish may be taken by fly in February, if weather and water suit, yet the fly-fishing season cannot be said to commence until after the 15th of March, as by that time the flies are become regular in their appearance. The best rise then is about the middle of the day, and in general they take home when they rise, and often under water, without breaking the surface, especially if there is a cool wind. Brooks, and the lower parts of rivers and sheltered streams, are the best places in the early part of the season. April is the best month. A fisherman cannot well go out in it without having sport, unless floods or excessive stormy weather happen. The rise is then earlier, stronger, and continues later; and observe, in frosty days the flies do not appear so early, or continue so long, as in mild weather. It is much the same in May, unless the sand flies are strong on. In June, early and late is the proper time, except on windy days, for then the green drake or the fernshaws are abundant all day. July, and most part of August, the late and early fishing continues, except in the days when the shorn and ant flies appear numerous. After the first heavy flood in August, the evenings and morning get cool, and the rises of the fish during that month, and in September and October (which are both good months), shorten in the same proportion as it increased in March and April.

To speak generally, the more cloudy the day, and the stronger the wind, the better (so you can manage your tackle), and also if against or across the stream. The wind inclining from the west to north-north-west, or from south

to south-east, I usually prefer, as I often find the south-
westerly winds bring on heavy rains and floods, and when
they are approaching fish will never take well, though
perhaps they will often rise at your fly, and a fisherman
is apt to suppose his fly is not right, when the cause lies
elsewhere; however, fish will sometimes rise and take
wonderfully during rain, but then it is in sudden passing
showers only.

Fish never rise well if the water is increasing with freshes
off the hills, from previous rain, or the melting of snow,
though the river be not foul.

When a fish rises at your fly, be sure not to strike till he
has taken it, more especially if it be a large fish, or if in
windy weather; I myself missed numbers, and seen many
others do the same, from the common fault of striking at
the moment of the fish rising.

If a good trout or two takes your fly, depend upon it. It
is right, and don't change it for a few false rises; however,
notwithstanding this remark, if you have been successful
with one fly, and at last find it generally refused, you
may conclude the fish are glutted with the kind you are
throwing, and seeking another, which you must endeavour
to discover. This often occurs when any fly is very strong
on, and I have frequently in the time of the March Brown,
and in the midst of the flights of the purple, taken many
with a Light Blue Dun fly.

In windy weather, and low water, fish rise mostly at the
slow ends of streams, or on the long flats of deep water, if
not too deep; you may then let your fly be just under the
surface, where it will be often taken unperceived by you, as
the roughness of the water prevents you from seeing the rise;
and therefore always in such days, remember to strike before
you attempt to draw your fly away to make another throw, or
you will often tear your hook out of a fish's mouth, or break
your tackle by the weight of one so hooked. In bright calm

days, they rise in or by the side of rough streams.

At the first clearing of the flood, the trouts are found in the shallow sides or end of a stream, and on the fords, should any wind be stirring; but if you remark in what sort of place you take your first good trout or two, it will tell you where to find the others, all day long, provided the water and weather continue the same.

Various rivers differ much in many little particulars. In some shallow swift brooks or rivers, fish will rise best just when the floods first begin to clear, and you will see the stones appear; in others, that are deeper or slower, they will not move much before the second, or perhaps the third or fourth day of clearing. Also, some particular wind will touch on one river, and will not ruffle another, according to the course they run, or how they are sheltered; rain, likewise, from one point of the wind will rise one river and not affect another.

On some rivers one sort of fly is more prevalent than another, and in their season must there be attended to. From these and such like remarks, you will be able to judge when and where you are likely to have sport, and the more so, if you have observed the state of the wind and water when you have been particularly successful at any one of them.

If you are accustomed to sport on one particular river, you may always know where to raise fish, for wherever you have rose or taken one before, in the same places you will find others, provided the weather and water are nearly the same. Always throw near where froth lies, and also on the current it swims down in; also, just below where any rivulet falls into another, or where a mill water comes in, or just below a weir; and never neglect to throw in difficult places, which fearful anglers pass, for there always lie good fish.

If you have a rise, and you miss it, either by your striking too soon, or the fish missing its spring, by the fly being drawn out of the natural current it would take, you may, if a small fish, throw almost directly over him again; but if a good one, don't venture near him for at least half an hour.

Be very cautious in approaching the water, for if you are once seen, all chance of success is over. Sometimes throw up a stream, and sometimes down, as you can be best concealed. Also, fish always your own side of the stream first, (if it be anyways broad) before you approach to throw over to the other side of it. The shadow of yourself or rod destroys all sport. Either kneel or stoop, or throw from behind banks or stumps; in short, take all the advantages that may offer, to gain the grand point of being out of sight.

Of course, have with you half a dozen flies which are in season, some larger and some smaller, of the same kind, that you may alter the size agreeable to the fullness of water, or state of the weather. If you may take any when out, catch the natural fly, kill it, by squeezing its head, and retire into some calm snug corner, where, seated upon your basket, try your skill, remembering to make your artificial in colours rather under the bodies of the natural, that is, your yellows, &c. not so bright; your dark ones a little lighter; and pay strict attention to what colour your feather carries in the water, for some get lighter, and others much darker, when wetted; and always take some of the natural flies home, that you may copy them at your leisure; you may find them in the eddies and on the froth.'

SALMONIA
Sir Humphry Davy (1828)

Davy, who is perhaps better known for the miner's lamp which bears his name, is also remembered by flyfishermen for his book *Salmonia*, which brought the River Teme at Leintwardine and Downton into the literary limelight, although there are also passing references to the Usk, Lugg,

Clun, Wye and Dee. It was written when the author was suffering 'some months of severe and dangerous illness' and is penned in a conversational style, similar to Walton and Cotton's *Compleat Angler*. The discourse is between four characters:

SALMONIA:
on
DAYS OF FLY FISHING.
in
A SERIES OF CONVERSATIONS.
with some
ACCOUNT OF THE HABITS
of
FISHES BELONGING TO THE GENUS
SALMO.

BY AN ANGLER.

—— " Equidem credo quia sit divinitus illis
Ingenium."

LONDON:
JOHN MURRAY, ALBEMARLE STREET.
MDCCCXXVIII.

Halieus – an accomplished fly-fisher
Ornither – a sporting gentleman
Poietus – a lover of nature
Physicus – uninitiated as an angler

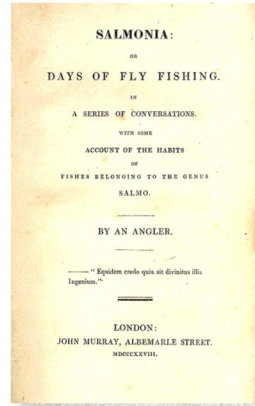

The book is laid out as a series of nine days of conversation and the first mention of the Welsh Borderlands is in the *Second Day* – in reality a chapter devoted to trout fishing, with references to early season fishing on the Usk and mayfly abundance on the Teme at its confluence with the Clun.

The *Seventh Day* is a chapter devoted to grayling fishing, and starts with a study of possible origins of the fish in Europe, followed by an account of catching grayling at Downton on the River Teme, then by an extensive account of the fish's distribution in English rivers.

There is a section, *Baits for Grayling*, which gives a detailed account of suitable flies through the months of the grayling season from March to September.

The *Eighth Day* covers natural history and has a detailed section including illustrations, outlining a number of *Phryganeae* (stoneflies) and *Ephemerae* (upwinged flies) together with their imitations – all of which have relevance to the trout and grayling fishing previously described.

This extract comes from the chapter *Seventh Day* and extols the merits of fishing for grayling on the River Teme at Leintwardine:

SCENE – Leintwardine, near Ludlow
TIME – Beginning of October
CHARACTERS – Halieus, Poietes, Ornither, Physicus

HAL.—You have reached your quarters. Here is your home – a rural, peaceable, and unassuming inn, with as worthy a host as may be found in this part of the country. The river glides at the bottom of the garden, and there is no stream in England more productive of grayling. The surrounding scenery is not devoid of interest, and the grounds in the distance are covered with stately woods, and laid out (or rather their natural beauties developed) by the hand of a master, whose liberal and enlightened mind ever condescended to regard the amusements of the angler; and he could hardly have contributed to a more effectual manner to their comforts, than by placing the good people, who were once his servants, in this comfortable inn.

PHYS.—Are we to fish according to any rule, as to quantity or size of fish?

HAL.—You are at perfect liberty to fish as you like; but as it is possible you may catch grayling of only this year, and which are no longer than the hand, I conclude you will return such pigmies to the river, as a matter of propriety, though not of necessity.

POIET.—This river seems formed of two other streams, which join above our inn. What are the names of its sources?

HAL.—The small river to the left is called the Teme, or Little Teme, and though the least stream, it gives name to the river: the other, and more copious stream, is called the Clun. The Little Teme contains principally trout; the Clun both trout and grayling: but the fish are more abundant in the meadows, between this place and Downton, that in other parts of the river; for above, the stream is too rapid and shallow to be favourable to their increase; and below, it is joined by other streams, and becomes too abundant in coarse fish …

POIET.—What flies shall we employ?

HAL.—I recommend at least three; for the grayling lies deeper and is not so shy as the trout; and, provided your link is fine, is not apt to be scared by the cast of flies on the water. The fineness of the link, and of the guts to which your flies are attached, is a more essential point, and the clearer the stream, the finer should be the tackle. I have known good fishermen foiled by using a gut of ordinary thickness, though their fly was of the right size and colour. Very slender transparent gut of the colour of the water is one of the most important causes of success in grayling fishing. Let me see your book: I will select a fine stretcher. Now, for the lowest fly, use a yellow-bodied fly, with red hackle for legs, and landrail's wing; for the second, a blue dun, with dun body; and for the highest, the claret coloured body, with blue wings; and let your first dropper fly be about three feet from the stretcher and from the other dropper, and let the hanging link which attaches them be 3½ inches long.

PHYS.—There are several fish rising; I shall throw at that opposite – he appears large.

HAL.—It is a trout and not a grayling.

PHYS.—How do you know?

HAL.—By his mode of rising. He is lying at the top of the water, taking the flies as they sail down by him, which a grayling scarcely ever does. He rises rapidly from the bottom or middle of the water, on the contrary – darting upwards, and, having seized his fly, returns to his station. There! A grayling has risen. I do not mean, however, that this habit is invariable; I have sometimes seen trout feed like grayling, and grayling like trout, but neither of these fish emit bubbles of air in rising, as dace and chub do.

PHYS.—I have one! He has taken my blue dun, and must

be a small one, for he plays with no vigour.

HAL.—He is about ¾lb – a fish of two years and a half old – very good for the table. I will land him if possible.

PHYS.—There! He is off!

HAL.—This happens often with grayling: their mouths are tender, and unless the hook catches in the upper lip, which is rather thick, it is more than an equal chance that the fish escapes you.

PHYS.—Here, I have another, that has taken the stretcher, and as it is a larger hook, I hope he may be held. He is likewise a larger fish – but how oddly he spins! This, I suppose, must be owing to his large back fin, by which the stream carries him round. There he is: he has quite twisted my link; it would not be amiss to have swivels for this kind of fishing.

HAL.—It is a fish in good season – dark above, fair below – and weighs, I should think about 1¼ lb.

POIET.—How well they rise! At that moment I had two on my line: one of them is gone, but I hope I shall land the other.

HAL.—Fish with activity while the cloud lasts. I fear the sun is coming out, when it will be more difficult to take fish. I shall try the next pool, and I advise you to follow me and fish by turns – passing each other, and taking different pools below, so wend your way downwards, fishing whenever you see fish sporting. There is no better part of the river than that pool below you, and you cannot take a wrong direction. Immediately beyond Burrington Bridge you will find two excellent pools, and I advise you to go no further down to-day. If you take a fish approaching 2lb, keep him alive in the fish barrel for crimping; the smaller fish you can kill, and carry with some rushes in your basket; we shall at least be able to send a dish of grayling to the patron of our sport at Downton.

TROUT AND SALMON FISHING IN WALES
George Agar Hansard (1834)

Although Hansard 'pilfers' from *The Fly Fisher's Legacy*, with much wholesale verbatim plagiarism of Scotcher's 1820 text, there is some worthwhile original material especially in the descriptions of a number of salmonid fish including *The Common Trout* and *The Grayling*.

Of the trout he writes 'for brevity's sake I shall range the trout under the consideration of the first classes of fish. For that end I must signalise his vivacity and vigour, his activity and courage, how natural they spring from the nature of this fish.'

He concludes his description of trout with a short poem:

> *The generous trout, to make the angler sport,*
> *In deep and rapid streams will oft resort,*
> *Where if you flourish but a fly, from thence*
> *You hail a captive, but of fish the prince.*

Hansard states that grayling 'are abundant in the upper portion of the Severn … they are also found in the Wye and its tributaries; very plentiful in the Lugg, and also in the Dee', and then he quotes Franck (a contemporary technical expert on fishing): 'umber or grayling is an amorous fish, that loves a frolic as he loves his life, whose teeth water after every wasp, as his fins flutter after every fly.'

> *Umber or grayling in the streams he'll lie,*
> *Hovering his fins at every silly fly;*
> *Fond of a feather; you shall see him rise*
> *At 'emmets, insects, hackles, drakes, and flies.*

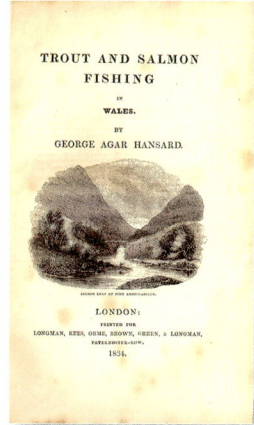

As far as can be judged the *Principal Angling Stations* section is also original and gives a county-by-county Description of the *Most Celebrated Angling Stations in North and South Wales*.

The entries for the principal rivers and lakes of the counties of Brecknockshire, Radnorshire, Montgomeryshire, Merionethshire, Denbighshire and Flintshire all fall within our region. Included are details of 'Fishing Stations' on the rivers: 'Wye, Uske, Irvon, Llynfi, Elain, Ithon, Eddwy, Machwy, Lug, Severn, Vyrnwy, Dee, Clwyd, Tannat, Ceiriog and Alyn, as well as on the lakes: Llangorse Mere, Llyn Tegid (Bala), Llyn Tryweryn and Llyn Alwen.'

There are especially relevant entries for: Crickhowell, Brecknock, Glangrwny and Tretower on the Uske; Aberedw, Builth on the Eddwy and Wye; Llandrindod on the Ithon; Michael Church on the Arrow; Presteigne on the Lug; Llanidloes, Bettws and Newtown on the Severn; Llan-yn-Mochant on the Mole/Tannat; Llandrillo, Llansanfraid Glyn Dyvrdwy, Llanwchllyn and Llangollen on the Dee; and Llanymenech on the Vyrnwy. (All spellings as in the book.)

A BOOK ON ANGLING
Francis Francis (1867)

Francis Francis was editor of *The Field* and an avid all-round angler. *A Book on Angling* (described on the title page as *A Complete Treatise on the Art of Fishing in every Branch*) is the result of a lifetime of experience with the rod.

In the preface to the first edition he outlines that it was his 'ambition to catch every species of freshwater fish, from the minnow up to the salmon, which inhabits our British waters. That satisfied,

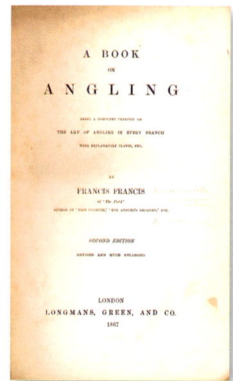

my next desire was to write a work, which should contain within one volume the fullest and most varied information upon angling.' The result is forteen chapters long and was regarded by many as the definitive work of the time.

The chapter on flyfishing concentrates on trout fishing and looks into selection of the rod, casting, selecting casts of flies, how to fish the stream – up or down? The section on weather predominantly concentrates on when the angler should go flyfishing, and is delightfully summed in a piece of doggerel:

When the wind blows from the west,
It blows the hook to the fish's nest;
When the wind blows from the south,
It blows the hook to the fish's mouth;
When from the north and east it blows,
Seldom the angler fishing goes.

Among the 72 artificial trout flies detailed are a number of patterns from Mr James Ackers, president of the Leintwardine Club on the Teme near Ludlow, whose waters the author knew well. The flies are described in order of appearance during the season from March to September. However it is the section on grayling fishing that is of special interest since it is centred on Worcester and Shropshire streams, the tributaries of the Severn. There are descriptions of various ways of taking grayling: 'by the grasshopper, by the gentle or maggot, by the caddis bait, or by the worm.' The most effective method advocated is with the grasshopper.

There are descriptions of a number of patterns and a full-page plate of artificial grubs which were developed for use on the Leintwardine Club's water. One, looking like a gooseberry, is strangely called the Grasshopper, and another is more appropriately called the Wasp Grub – it is interesting to note that both are not far removed from some of the nymph patterns in use today.

When describing how to fish the grubs, the author quotes Mr Wheatley, the Leintwardine guru of this kind of fishing, who suggested he: '(used) as much line as you can conveniently work ... pitch your bait in every likely place especially every deep eddy ... working it up and down, sinking and drawing ... never allowing it to remain still an instant ... at every touch strike pretty smartly, but not violently ... October and November, when the lure is deadly.' (Sounds like yet another early-days description of Czech-nymphing.) Wheatley also makes reference to the use of a float in conjunction with the lure. (An early 'strike indicator'?)

The Grasshopper was so effective that it was only permitted for a short period of time each season – the two days before and two days after the Leintwardine Club dinner!

The penultimate chapter gives a comprehensive illustrated account of *How to Dress the Trout Fly* – complete with dubbing, wing and hackle preparation.

This extract is taken from Chapter VIII.

'Grayling should not be fished till August; they are not worth eating before that, and not very good then. A September fish is better than an August fish, October better than September, and November best of all. All through the winter, on a warm sunny mid-day, you may get sport; and even if it not be a warm sunny day, you need hardly despair, as the fish are in condition in winter, and must needs feed at some time, though certainly a glimpse of sunshine serves to bring out the flies, and to bring up the fish wonderfully.

There are various ways of taking the grayling – by the grasshopper, by the gentle or maggot, by the caddis bait, or by the worm, but I hesitate to notice them, as the grayling is such a sporting fish, and so free to rise to all comers, that it is a disgrace and shame to treat him like a poacher, with worms and such abominations. Still, as in an angling book one has to consult everybody's tastes but one's own, I suppose I must give the information, or it would be considered an 'hiatus,' though not perhaps *valde deflendus*.

The most slaughtering way of fishing for grayling is with the grasshopper. The grasshopper, so-called, is not a grasshopper at all, and though actually an artificial bait, in nowise resembles a grasshopper; why it should have been called a grasshopper any more than a gooseberry, which it more resembles, I cannot conceive. No matter; this is the grasshopper. Take a No. 5 or 6 trout-hook; lap round the shank some lead, enough to sink it pretty quickly; over this wind Berlin wool of various colours, chiefly green, with a few turns of yellow or red, or both.

With as much line as you can conveniently cast and work, pitch your bait into every likely place, particularly into every deep eddy and swirly hole, working it up and down, sinking and drawing with constant short jerks of the wrist, never allowing it to remain still for an instant, until the whole of the water be thoroughly searched; at every touch strike pretty smartly, but not violently, and disturb the water as little as possible in landing your fish, as in October and November, when this deadly lure is chiefly used, the fish are often congregated in good numbers in any favourite hole, and with caution many may be caught before the rest are scared. Wheatley recommends a float as an addendum to this process – out on it! And he also recommends the point of the hook to be tipped with a bit of worm or a maggot, to flavour it.

To give some idea of the deadly nature of these baits on some streams, I have known instances where by the use of it, large twenty-five or thirty pounds baskets have been filled and emptied three times over in one day's fishing by a single rod, and they are always the best and largest fish. It is quite incomprehensible, as on other rivers they take no more notice of the bait than they would of a turnip; its use being confined to the Worcester and Shropshire streams – the tributaries of the Severn, in fact. It has often been tried in Hampshire, and has not yet succeeded, as far as I know, I dare say it would do in the Derbyshire Wye, but only fly is allowed there fortunately. At Leintwardine, on the Teme, it was allowed for a short time, and the slaughter made of the grayling was positively dreadful, and it was again prohibited, save for about four days in the year, that is, two days before and two after the annual dinner at Leintwardine, as a sort of bonne bouche for those who go down to the dinner. Tremendous bags are made then, but it is found that its use spoils the fly-fishing, as does the minnow with trout; and it has been clearly proved there that when it is not used the big grayling rise much more freely to the fly. It is certainly an artificial bait, and that is all that can be said for it; if it be used, some restriction should be placed on it.

Grayling are also fond of the maggot or gentle, and may be whipped for with them, the bait sinking to even mid-water at times, or a very light quill-float, with about three shots – a tripping bait – a few gentles being thrown in now and then as ground-bait. A Nottingham line and reel may be employed. A red worm may also be used either in the same way or with a free line, as for trout, and that certainly is the more sportsman-like plan of the two. All these plans, though possible, are not to my mind legitimate, as there is scarcely any reasonable water or weather when grayling will altogether refuse the fly; and though, in a book in which it is my desire to give the fullest information upon every style of angling, I feel bound to mention these methods, I do not feel disposed to enlarge much on them, as I certainly would never resort to them myself. Sometimes a grayling may be taken with the minnow, but it rather an accident than otherwise. In like manner barbel and chub take a minnow or small gudgeon, but no one would fish thus for them. It is needless to say fish fine for grayling, as if you do not you will soon learn to. A wee silver dun with a tinsel body, and the lightest blue hackle, is a prime favourite everywhere. '

FISHING REMINISCENCES
Archdeacon Lea (1892)

In 1892 Josiah T. Lea organised the printing of 100 copies of *Fishing Reminiscences* by his father, the late Archdeacon Lea, for 'distribution among his most intimate friends and relations.' The reminiscences are in the form of ten papers, each one the account of a specific day's fishing experience. The final three of the ten are of particular relevance to those who fish the Welsh Borderlands.

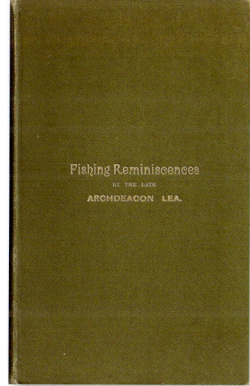

A Day on the Dee gives a graphic account of the antics of coracle fishers on the Dee near Llangollen as well a how to fish with 'a shilling's worth of flies of the season from a local fisherman.'

A Day at Leintwardine includes 'pleasant wanderings by the sparkling Teme', which the author reckons is one of the best rivers in England for trout and grayling, though he concedes there are better grayling in the Lugg! There is a vivid description of an August day on the Leintwardine Club water, prior to its lease expiring in 1869, in which 36 fish were caught – 33 grayling and three trout.

A Day on the Severn outlines a day trout fishing with a minnow from a punt floating down the river at Bewdley. There is a delightful account of the excitement surrounding the catching of a 3lb 3oz trout which is one of eight fish caught in nine runs down the river and which was reported as 'an unusual amount of success.'

A SHROPSHIRE LAD
A. E. Housman (1896)

A Shropshire Lad, Housman's famous book of 63 nostalgic verses, has not been out of print since its first publication. Reference is made to these verses in some of the other books in this review and so it seems appropriate to include it. The verses testify to the trials and tribulations of life set in 'a land of lost content' – Shropshire! Although not known to be an angler, Housman wrote endearingly of the region, as in verse XXVIII of *The Welsh Marches*:

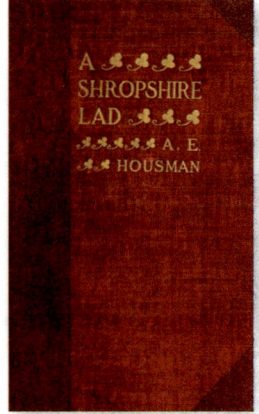

> *In my heart it has not died,*
> *The war that sleeps on Severn side,*
> *They cease not fighting, east and west,*
> *On the marches of my breast.*

and of *Western Brookland* in verse LII:

> *Far in a western brookland*
> *That bred me long ago*
> *The poplars stand and tremble*
> *By pools I used to know*

He makes reference to other rivers of the region in verse XXVII:

> *The land where I shall mind you not*
> *Is the land where all's forgot.*
> *And if my foot returns no more*
> *To Teme nor Corve nor Severn shore,*

And verse L has an idyllic reference to places and rivers:

> *Clunton and Clunbury,*
> *Clungunford and Clun,*
> *Are the quietest places*
> *Under the sun.*

> *In valleys of Springs of rivers,*
> *By Ony and Teme and Clun,*
> *The country for easy livers,*
> *The quietest under the sun.*

AN OLD MAN'S HOLIDAYS
Edward Marston (1900)

An Old Man's Holidays is the fourth book from this prolific author who wrote seven books between 1887 and 1911 on fishing and the countryside. This book has 16 chapters of holiday sketches and fishing, and the Welsh Borderlands feature in three of them.

In the chapter *On the Ithon, Llandrindod Wells*, the author tells of a week of fishing forays in July 1898 at locations still recognised today such as: Shaky Bridge, Lovers' Leap and Alpine Bridge. He describes this valley as 'an oasis among the hills.'

Following on from this week of fishing, Marston moved fifteen miles up the Wye valley to a base at the Elan Valley Hotel near Rhayader. The chapter *The Elan Valley and Birmingham Waterworks* depicts two frustrating days of sport on the Elan where the author blames the Birmingham Corporation for ruining the fishing prospects!

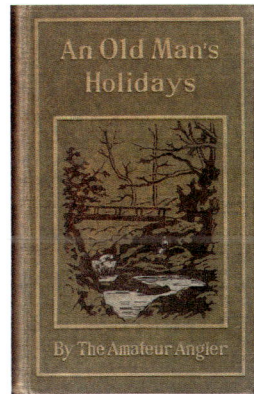

The chapter *In Pursuit of Mayfly* refers to the River Arrow in early June, which is elaborated in one of his later books *Fishing for Pleasure and Catching It* (1906) reviewed later in this chapter.

FISHING IN WALES
Walter M. Gallichan (1903)

Fishing in Wales is the first of three books by Gallichan that are relevant to this review. Although it talks about fishing throughout the whole of Wales, it gives particularly good coverage of the Welsh Borderland rivers and streams. There are specific references to the Dee around Corwen and Llangollen (complete with coracle fishers); to the Tanat near Llangynog; to the Ceiriog near Dolywern; to the Usk from its source to Abergavenny; to the Wye and its tributaries – the Irfon, Cammarch, Ithon, Monnow, Arrow, Teme, Lugg and Pinsley. Throughout the book there are references to an abundance of trout and grayling in these good rivers and streams. There are also passing references to flies but a lack of detail with regard to their patterns. There are also interesting references to suitable accommodation opportunities.

FISHING FOR PLEASURE AND CATCHING IT
Edward Marston (1906)

This was Marston's sixth book, and contains anecdotal stories of various fishing holidays, three of which are on the rivers and streams of the Welsh Borderlands. Referring to the Lugg he states in the chapter *May Fly Fishing in Herefordshire in 1903* that there is 'an ancient reputation for the quality of trout fishing and in bygone days it was a great privilege to fish its waters.' He fished it with success beneath Dinmore Hill in Herefordshire and also at Kingsland 'during a cold fishless June with the wind persistently in the Northeast preventing mayfly hatching.'

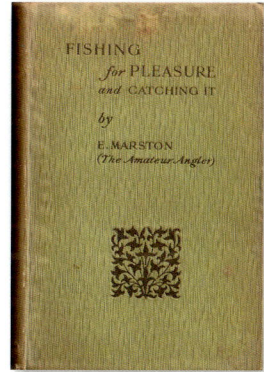

He mentions in the chapter *On the Ithon (a Scramble in the Woods)* that there are seven miles of excellent fishing to be had on this 'most tantalizing, rod-breaking, stream' in the vicinity of Shaky Bridge.

Other Welsh Borderland streams mentioned in passing are the Teme and Corve in the Ludlow area and the Arrow where he reports that in 1905 four trout fishers took 'nineteen-and-a-half brace' in one day.

THE TROUT WATERS OF ENGLAND
Walter M. Gallichan (1908)

The Trout Waters of England – A practical guide to the fishermen for sea trout, brown trout and grayling is really the companion volume to Gallichan's earlier *Fishing in Wales*. In this book the author takes the reader on a whistlestop tour of 'open' trout fishing in fifteen areas of England: 'that is to say … without fee in some cases; while in none of the quarters will he find it necessary to expend much money upon his sport.'

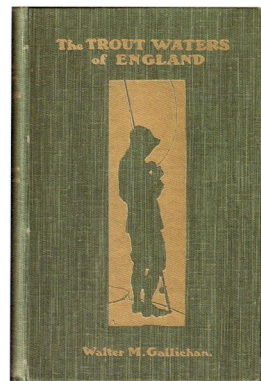

Our interest lies with the chapter entitled *On the Welsh Border*. It opens with: 'The Wye and several tributaries, the Severn tributaries, and the Usk and its affluents are trout streams of considerable importance.' The remainder of the chapter expands on this by looking more closely at the fishing opportunities in each catchment within England, in which he interestingly includes Monmouthshire.

The Wye, from where it enters England near Hay-on-Wye, he declares 'is not a prime trout river but that its tributaries the Monnow, Trothy, Lug and Pinsley Brook certainly are.'

Of the Severn he declares 'that it is only in the upper (Welsh) reaches that trout abound but that the tributary rivers Teme and Letwyche are good for trout and grayling while on the Vyrnwy … there is fair fly-fishing for trout, grayling and chub.'

The Usk he states, 'is, par excellence, the trout river of the district', a point of view shared by many who fish it today. He recommends Abergavenny and Usk as suitable bases and informs the reader that the Usk 'is an early river, and in a mild March and April the trout rise well to duns of various dressings.'

CLEAR WATERS
A. G. Bradley (1915)

Arthur G. Bradley lived in the heart of the Borderlands and was author of many books. He had a lively personality and enlivened his pages with many delightful anecdotes. *Clear Waters*, sub-titled *Trouting days and trouting ways in Wales, the West Country, and the Scottish Borderland*, has three chapters that merit closer attention. *The Welsh Dee, The Welsh Borderland* and *Elan Lakes – Wild South Wales*.

The chapter titled *The Welsh Dee* starts romantically at the river's sombre birthplace, where the infant Dee comes breaking out at the foot of one of the Aran Mountains, soon to be joined by two other 'impetuous streams' on their way to Llyn Tegid (Bala Lake). We then concentrate on the seven miles of river from Llansantffraid (or Carrog) to the Chain Bridge at Berwyn just upstream of Llangollen, where we learn that the river has good March Brown fishing with 'vistas of woodland and fretting waters' but that the 'trout retire early in the season.' There follows an elaborate account of *cwrwgle* (coracle) fishing around Llantisilio with Evan Evans lifting twenty pound baskets from a coracle on an April evening.

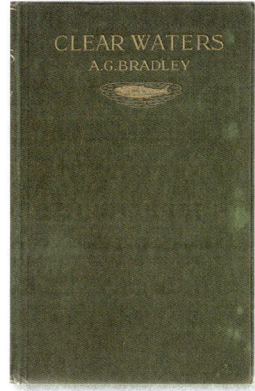

Bradley goes on to state that Borderland rivers and streams have similar characteristics and includes the Lugg, Arrow, Teme, Monnow, Honddu, Corve, Onny, Rea and the Camlad in his analysis. He declares that they show a strong family likeness and that 'the breed is one of quality.' On the whole he considers them to be wet fly rivers but with some excellent dry fly opportunities.

Reference is made to the Lugg (and Arrow) rising in the wilds of Radnor Forest and flowing through 'bosky gorges' and on towards the pleasant pastures of Hereford, but below Leominster deteriorating as a trout stream.

Of the Teme Bradley states that it 'has scarcely a dull mile and is always beautiful.' Ludlow is noted for its stately pose and old-world charm.

The Onny he describes as a bewitching little stream but not rated in the same class as the Teme or the Lugg, but it is renowned for large bushy flies with overgrown red and blue dun hackles, a feature common to whole region.

The chapter ends with reference to the Honddu around Llanthony Priory in the heart of the Black Mountains, where the Priory Inn water is reported to be thickly fringed with bushes. Those who fish it today as a 'Passport' beat of the Wye and Usk Foundation would agree.

In the chapter *Elan Lakes – Wild South Wales*, Bradley claims that Birmingham, 'the murky metropolis of the Midlands' is responsible for the transformation of the Elan and Claerwen valleys by way of four lakes, each with large populations of native and stocked trout. Passing references are made to a mountain lake, Llyn Carw, and the remote twin lakes of Cerrig-Llwydion, as being worthy of a visit for their handsome trout.

The young poet, Percy Bysshe Shelley, came to Cwm Elan after being expelled from Oxford, and later eloped there with his sixteen-year-old cousin Harriet Westbrook to settle at Nantgwyllt House, now lying deep under the waters of Caban Coch reservoir. Needless to say he poetically recorded his personal turmoil:

When mountain, meadow, wood, and stream
With unalloying glory gleam,
And to the spirit's ear and eye
Are unison and harmony.
The moonlight was my dearer day;
Then would I wander far away,
And lingering on the wild brook's shore
To hear its unremitting roar,
Would lose in the tidal flow
All sense of overwhelming woe.

The chapter continues with reference to Rhayader – the name a derivative of the Welsh *Rhaiadr Gwy*, meaning the cataract of Wye – as having 'excellent and snug headquarters for fishermen.' Trout fishing on the Wye from here up to its source is deemed pretty good, especially in the locality of Llangurig ('a veritable little oasis in a fine, wild country'), which surprisingly is only five miles from the little sheep town of Llanidloes on the banks of the Severn where the trout fishing is excellent. We are also told that the 'twelve-mile stretch of the Wye from Rhayader downwards is, I think, as beautiful as any of the sections into which the queen of English and Welsh rivers naturally falls.' In the heart of this stretch is Builth where the Wye has inspired many poets including the great Welsh poet, Dafydd ap Gwylim. His poem Sweet Wye may have lost a little through translation into English:

> *Sweet Wye, with thy waters as white as the snow,*
> *Now dark as the thunder-cloud's banner of woe.*
> *Oh why should we wander beyond thy wild stream,*
> *From the land of the harp and the bard and his dream!*
> *The streams of the Saxons are languid and dead,*
> *Like the mist on the mountain when summer is fled.*
> *With thy wild, thronging billows, now softened, now shrill,*
> *Like the laugh of fair children that sport on the hill,*
> *Now all glowing with light and all snowy with foam,*
> *Like the maids of the land of my heart and my home.*

Bradley concludes the chapter with references to the upper Severn around Llanidloes, the Teifi and the Towy.

This extract comes from the chapter *The Welsh Borderland:*

'I always think of the streams of the Welsh Border, that is to say, of the English counties bordering Mid and South Wales, as in a class by themselves. This is in part, perhaps, but not I think wholly, a mere personal caprice, come of frequent intercourse with them. They all have much the same characteristics, and as a group come midway, as it were, between the frankly impetuous streams of Wales and the slow-moving waters east of the Severn. The Lugg, the Arrow, and the Teme, the Monnow and the Honddu, the

Corve, the Onny, the Rea and the little Camlad, the only
river this last which runs from England into Wales, may
be accounted a fairly exhaustive list, and if you know them
all you may consider yourself to be on terms of tolerable
intimacy with what is often but not quite accurately
designated the Marches of Wales. A strong family likeness
runs through them all, but the breed is one of quality, not
of that common order which satisfies people to the east of
the Severn and south of the Trent and artists who cannot
paint fast waters. The fish, too, speaking broadly, like the
scenery, come midway between those of Wales and of the
slow waters of low-pitched England, and average from a
quarter to three-quarters of a pound. Though essentially
wet-fly rivers, some of them are excellent for dry-fly fishing,
if you prefer that method. Practically all of them rise in the
Welsh mountains and carry their native impetuosity into
English valleys, whose oftentimes gentle gradients succeed
in partially curbing it and creating that compromise
between the rapid and slow river which is the ideal of many
trout fishermen. Lastly, some of them, notably the Teme
and Lugg, are also natural grayling rivers of the first order.

As an item of useful information it may be noted that
the whole of them are preserved by owners, lessees or
members of clubs. There is very little hotel water and
scarcely any free or association fishing. I myself have fished
here and there at different times on all these streams, but
more frequently of recent years upon the Lugg, though
more often to be sure in quest of its grayling, rather than
of its trout. There is probably no better portion of the
Lugg for a combination of trout and grayling than those
pleasant reaches by which it winds its purling way from
the battlefield of Mortimer's Cross to Leominster, where
it meets its smaller sister the Arrow. It is strange that its
upper waters should have been the scene of two historic
conflicts: the greater one just mentioned, which seated

Edward IV upon the throne and wrought such havoc among the Lancastrian notables; and that other less known one of Pilleth, which ushers in the first act of Shakespeare's Henry IV and marked the first formidable blow of the 'damned Glendower.' For the Lugg, like the Arrow, rises in the wild moorland of Radnor forest, and thence runs down towards Presteign, a babbling alder-shaded brook in a narrow vale, where below the hill of Pilleth, Mortimer's levies were rolled up in 1400 by the Welsh, and eleven hundred Herefordians bit the dust. Hence came spurring eastward to London and King Henry that "Post from Wales loaden with heavy news."

On leaving Presteign the little river has to fight its way through fine uplifted woody hills, to thread the bosky gorges of Aymestry, through which the Yorkist army marches to Mortimer's Cross and so out into the pleasant pastures of Hereford. The old grey tower of Kingsland church, which witnessed the fearful slaughter of that sanguinary day, and no doubt the heavenly portents which ushered in its fateful morn, rises significant and conspicuous above the woods and pastures of the now wide opening vale. The river seems here to attune itself to its gentler surroundings, slipping down between crumbling red sandstone banks from gravelly run to rippling pool, and thence into interludes of quiet and deep water. Trees overhang much of it on one bank or the other, occasionally on both, and as wading is neither customary nor desirable, the fishing has generally that flavour of difficulty about it which is or should be accounted to its credit. I doubt if there is a better bit of grayling water in the kingdom than this, or one where they rise more freely in the early autumn months. No worming is practised here as on the Border and in Yorkshire. There is no occasion for it. For when the water is clear in September and October, no matter what the wind's quarter or what like the day, the grayling is more or less ready to take the fly, and certainly no flies that I for my part ever offer them or have seen my friends offer are more effective than the red-tag and the mid-blue.

In a short week during each of now many successive years on this water, it is curious to remember when comparing it with any trouting record, that half a dozen fish is the nearest to a blank day recorded in my journal. And the Lugg grayling are strong and shapely, averaging like its trout about two to a pound. No reference to written data, however, is needed to recall many a good basket from this alluring stream. Several times while pursuing my homeward way across the big ox pastures to a certain hospitable roof upon the green slopes beyond, I have been thankful that the Lugg is not a wading river, and that the burden of waders and brogues is not added to the burden on one's back. Once or twice I have had to cut short my day from the fact that my tolerably capacious creel would not hold another fish. And it may be remembered that there is no object to sparing grayling whatever might be desirable in some waters with regard to trout. They can always more than maintain themselves against any onslaught of the fly-fisher. Moreover, where the trout shares their water one feels that the more grayling fairly killed the better, as the less noble tenants of the stream are apt in this case to be over pushful to their betters. In the north, as we shall see, the grayling has in this way worked havoc. But I think in stream like those of Herefordshire, where nature has placed these kindred breeds side by side, she somehow preserves the balance. Still a vague and no doubt erroneous feeling that a captured grayling makes room for an extra trout removes any compunction to basketing just as many as you can catch, or on those occasions hinted at, as you can carry – even to keeping the little ones.'

THE TROUT ARE RISING
B. Bennion (1920)

Bertie Bennion ('B.B.' of *The Field*) wrote *The Trout are Rising* in which he tells of times spent fishing in England and South Africa. There are five chapters of particular interest and relevance to those who fish the Welsh Borderlands. He left Britain for South Africa in the early 1900s to work for mining magnate Sir George Farrer as his personal secretary. The job seemed mainly to entail organising and accompanying Sir George on frequent fishing trips around Southern Africa. Later he became a newspaper journalist and contributed to several fishing magazines including various *Hardy Guides*. He wrote a second book about general fishing in South Africa in 1923.

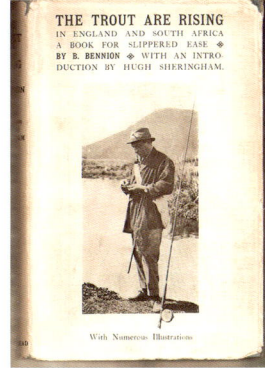

The chapter, *By Severnside in Shropshire* recounts tales of coarse fishing on the Severn near Cound and Shrewsbury and further judges how the river cannot be acclaimed as a trout-full river but that 'grayling find the river much to their liking where it has sandy, gravelly beds.' The chapter concludes by suggesting that 'a July day in a Severnside meadow ought to help a busy man learn the art of resting.'

A Tributary of the Severn describes a number of trout fishing locations on the River Tern, described as a 'good trout stream' close to Market Drayton.

Weeks in Worcestershire describes Tenbury as 'the town in the orchard' and recalls days of fly and bait fishing for grayling thereabouts.

On the Fords of Teme outlines some successful grayling forays on the river with different sets of companions. With a tip-off from a certain 'visitor from Stroud', the author has 'an hour of rare delight' at the tail of a likely ford having put on a Green Insect. In the company of 'the Major' and another demobilised officer the party fished for grayling at 'every moment possible, fished again at meals and again in the smoking room.'

Bennion goes on to quote from Lord Grey's *Fly Fishing* stating: 'Dry fly fishing – the effort, in short, is to make the trout notice the fly without noticing anything else' and the same principle, he asserts, applies to grayling.

A Memory of the Lugg relates the events of a November day grayling fishing on the Lugg near Mortimer's Cross close to the scene of the battle which secured the throne for Edward IV. The Major, we're told, caught 'a good sized glittering grayling' on the first cast whilst the rest of the party were still tackling up. Some sound advice in the form of definite instructions from the riparian hostess of the beat were given but not necessarily heeded: 'If the grayling are rising, put the dry fly on; if they are not, then fish wet.'

This extract is from Chapter IX in *The Trout are Rising* and is called *On the Fords of Teme*:

'So far, I must confess that, though I had occasionally employed the dry fly when necessary, the wet fly had appealed to me more and I regarded myself as first and foremost a wet-fly man. But now I began to feel the genuine dry-fly enthusiasm, though far be it from me to institute comparisons or to dogmatize as to preferences. On this point two golden sentences from that charming and highly educative book, *Lord Grey's Fly Fishing,* may appropriately be quoted. "I have," he says, " at various times started in my own mind so many theories which have been suggested by experience and afterwards upset by it, that I do not desire to press anyone to accept an opinion unless there is anything in his own experience which goes to support it. There is only one theory about angling in which I have perfect confidence, and that is that the two words, least appropriate to any statement about it, are the words 'always' and 'never'."

Touching dry-fly fishing, he sums up the art in these words: "The effort, in short, is to make the trout notice the fly without noticing anything else. It is in this that the fine art of dry-fly fishing consists." Obviously the same principle applies to grayling, although of the two fish the grayling is far less shy.

The time the visitor from Stroud and I had together by the waterside that day, from early forenoon until 4 o'clock, had its sparkling interval. During those days the wise thing was to be at the waterside soon after breakfast. Early in autumn 10 a.m. is a good time for beginning, later 11 o'clock, or even midday, will be soon enough. One can go on fishing as long as there is any encouragement to do so, maybe until dusk in mild weather. If the season is not too advanced and if the water is right, grayling are almost sure to rise cheerfully at some time of the day. If they are not rising, and you wish to fish, then put on the wet fly (three flies if the river suits); if on the other hand they are rising, then fish dry. Why, the grayling then are calling to you! Sometimes a particular fly must be used, if any business is to be done. Sometimes practically any grayling fly, especially when tipped with a dash of colour, will attract them. But you never know. The grayling is a challenge to study. You think you understand this game fish, and then you realize that you are contemplating a mystery. That is, perhaps, why the grayling is called the 'Lady of the Stream'.

That morning the Stroud angler had started at the far end of the association reach, in the Newnham Bridge direction. I had gone a little higher up, to within sight of Boraston Church, with its quaint spire. I had done nothing. When I had worked my way down I saw him, bewadered and in the water, supremely happy. Grayling were rising all round him. He had struck a gravelly ford such as the fish love. Already he had a nice bag, and he deserved it, for he cast his short line very prettily. The grayling sometimes missed or refused the fly, but they kept coming. He would have been a good study for a "Picture of a Happy Grayling Fisherman."

"Put on the green insect!" said he, briefly, in a moment snatched from his business, as it were.

"Thank you," I said, "I will," and I did. Hurrying on I came to a likely ford, established myself at its tail where the deeper water was beginning, and where a short line was not only valuable but imperative. And then I had an hour of rare delight. Perhaps the sport which I enjoyed, good though it was, was not the chief part of my enjoyment. It was quite as much the behaviour of the dry fly, the Green Insect, that kept me rapt with attention and appreciation. The fly sat on the water, now like an imitation of a greatly reduced hedgehog, now like a miniature Busby! However absurd the two comparisons, they are what that floating dry fly, that green insect, put me in mind of at the time. The current was rapid, and, as soon as the fly alighted on the water, off it went! I positively laughed with enjoyment. Then all of a sudden a grayling would glide up from the bottom like a ghost, and maybe it was hooked – maybe not. It mattered little. Moreover, it would probably come again. When in the humour the grayling will several times to the same fly. It was a busy time, and, when the rise was over, I left the ford, still chuckling to myself. That was a good day. The rise was not a long one, but it was brisk while it lasted. We both got a bag, the man from Stroud a bigger one than I.'

FISHING IN MID-WALES
Walter M. Gallichan (1939)

Walter M. Gallichan was an enigmatic character; one of the first professional angling journalists and a prolific writer on the subject of fishing.

Fishing in mid-Wales is a charming, if short, 55-page book, packed with a significant amount of useful information for the Borderlands flyfisher. Gallichan relates a number of fishing tales of when he was based at various hotels in the region, mentioning early spring wet fly and summer dry fly forays on the Ithon (and its tributaries) at Pen-y-bont and Llandrindod Wells, as well as the Wye above Rhayader and below Builth Wells. In this context he states: 'For brook fishing in beautiful scenery I recommend the Edw.' Also the Irfon which 'rises in one of the wildest regions of Wales … with rocks and rough going in parts of the banks' and there is a short entry on the Lugg near the 'old world village' of Presteigne.

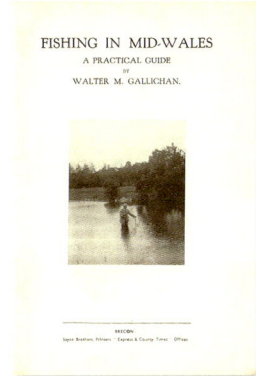

'Small hackle flies' are frequently referred to throughout the book and Gallichan includes a list of flies he has found successful on the Wye, Ithon, Irfon and tributaries. They are Blue Dun, Greenwell's Glory, Brasil, Olive Dun, Wickham, Mayfly, March Brown, Alder, and his own 'Gallichan's Six' – Black Gnat, Borderer, Grizzle Dun, Olive Quill Gnat, Orange Dun Hackle, and Whirling Dun.

There is a section devoted to the Birmingham Corporation reservoirs in the Elan Valley where he says that the trout 'are numerous and strong.' In the mid-1930s fish were taken to seven pounds plus! Llangorse Lake (Llyn Safaddu) the largest natural expanse of water in South Wales also has a brief mention. The final section on the *1939 Rules, Regulations and Permits* on the rivers and lakes mentioned in the book makes fascinating reading.

This extract is from Chapter VII of this short practical guide to fishing in the Welsh Borderlands:

'This river rises in one of the wildest regions of Wales, on the fringe of the Forest Fawr, near the little village of Abergwessin. A mountain road from Llanwrtyd to Trega-ron is on the left bank of the stream for some miles above Llanwrtyd, passing a narrow gorge known as the Wolf's Leap. Trout are abundant throughout the whole course of the Irfon, and there are two fisheries open to hotel visitors at Llanwrtyd Wells and Llangammarch Wells.

The Irfon (sometimes spelt Yrfon) rises quickly after rain in the hills and hurries down to Llanwrtyd in a very lovely setting. In flood, the stream is peat-stained, and when the water is fining, it remains slightly stained for some days and is in good order for the fly.

I have spent charming days on this river, both at Llanwr-tyd Wells and Llangammarch, and have made some good baskets in spring and early summer, with dry or wet fly. Visitors to Llanwrtyd have some miles of open water above and below the Dolecoed Hotel, and from the Abernant Lake Hotel downwards is a well-stocked length. With a short rod, a fine tapered cast and a small dry fly success waits the skilled angler, even when the river is at low summer level.

Abernant Lake has a fleet of rowing boats, and there are some big chub in the water, that take the fly. The Irfon below the Hotel has many fine runs and long glides down to Llangammarch Bridge. There is a tributary, the Dulas, which may be fished by guests at the Lake Hotel.

Some years ago, I fished a charming little brook that flows down from the golf links at Llangammarch. It holds plenty of small trout. The main river has a good number of big trout and an abundance of three-quarter and half-pound fish.

Salmon ascend this part of the Irfon from the Wye.

The lake at Llangammarch Wells, near the Hotel, is stocked with trout. The Irfon flows on through beautiful glen scenery towards Garth. Further down the water is privately owned. The lower reaches belong to Lord Swansea and the fishing is private.

Throughout its course the Irfon is well preserved, and a Wye conservancy bailiff lives by the riverside. My friend, Fred Shaw, ex-champion fly-caster of England and author of angling books, speaks highly of this river. He points out that it is an error to suppose that the Irfon cannot be successfully fished with the dry fly. Although the river has many rough, tumbling runs, there are pools admirably adapted for fishing with the floating fly.

The same cannot be said for mountain streams in general, especially in the height of summer. I have seen Shaw take trout with a dry fly on more than one swift, rocky brook, when we were staying at Lake Vyrnwy some years ago, and he astonished some of the 'regulars' who declare the dry fly is useless in sharp streams. There is an art in preventing the drag, when fishing across the stream, which can be acquired by practice. This mode of 'staggering the line' is used with good effect on the Ithon by Mr Dixon and other experts.

The flies that I have recommended for the Wye and Ithon will kill on the Irfon. Where permitted, the natural minnow is often attractive in high water, and so is a small fly spoon in the runs. Occasionally, a big chub will take the spoon.

The Irfon is a very interesting stream for those who are not daunted by the problems that always face the angler in impetuous waters, with rocks and rough going on parts of the bank.

Mr Bradley, the well-known writer of travel and historical books upon Wales and its rivers, has written enthusiastically of this river; and it was an article by him in *The Field* some time ago, that urged me to pay my first visit to Llanwrtyd Wells.'

A DICTIONARY OF TROUT FLIES
A. Courtney-Williams (1949)

A Dictionary of Trout Flies grew out of an earlier book by Courtney-Williams *Trout Flies: a Discussion and Dictionary* (1932). It is an all-embracing definitive work giving dressings of hundreds of flies with anecdotal notes on each one.

Our interest is alerted when in the introduction he states that included in those rivers it had been his good fortune to fish were the Usk, Teme, Corve, Lugg, Onny, Clun, Tanat and Dee. He declared himself a Borders fisherman and many of his most enjoyable days were spent on minor Welsh waters, streams such as the Alwen, Ceiriog, Monnow and Irfon.

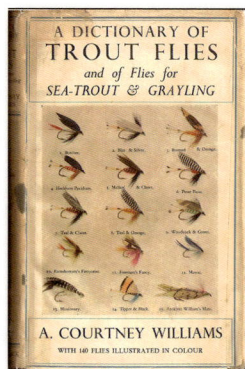

From his own experience he is 'sufficiently optimistic to believe that details about some of the lesser-known fly patterns such as the Grey Duster, Dogsbody, Welsh Partridge and Paragon will enable anglers to tie flies which will account for many a good fish.' (All four of them happen to be Welsh Borderland patterns.)

In Part One, Section I, *On Catching More Fish* there is a passing reference to Canon Eagles' 'natural gift for catching fish armed only with two fly patterns' – his own Herefordshire Alder and the Grey Duster.

Section II, *On the Importance of the Fly*, opens with a description of the same Canon Eagles with his 'crude gear' catching an incredible number of fish each year: 'His great gifts included skill, patience … but perhaps more than anything else, it was his ability to select the right fly which gave him so much success.'

In Section V, *On Fly-fishing Methods* there is a charming reference to the Rev. Edward Powell's two forms of flyfishing, 'the first as it is (or should be) practised on most rivers and the second as it is practised on the chalk streams; and the two styles are poles apart.'

Reference to the Rev. Edward Powell is also made in Section VII, *On Flies and Fly-dressers* where Courtney-Williams writes about him as 'the rector of a small Shropshire parish ... a very expert flyfisher ... most of his patterns are of the impressionistic variety ... the results he secures are sometimes devastating in their efficiency.'

Part Two is entitled *A List of Natural and Artificial Flies* but it is much more than that, for at each entry you not only find the details of the dressing of the pattern in question and its variants, but also a potted history of its origins and in many cases additional information about the originator and the natural fly of the same name.

If one scans the Index there are numerous references to the Welsh Borderlands through the entries of twenty artificial flies, seventeen personalities and fifteen rivers of the region.

FISHING FANTASY: A SALMON FISHERMAN'S NOTEBOOK
Jack Hughes-Parry (1949)

From the subtitle one might be justified in questioning this book's inclusion. However the Hughes-Parry family lived and fished the Dee in the Llangollen area for generations and the book contains a couple of relevant chapters. There is an informative one on *Fishing from a Coracle* and another simply entitled *Trout Fishing*.

The *Trout Fishing* chapter opens with a delightful comparison of 'pukka dry

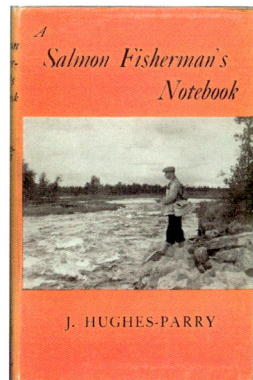

fly fishing' on the Test, Itchen and Kennet, with the 'ordinary middle-sized rivers of Wales a very different state of affairs.'

The pros and cons of when to use dry and wet flies is quickly followed by a wonderful description by the author of the modern day 'duo' system: 'I firmly believe that a cast consisting of a brown nymph-like fly fished *wet*, with a largish grey Badger Hackled fly some one foot or less from it, fished *dry* as a dropper, will beat both the plain dry fly or the wet fly when fished alone, especially on small brooks.'

The relevant section of the chapter concludes with the author advocating the use of only eight flies – four dry and four wet – to cover all eventualities on small streams:

Wet	Dry
February Red	*White Moth*
March Brown	*Feather Duster*
Greenwell's Glory	*Russet-coloured Palmer*
Coch-y-Bonddu or Invicta	*Black Gnat*

His own favourite cast he tells us is made up of a March Brown on the point and a Feather Duster on the dropper only nine inches apart except for when the heather fly is in evidence when he changes the dry to a Coch-y-Bonddu.

THE PASSIONATE ANGLER
Maurice Wiggin (1949)

Maurice Wiggin, a Black Country man, was literary editor and angling correspondent of *The Sunday Times*. In *The Passionate Angler* the reader is taken on 'a rambling record of hours and days gloriously mis-spent on various rivers and lakes.' Three chapters contain material of interest to the Welsh Borderland angler.

The chapter *Downstream from Bewdley* introduces the 'singular method' where trout are caught using a minnow and a line made of sewing cotton! More conventional flyfishing is mentioned but 'the casting is rather difficult – you really need to be ambidextrous to shoot a good line under the trees that cling to the tall east bank.' Apparently Bewdley trout are also 'stubborn risers rather than non-risers' making sport unpredictable at best. The Severn is described as 'a rude and reckless river, treacherous and shaggy … rough and brown and broken, and that is the sort of river I like best.' The chapter ends with some whimsical statements about 'the wild and wonderful uplands of the Welsh Marches.'

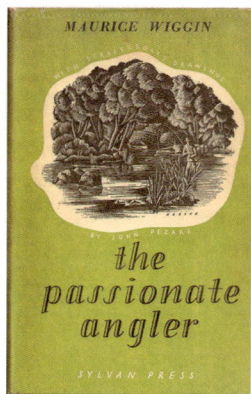

'You must cross the Severn to reach this paradise' which is a natural frontier … in the strictest historical sense, Englishmen have no right west of the Severn … there is still something in the air – some memory stirring of the days when this was truly border country … it is the loveliest country … full of nooks and corners … the lovely smoky country between Severn and Wye.'

The chapter *The Peacock's Tail* gives an honest account of a failed day on the Peacock Inn water at Newnham Bridge on the Teme near Tenbury Wells. A few beers in the pub, the stark realisation that fly boxes had been left at home and that there was only one fly, a Herefordshire Alder, to fish with. And then a wayward back cast snapped the point and barb off the fly hook. Every cloud has a silver lining though and the subsequent visit to Tenbury Wells led to a chance meeting with Ted Coombes in Cross Street where below the sign 'Shoemaker and Fishing Tackle' lay an Aladdin's cave of fishing tackle in an upstairs room.

Every angler, given good fortune, happens upon a secret

spot, or so we are told in the chapter entitled *Ashford Carbonell. Downstream from Ludlow on the River Teme*, Ashford Carbonell was the author's favourite 'secret spot.' It is a beat of only four hundred yards long, the top half of which is a glassy smooth glide between the bridge and 'the foaming half-moon weir' below which is a fast stickle racing away over gravel for a couple of meadows' length. The mill had ceased to function when the miller died and so now prospective anglers were 'scrutinised' by the miller's widow. An absorbing hour on the upstream glide is described, culminating with a small dace taking the fly. The chapter ends with the delights of the author's companion hooking and eventually landing a six-and-a-quarter pound pike on a 3X cast on a wet March Brown in the faster water below the weir.

All of the chapter headings in *The Passionate Angler* are graced by pen and ink drawings by Will Nickless. Nickless, a regular fishing companion of Wiggin, was a prolific artist who, from the late 1940s to the early 1970s, was responsible for thousands of black-and-white and colour drawings for comic books, magazines, advertisements, childrens' annuals and close to a hundred books. He also illustrated Maurice Wiggin's second fishing book including (no. 27 in this list), *The Angler's Bedside Book.* A selection of his illustrations was chosen from both books for the chapter headings in this book.

THE ART OF ANGLING
Kenneth Mansfield (Editor) (1957)

This massive work was published in three volumes and includes chapters by many fishing luminaries including Dick Walker on carp fishing and rod building, bass fishing by Donovan Kelley, tunny fishing by Eric Horsfall Turner, cooking coarse, game and sea fish by Ambrose Heath. Other contributors include W.A. Adamson, L. Vernon Bates, J.A.L.

Caunter, H.G.C. Claypoole, F. Cowburn, J.P. Garrad (Seangler), Edward Ensom (Faddist), F.W. Holiday, T.C. Ivens, L.A.J. Jackman, Peter Michael, L.A. Parker, B.A. Parmenter, Raymond Perrett, O.M. Reed, John G. Roberts, Coombe Richards, Michael Shephard, Peter Tombleson, C.F. Walker, A.L. Ward, Arthur Went and T.K. Wilson ... but very little of particular interest to the Borderlands angler except an extended chapter by The Rev. Edward Powell.

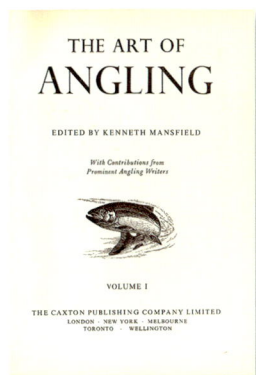

THE ART OF
ANGLING

EDITED BY KENNETH MANSFIELD

With Contributions from
Prominent Angling Writers

VOLUME I

THE CAXTON PUBLISHING COMPANY LIMITED
LONDON · NEW YORK · MELBOURNE
TORONTO · WELLINGTON

Here is Pastor Powell's entire chapter (chapter 9) *Dry-fly Fishing on Rain-fed Rivers* which is in Volume 3 of *The Art of Angling*:

'Personally I think that a better title for what follows would be *Normal Dry-fly Fishing*, for there is no doubt that, taking the British Isles as a whole, a chalk stream is a very abnormal thing, and to follow the advice and imitate the practice of those who have the misfortune to fish on no other kind of water is the most misleading thing that a beginner can do. Moreover it is a very easy mistake to make because eighty per cent of all dry-fly literature is based on chalk-stream practice, and its authors appear to take it for granted that what applies to Hampshire applies everywhere.

Nothing could be farther from the truth. The universal key which unlocks the mystery of the behaviour of all animate nature – bird, beast, insect, or fish – is food supply. Trout in chalk streams obtain their food in conditions so different from those in other rivers that for a chalk-stream man to fancy that a long experience of the Test will equip him to deal successfully with trout in, say, the Eden or the Teify is an error of the first magnitude.

Consider the following facts:

(i) The level of a chalk stream hardly varies throughout the year. Other rivers can become swollen to raging torrents in an hour or two or reduced to a mere trickle in a fortnight.

(ii) Chalk streams are nearly always as clear as gin. Other rivers are liable to solutions of mud so dense that underwater visibility is consequently reduced to practically nil.

(iii) The gentle gradient and absence of trees on a chalk stream encourage a dense growth of weeds. On other rivers the speed of the current makes it impossible for mud to settle and provide a root-hold and, in the few places where this is possible, the banks are often so bushed that sunlight, which is essential to weed growth, cannot penetrate. The result is that water-born flies who need mud and weed to breed in are far less numerous on non-chalk rivers.

(iv) The rapid rise and fall of "normal" rivers and the abundance in many cases of overhanging vegetation provide all sorts of land-bred provender, while the chalk stream fish have to depend far more on flies that are bred in the river itself.

(v) As a rule, owing to the placid nature of its flow, the trout in a chalk stream has plenty of time to examine each bit of flotsam before committing himself. On other rivers he often has to make up his mind in a split second or lose for ever the chance of a succulent mouthful.

(vi) The water in a chalk stream is always alkaline. On other rivers it is generally slightly acid and discouraging to shrimps and shellfish.

FLIES AND TECHNIQUES

The points just mentioned are only some of the considerable pinches of salt which the beginner should always remember to take with him when he consults the experts or the literature of the chalk stream. They will profoundly affect his gear and his tactics.

For instance, the principles on which he will make or select his flies will be quite different. Instead of nearly confining himself like the chalk stream fisherman to one "order" (the Ephemeridae) of insects, the "normal" dry-fly man will lay far greater emphasis on land-born things like beetles, ants, ichneumons, moths, and diptera. Moreover, exact imitation will be nothing like so important. In normal dry-fly fishing one seldom encounters dense fleets of one particular species as on a chalk stream. The trout one has to deal with cannot afford to confine themselves to any particular dish. If they did, they would starve. In order to get a living they have to vary their diet as opportunity offers.

Characteristics Of Flies For Rain-Fed Rivers

In view of the above facts, normal dry flies should, it seems to me, differ from those of the chalk stream in the following particulars. Firstly, they should be bigger in order to be visible to the fisherman and to trout living in water that is seldom clear and often turbulent; and generally, too, lying deeper than chalk stream fish because they are not expecting a regular supply of surface food and are therefore unwilling to make the highly skilled gymnastic effort of rising and returning to the same stance in a strong stream unless for a really worthwhile mouthful. Secondly, normal dry flies should be more buoyant as they have to ride out a far rougher sea. Thirdly, they should aim at suggestion rather than exact imitation.

In my opinion, too, the normal dry-fly man should, except in really low and clear conditions, use two flies about 2ft apart. This not only gives a trout lying in rapid water double the chance of seeing what you want him to see, but will help enormously to decide the question of what is the favourite dish on any particular day, there being usually no rises or natural insects to be seen.

Styles Of Fishing

Which brings me to the most important difference between the two styles of fishing. The normal dry-fly man must learn to "fish the water," as opposed to fishing the rise like the chalk-streamer. And when I say "learn" I mean "learn." It is the kind of knowledge which is only acquired by years of keen observation, applied logic, and passionate concentration. Nine times out of ten on a normal river there will be no trout to do three-quarters of your work for you by pushing his mouth out of the water and shouting: "Here I am." You must know where he is, with nothing to guide you but the look of the surface, for it is seldom indeed that the fisherman will be able to see far beneath it on any but chalk streams.

In my humble opinion this sense of watermanship is incomparably the most important qualification of the success- ful fisherman with the normal dry fly. There are only three ways of acquiring it. The first, and probably the most effective, is to have had the run of some local brook with a worm when young. The second, quite indispensable if you come to it after you are grown up, is to ingratiate yourself very humbly and politely with some expert (for there are few things which the successful fisherman values more than privacy and solitude!); dog him like a bloodhound; watch him like a cat; notice the kind of water he takes trouble over and the kind he omits; keep low and just out of reach of his back-cast, and reserve your questions for the lunch interval. The third is to remem- ber, as I have already said, that the key to the mystery is food-supply. Watch the surface and ask yourself, "Where, if I were a trout, should I take up my stance if I wished to see and catch with least effort the greatest number of surface-borne insects in the shortest time?" After years of practice, this weighing of probabilities becomes nearly automatic and instinctive; though the fisherman has a perfectly valid, logical reason for every cast he makes or refrains from making.

But, having learnt where to expect your trout, there always remains the great question: "What are you going to offer him?"

Selection Of Flies

My advice to the beginner is to start with one or more of the following general flies and to ring the changes on them until or unless you have reason to suppose that some natural insect is being taken on the particular day when you happen to be fishing:

The Doctor (suggesting beetle):

Hackle: Coch-y-bonddu cock
Body: Black wool
Tailquarter: White rabbit fur, dyed yellow in picric acid
Whisks: As hackle
Hooks: No. 14-10

The Paragon (suggesting sedge):

Hackles: Two – dark Rhode Island hen
Body: Rabbit face fur, very full. Equal quantities of the brown and the black rubbed up together
Whisks: Red cock
Hook: No. 16-12

The Ermine (suggesting moth):

Hackles: Two. Grey speckled partridge
Body: White rabbit fur
Ribbing: (Very distinct) doubled black sewing cotton, three or four turns
Tag: Pale orange wool
Hook: No. 14-10

These should all be stocked in several sizes. The heavier or thicker the water the larger the fly and vice versa. A fly of a full inch diameter when wound is none too big on occasion. These may be regarded as the stand-by of the normal dry-fly fisherman, but, of course, he must always keep his wits about him and notice the occasions when it will pay him better to imitate some special insect that happens to be popular at the moment. Among these he may expect the following in their appropriate seasons: dark olive, March brown, grannom, gravel-bed, black gnat, alder, light olive, iron blue, black-beetle, soldier beetle, red ant and needle. Many of these flies are described in detail later in this chapter.

Of course, if the river he is fishing is cursed with the mayfly he will probably want to use an imitation of it, though I generally find that the alder kills just as well at the beginning of the hatch and the ermine far better at the end. A charm of West and North Country fishing is that you are spared the long period of lethargy and repletion which affects so many English trout after the mayfly is over.

FISHING TACTICS

The tactics of normal dry-fly fishing will depend more than anything else on two great factors – the state of the water and the time of year.

Water-level and colour

On arriving at the waterside, the first thing to do is to note the level of the stream. If it is high and even if coloured in moderation, there is no occasion to lose hope. Remember that a trout can see through an amazing amount of mud and withstand a surprising force of current, but what defeats him is a combination of the two. It is no good spending your time thrashing Niagaras of pea soup. Concentrate on the lips and edges of pools – the lips because the water is shallow and the edges because they are slow. If you know your stream well, remember that the good stretches will probably be too heavy in a flood and that the dead stills you have been accustomed to pass by will now very likely be moving at precisely the right pace to pay a trout to occupy them – viz. fast enough to carry a succession of edibles past or over his nose but not so fast as to exhaust him.

In Wales and the West Country, where most of the rivers are fed by peat water, a half-flood in June, July, or August is an advantage rather than a handicap. Such streams flowing over a rocky terrain carry very little mud in suspension. They go very black but that is due to stain, not solids, and if I had to choose the ideal time for fishing them with a dry fly I should pick a half-full river running down after a flood in one of those three months.

Baits

It is well to remember, too, that at this time of year in normal rivers the hatch of *Ephemeridae* is negligible compared with the colossal multitudes of land and tree insects. It is instructive to catch hold of an oak or alder bough in July or August and give it a shake. The profusion of life disclosed takes one's breath away. Imagine, then, the opportunities for mixed grill enjoyed by trout who have the sense (and most of them are sensible in the extreme, as the beginner will soon discover) to lie quietly in the shade beneath overhanging branches, especially if there is an occasional puff of wind. Insects are sure-footed things – three times more so than we are, to be exact – but even they are liable to make a false step in gusty weather.

Of course, many of these insects are too small to imitate successfully (I have been trying for thirty years to make a

satisfactory copy of the aphis and so far failed) but there
are always beetles and moths and even caterpillars. I shall
never forget a glorious hour I had on a Welsh river some
years ago. It was a typical mid-summer anticyclone. The
sun was fierce and persistent; the river was in the last
stages of desiccation. For hours I had been flogging the
likely places without result, when I arrived at a spot where
a clump of oak trees leant far out over a slow, deepish
stream running along at the foot of a rocky cliff. I had had
almost enough and sat down on the opposite bank idly
watching the water. Suddenly, to my astonishment, the
surface of the river under the boughs was disturbed by five
or six practically simultaneous rises of what looked like
good fish – the first rises I had seen in about four hours'
fishing. I watched for about five minutes, but there was no
repetition. There were no naturals on and not a fish stirred.
And then, for no apparent reason, it happened again. I was
completely at a loss. I had never seen anything like it. It was
not until I was watching open-mouthed the third exhibition
that I twigged it. Each concerted rise had coincided with a
puff of wind. Of course: caterpillars!

Fortunately, I remembered that the previous season I had
tied as an experiment some lures which were intended to
suggest this very idea. No particular species, of course, but
an epitome of all caterpillars – emerald-green wool body
ribbed with a strand of picric yellow wound on a thing
like a miniature two-hook Pennell-tackle and finished off
with a black head. It acted like a charm. Before I left the
oaks I had six good fish in the basket, two or three of them
three-quarter pounders. I am aware that by no distortion
of language could this be called dry-fly fishing. They were
well sunk and they were certainly not flies, but I hope that
my readers will allow that the end justified the means, and
my story does illustrate my point that however low the
water or fierce the sun there is always hope under trees.

The time and the place

On the other hand, if the sun is blazing and there has been no rain for weeks, remember first that trout must have oxygen and secondly that they hate glare, so concentrate on rapids and rocks and places where trees or banks cut off the direct rays of the sun, and see that you make the most of the hours when he has lost most of his power – 7 to 10 p.m. G.M.T.

In high summer, most natural things go into siesta during the afternoon, and the fisherman will not lose much if he follows their example, say, from 3 to 6 p.m. My advice to anyone over fifty is to make the most of this providential arrangement, to come out of the water and either lie down in the shade with a thermos, or, if he has a car, to buzz back to his base and have a leisurely tea and start fishing again at about 6:30pm. He-will feel like a giant refreshed and find himself as keen as he was in the morning and ready to carry on till dark.

Broken water

The other type of water to concentrate on in hot, low conditions is that which is tossed and broken by rocks. The reason for this is that only in rough, broken water do the trout get a sufficient supply of oxygen. Time after time my day has been saved for me by skipping out favourite places and making the most of cascades and boulders, but here again the fisherman must modify his technique to suit the conditions. I observe that nine people out of ten pass by such places as utterly unsuitable for a dry fly, whereas, did they but know it, they are a godsend in a drought. The reason for this mistake is that they have been brought up or chalk stream literature, and chalk stream flies in such places are practically useless. To begin with, they are so small that the trout can't see them; secondly, you can't see them; thirdly, even if the trout could see them he would not be such a fool as to make the difficult and exhausting effort of leaving the shelter of his pet boulder – timing his interception and returning to his stance without being washed away – all for the sake of some split-winged dun on a 00 hook. It would just not be worth the trouble.

So, having reached your cascade, put on a couple of large suggestions of beetle, moth, or sedge, and fish carefully all the bays and pockets and backwaters and, in fact, everything that is not a raging torrent, and you will be surprised very often at the vitality and initiative of its inhabitants compared with the half-doped lethargy of the trout population in other places.

Trees, then, for shade and a steady food supply, and rocks for oxygen. These are the two chief features for which the normal dry-fly fisherman in a drought should search by day. But there remains, thank heaven, the evening, and that requires a very different approach.

The evening hours

Soon after sunset, generally after a hot, still day, there sometimes occurs on many normal rivers as well as on the chalk streams a mysterious phenomenon known as "The Evening Rise." Certain stretches of the stream, which in all appearances were dead and untenanted during the daylight hours, suddenly come to life, and for a period of half an hour or so literally boil with madly rising trout and fill the novice with a corresponding frenzy of excitement. Unfortunately, it is generally quite impossible to see what they are rising at, and by the time you have changed your flies two or three times the whole thing stops dead like turning off a tap. If he is lucky enough to land a fish at all, the beginner will be wise – though it is almost more than flesh and blood can stand – to stop fishing altogether and disgorge his victim. If he can only identify the fly which is causing all this mass hysteria and is able to copy it, he should do well the following evening and perhaps for another week if the evening rise is repeated, but even the oldest and most experienced hand generally finds himself guessing on these occasions.

I remember telling the great Dai Lewis how helpless I felt, and asking his advice on how to deal with an evening rise. His reply was: "I don't know. Nobody knows, and what a good thing! If anybody found-out, the river would soon be skinned." But one tip I did discover and I hand it on to my readers with my blessing. It is this. Don't make the mistake of leaving the river when the evening rise is over. Take off your minute Pheasant Tail, or whatever you tried for the fun and games now finished, and tie on a whacking great Ermine or Paragon of not less than a full inch diameter, oil it and throw it under the opposite bank, working it towards you on the surface in a series of jerks. Keep this up is long as you can see and the chances are you will get some memorable shock. The fish who fall for this method are generally big ones. Three times out of four they miss it, but even if they do you have had your thrill, which equals, if it does not surpass, anything in the whole of fishing.

GENERAL HINTS

Finally I venture to add some general hints, the results of more than half a century of experience, which I hope may be of some help at any rate to the beginner.

(i) However keen (or young!) you are, never omit food. It doesn't pay. Make a point of taking nourishment of some sort, even if it is nothing more than a couple of sandwiches and a banana every four hours.

(ii) Remember the farther you go up a river the

quicker the water runs down. So if the bottom of your river is impossible, the top beats may be quite fishable. Discoloration, too, may be due to an isolated thunderstorm affecting one small tributary only, with the result that all the main river above the junction is unaffected. As a rule, though, tributaries become fishable after a flood before the main river does.

(iii) Always wade when possible. Keep low. Try to perfect the back-handed cast flat over your left shoulder. Remember that you have knees as well as feet. All these things help to make you less visible.

(iv) Always carry in the bottom of your basket a short length of bamboo or elder wood with the pith removed, with one end shaped with a knife like a very narrow, elongated spoon. Insert this gently as far as it will go down a trout's gullet. Give it a half-turn and then remove it. The contents will show you what was on the menu for his last meal.

(v) Remember that there are two kinds of light – diffused and reflected – and if you want to see your fly, be careful in the first case of colour, in the second of opacity. Diffused light occurs when anything – trees or rocks or banks – interpose between the sky and the river and renders the water transparent to the eye of the fisherman. Reflected light makes it impossible to see anything except the surface. In the latter case it is necessary for visibility that your fly should be opaque; in the former that it should be of the right colour. The most visible colour, in diffused light is, of course, pure white, but next to that, for some reason which I do not understand, is orange. In reflected light, because of their comparative opacity, hen's hackles are far more visible than cock's. The obvious thing to do, then, if you are using two flies, is to tie one on that is visible in reflected light and one that stands out when it is diffused.

(vi) Lastly, when fishing a big river in a wind it pays

handsomely to visualize in your mind's eye the course of the river and note the places which owing to cliffs or trees or the direction of flow are likely to feel it least. It is possible to get quite a good day's fishing even in a full gale if you will concentrate on such places and omit the rest.'

Although the following excerpt, *How I Beat My Father* does not in fact come from any of the books listed here, it is an obvious choice to follow-on the Rev. Powell's chapter as it is by his son Michael Powell. It first appeared in *Grayling*, the journal of the Grayling Society, in the spring of 1999:

'September! That for me was the month for grayling in the few days before term began. Being away at school during mid-summer meant that I missed the best part of the trout season; April anyway was often too cold or the rivers too high; in August there was often a drought and the fish weren't moving; but September – that was the time for grayling. Each year during that month my father took two nights away on the Teme, which meant virtually three days fishing; and I went with him. It was the time of the hop pickers, which somehow made things more exciting. Whole families used to come from the Black Country to the Teme valley, housed in wooden huts called barracks, for the few weeks of the picking season. It was a kind of paid holiday; but when we asked if they liked Worcestershire, I remember they said they would sooner live in Dudley! The hop fields are still there, stretching as far west as Tenbury. But the picking is now mechanised, no longer labour intensive and the barracks are no more.

We usually stayed at Newnham Bridge, in a pub next to the River Rea, the deepest tributary of the Teme which used to hold the heaviest trout and a few grayling a mile or two from the junction. We would concentrate on the fords of the main river. Here the middle Teme has long stretches

of flat water devoted to many sorts of coarse fish, with
swifter water every hundred yards or so. Here the grayling
were, and still are, to be found, and a few trout. I have read
somewhere that grayling do not shoal together until the
really cold weather begins. This may be so in northern rivers,
but my experience is that any time from the late summer
they shoal in any river where there are plenty of them; and
it was certainly the case in those distant days. The best of
the fords on the Teme we called the White Railings stretch,
where the river runs right alongside the main road (the
A456). If you look closely and clear away the undergrowth,
I think you can find some of those railings still. This is the
stretch where my father turned me loose in 1934.

At that time I had been fly fishing for just two years.
Before that I had been trained by using an upstream worm,
and by watching the expert. My rod was a 7ft greenheart
from Hattons of Hereford. Both of us, father and I, were
just emerging from just using mainly wet fly, to all year
round use of predominantly dry. So I started with two wet
flies, probably a Red Tag and a Green Insect and had the
odd take. However, this was the year when my father was
creating the Orange Otter (nothing to do with the river in
Devonshire by the way) and I soon changed to this fly and
stayed with it. The eventual tying was a ginger red cock's
hackle one third of the way down the hook from the eye;
and the body in two sections made of soft under pelt of otter
fur, dyed in a very idiosyncratic way. He used a mixture
of red ink and picric acid, boiled on the stove in his study.
Nowadays, of course otters are rightly protected and picric
acid is a substance which chemists refuse to sell. Seal's fur
is altogether too springy, perhaps stoat's fur might do. Reg
Righyni suggested to me that the Orange Otter resembled
a salmon roe! But we fished it dry and I don't think that ova
float, nor are available in September. Possibly the fish took it
for a soldier beetle or some kind of ant. I have a theory that

grayling are particularly fond of beetles, hence the success of the Red Tag and the Treacle Parkin.

Well, on that red-letter day grayling took the Orange Otter almost without hesitation. I think it is a pretty good fly still. I fished the White Railings stretch slowly and I think for a boy my age (fourteen) pretty carefully. It was a wonderful rise (to what in the natural world I wonder). They were showing upstream and also in the water below where I had been wading. Until that day my largest bag had been nine small Welsh trout; on this occasion it was thirty-four grayling to a pound and a quarter and two trout. My father's diary, which I still possess, has a lot to say about the **Orange Otter** and its success on that day (Sept 12, 1934) for both of us. But practically nothing about the remarkable catch made by a boy of my age! He was, I'm afraid, obsessed by numbers and was rather peeved to have been beaten by his inexperienced son. As a matter of fact, I have never caught as many as he did until one day when he was over seventy and a northerly gale at Tregaron drove him from the Teifi, and I returned later with a respectable bag.'

ROD IN HAND
Cyril V. Hancock (1958)

Cyril Hancock was the angling correspondent on the *Birmingham Post* and a member of The Greenwell Club. In 1959 he published *Rod in Hand: an Angler's Moods and Memories*. He was an avid Welsh Borderlands stream fisherman and has six fly patterns to his credit. His book includes three chapters of particular interest to the Borderland flyfisher.

In the chapter *Western Brookland* he

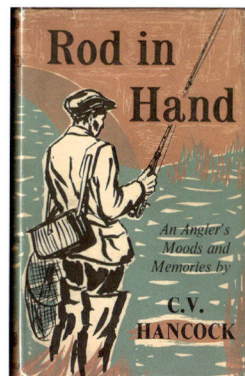

recalls fishing trips on the Teme, Onny and Clun intermingled with verses from A. E. Housman's *A Shropshire Lad*. He admits to being 'an unashamed collector of rivers' and later on proclaims that 'in nearly all forms of fishing knowing the water is a big factor in success ... the enjoyment of fishing new waters is a varied bag of experiences and memories.'

He passionately writes of days of salmon fishing on the Dee in the chapter *Fairy River* and of trout fishing he says that, except early in the season, Dee trout 'are seldom easy ... teams of three wet flies become useless as spring advances' when the better fish 'retire under the trees.' The flyfisher who scores then is generally one who has practised casting 'a crafty fly, dry or wet, into these haunts.' He recommends fishing the river 'before noon and at sundown' with 'a little Badger Hackle or Knotted Midge useful in the mornings, or a Red Tag' and he goes on to admit that Dee trout are 'far harder to catch than those of Welsh Border streams.'

In the chapter *Grayling Time* Hancock recalls autumn forays on the Lugg, while claiming that 'in October the Welsh Borderland is at its loveliest ... this is true grayling country ... in the Welsh Borderland grayling belong. Monnow, Lugg and Arrow, Teme, Onny and Clun, Vyrnwy and Tanat – here, surely, is the grayling's home.' Reference is then made to 'Mayfly blossom' on the Leintwardine Club water on the Teme – this is nothing to do with the blossoming of the May tree but the abundant rise of fish to the fly. A description of a perfect day for grayling fishing is given with 'a white frost ... the late October sun shines warmly and quickly turns the white meadows to green again. The water is in good order and the grayling are sure to rise with abandon.' He advises the flyfisher that 'in early autumn, though, it pays on Border streams, to fish a suggestion of the natural fly (such as a Blue Upright or Silver Twist) ... as autumn advances ... nine days out of ten fancy flies pay best (such as Red Tag, Apple Green (beloved on the Teme) and the several varieties of the Witch.'

The chapter *Flies in Trumpery* opens with the not unlikely scenario of a lost fly box and the golden opportunity it presents to start a fresh collection of flies. Hancock then weighs up the pros and cons of the 'one fly' fisherman citing the Hackle Hare's Ear on the Onny, Hereford Alder on the Lugg, Pheasant Tail on the Ithon, Grey Duster on the Alwen and Dogsbody on the Usk as examples.

On the Welsh Borderland streams he advocates that 'it usually pays to use big hairy patterns, dry and wet alike, such as would shock both south and north countrymen … a sound general rule is: The smaller the brook, the bigger the fly.'

He lists his selected top twelve dry flies which are: Gold-Ribbed Hare's Ear, Powell's Paragon, Pheasant Tail, Hereford Alder, Coch-y-bonddu, Powell's Moth, Iron Blue, Knotted Midge, Badger Hackle, Coombes' Blue Variant, the Fore-and-Aft Mayfly and the Midget Mayfly. All but the Iron Blue are hackle flies. For wet flies he recommends two of his own patterns, the March Brown and the Pet.

DOWN ALONG TEMESIDE
Richard Holding (1963)

Down Along Temeside began as a book largely about angling but soon outgrew this limitation; it contains reminiscences and anecdotes of the Holding family holidays based at a self-constructed wooden building beside the Teme at Orleton affectionately called 'The Hut.' There are stories about fish, fishing and life in the middle Teme region (from Eastham to Stanford Bridge) in the first half of the twentieth century. 'For two or three

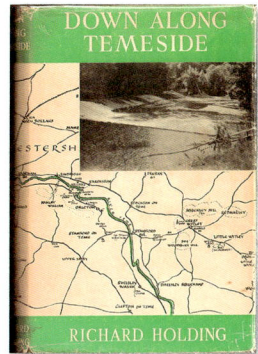

years the fishing thrived but then began a long chapter of decreasing returns. Up to the middle twenties there were still plenty of trout and grayling but soon the steady decline in their numbers became woefully apparent ... As the fly-fishing declined ... the number of trout steadily declined. Then the grayling seemed to have completely disappeared.' The anglers had to go 'further afield into the Welsh Marches for trout-fishing on the Lugg, on the Clun and the Monnow.'

In the second edition of the book (1989), the Monnow features as the subject of two of the author's delightful poems: *The Trout* and *Border Monnow*. This edition also contains many more of the author's poems of which *Trout Season* and *The Song of the Red Tag* are of particular interest to those who fish.

THE ANGLER'S BEDSIDE BOOK
Maurice Wiggin (Editor) (1965)

The Angler's Bedside Book is, according to the introduction, 'a collection of new writings specially commissioned from some of the liveliest and most knowledgeable angling writers of our time.' C. V. Hancock's contribution, *The Land of Teme and Gleam,* is of special interest to us – a beautifully crafted piece succinctly describing flyfishing on the rivers and streams of the region. The 'Gleam' in the title comes from the Welsh word *Llugwy* (meaning gleaming) from which is derived the English word, Lugg. The piece opens by explaining that the bleak eastern sides of the highest mountains of Wales is where the big rivers rise – the Dee, Severn and Wye, and their tributaries, the Teme, Lugg and Monnow which also have their springs in these foothills.

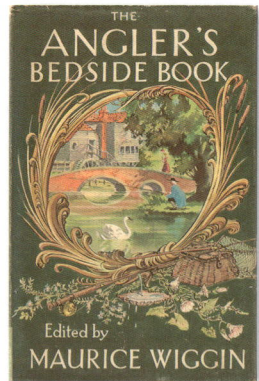

'For a fly-fisher for trout and grayling the Border counties of Salop, Hereford and Monmouth compose a delectable land.' Hancock goes on: 'streams of this Borderland clearly belong to one family, neither tumbling mountain streams, nor placid Midland brooks, they are of the Border, Borderly.' In this region, we are told, not only does the fisherman have his eyes open to nature about him but also to history – like the bloody battlefield of Mortimer's Cross and Leintwardine's Roman station at Bravonium.

Generally 'a pounder is a trout to display' and the 'brooks beauty compensates for the size' (or lack of!) Historically this used to be wet fly country, epitomised by the prodigious catches of the Eagles family based at Longtown. Nowadays the dry fly predominates and few wet flies are ever cast. The region has a long tradition of fly dressing, with the likes of Bowlker and Brookes (Ludlow), Ted Coombes (Tenbury) and the Rev. Edward Powell (Munslow), as just a few of the best known tyers. In conclusion we are given details of the author's dry and wet fly preferred selection for a Border fly box. Red Tag, Blue Variant, Coch-y-bonddu and Double Badger for dries and his favourite wet-fly team with a Red Tag on top, then Brookes' Fancy, and on the point his own charming Droitwich.

ENGLISH AND WELSH TROUT FLIES: ESSAYS AND ANALYSES
W. H. Lawrie (1967)

In the preface of *English and Welsh Trout Flies: Essays and Analyses*, the author states that his book has 'three-fold purpose, namely, to record some of the very excellent lists of trout flies not readily available to the average fly-fisherman; to provide a small reference book of English trout flies; and, finally, to seek to draw from analyses findings applicable to the advancement of contemporary trout flies.' He goes on to say that 'the writing of this book has served as a reminder of the long and fascinating history of fly-fishing and fly-making.' The book is remarkably informative and goes a long way towards fulfilling that three-fold purpose and has two specific chapters of relevance to the Welsh Borderland flyfisher.

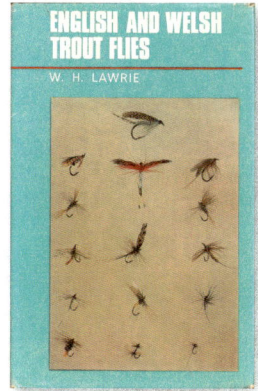

The chapter entitled *The Origin and Design of the English Trout Fly* outlines the concept of classical periods of the art of fly dressing when there was precious little development, and periods of advance and innovation when new patterns and styles are experimented with. This is admirably illustrated with reverse, sloping and hackle winging styles.

The chapter *Usk Flies and Favourite Welsh Patterns* examines the style and origins of the Usk wet fly, designed typically with short body, slim wings and sparse hackle, capable of sinking fast and making it ideal for Usk style wet fly fishing with quick and repeated casting across and slightly upstream – a method long used for wet fly fishing on the Tweed. The possible links between the flies and fishing styles of the Usk and Tweed are considered, suggesting that during some uprisings on restrictions of fishing some Scottish river watchers were brought in to oversee the Usk valley fishing and that some may have settled in the area bringing their fishing styles and methods with them. Details are given of a selection of eight wet flies belonging to one such settler, Mr Acheson, who became an Usk river keeper. Reference is also made to other early Usk patterns including Ogden's two March Brown patterns dating from 1879 and nine earlier flies from Lascelles.

In other chapters the following topics are covered: the

historic reintroduction of wet fly fishing – and hence nymph fishing; the ingenuity of the fly-dresser with 'bottle-brush' and 'V'-trimmed hackles; the recommended use of 'reverse-dressed' flies by Alexander Mackintosh for downstream fishing dating from 1806; the importance of high quality fly dressing materials, and the importance of 'local design', illustrated by, among others, the Usk and Teme patterns.

FLY FISHING ON THE USK – AN HISTORICAL APPROACH
David John (1968)

In 1968 the Brecknock Museum published a booklet, *Fly Fishing on the Usk – an Historical Approach*, written by David John. Within its compact thirty pages there is an incredible amount of valuable information.

There are a number of interesting sections: *The Fish* in which there is a detailed account of the life cycle of salmon followed by briefer accounts for brown trout and sea-trout/ sewin. He tells us that brown trout in autumn, when moving upriver to spawn, are known in Welsh to be *twps y dail* – meaning 'fools of the leaves' or 'Autumn fools.'

The Equipment of Fishermen examines the merits of different rods (whole cane and split cane), summarises the benefits of the reel over line winders, and praises the benefits of dressed silk lines.

In *Trout Flies*, three types of fly are considered – the imitative dry fly, the flashy silver/gold-bodied flies and the nymph patterns – and their relative merits given.

The role of the Usk is mentioned in *John Lloyd of Dinas and the use of waders.*

A variety of Conservation Problems are aired as well as the problems associated with *Pollution: Extraction and Reservoirs.*

The section on *Fly-tying* looks at salmon flies in detail before considering the development of Usk-style trout flies and the possible Scots influence on fishing on the Usk and concludes with a detailed description of tying and history of the Coch-y-bonddu (of which he cites Courtney-Williams, identifying it as an imitation of the garden chafer or June bug).

The *Conclusion* to this booklet epitomises flyfishing and fly-tying admirably and warrants being quoted in full: 'Flyfishing and fly-tying are really all part of one thing, the catching of fish by the most exciting means known. Together they provide an absorbing occupation all the year round. They have at least done so for many people in the past and it is to be hoped that they will continue to do so for many people in the future.'

SMALL-RIVER FLY FISHING FOR TROUT AND GRAYLING
James Evans (1972)

Well-known fishing writer John Goddard states in his foreword, 'the author has written a classic that will be looked upon as a leading guide for this type of fishing for many years to come.' This sentiment still holds true nearly forty years later, since this book is a masterpiece on the tactics and techniques required for those wishing to flyfish small rivers, brooks and the upper reaches of larger rivers – all of which abound on the Celtic fringe.

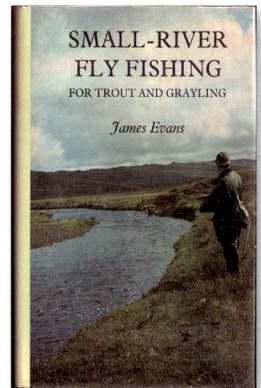

James Evans lived in Luston and built up a very sound

and extensive knowledge of fishing in the region. He was president of The Gamefishers Club and was responsible for creating ten Border fly patterns.

If I had to select only one book on Welsh Borderlands flyfishing to take with me to my Desert Island this would be it, and I urge anyone genuinely interested in this specialised branch of fishing to try to obtain a copy for reference. This is the first book specifically written on the tactics and techniques of Borderlands stream flyfishing and each chapter is packed with useful advice and invaluable snippets.

In the chapter *Terms of Reference* we are carefully shown the differences between chalk streams and rain-fed streams in respect of their hydrology, ecology and fishing methods. Appropriate methods of casting (side, flicks and switches) are touched upon as are pollution and water abstraction.

The chapter *Tools for the Job* gives dated, but still relevant, information on the requirements for rods and rod handles, lines, leaders and a full range of accessories.

We are informed at the start of the chapter *Natural flies* that 'general artificial patterns are best on Border streams' owing to the dearth of regular hatches of flies, the paucity of food supply and 'water speed and turmoil.' Without getting bogged down with detail we are given a comprehensive run down of the natural flies likely to be found – stoneflies, sedges and up-winged flies – and matching artificials.

In the chapter *Some Thoughts on Casting* many technical points are examined and the benefits of ambidextrous casting are considered and he gives us a fantastic account of upstream nymph and wet flyfishing.

The art of reading the water is beautifully illustrated in the chapter *Watercraft* and the intimate details of a 'typical Border pool' are graphically portrayed.

The chapter *On Fly Dressing* opens with the notion that 'parcels are tied; fishing flies, provided they do not look too much like parcels, are dressed.' The benefits of dressing one's own flies are given before an examination of the equipment and materials for fly dressing is given.

The chapter on *Artificial Flies* contains some fascinating material. In the first section, *The Reversed-hackle Dry Fly*, the author outlines his 'chance' introduction to this style of fly by way of a magazine article on the Fore-and-Aft Mayfly by David Jacques, from which he developed his own Border Mayfly pattern. In essence these flies are dressed back-to-front (i.e. with the hackle at the bend, not the eye end of the hook), and have no tail or wing. They sit more naturally in the water film than normal hackled flies and are superior floaters on faster flowing and broken water.

The second section of the chapter, *Border Patterns* contains the dressing of sixteen of the less well-known Border patterns and variants of dry fly; a synopsis of *Nymphs for the Borders* (four patterns) and concludes with a most interesting section on *Upstream Wet Flies* complete with their hackles facing forwards.

The short chapter on *Grayling* is packed with details on the ecology of the species and methods for catching them.

The final chapter, *Water Improvements,* looks into the ways of improving the nourishment for fish by attending to the wellbeing of the fishes' food supply organisms. Strategies mentioned include the introduction of weed, and stream bed management using groynes or 'croys.'

Here is an extract from Chapter 1, *Terms of Reference:*

'Now let us look at a "rain-fed" stream.

By definition it is a subject on the vagaries of the weather: heavy rain followed by dry spells make it go up and down like a yo-yo; the rain does not need to occur in the locality in which one is fishing, for a cloudburst in the hills among which the stream has its source can later in the day bring up the level dramatically as one watches;

however, if the rain is local it can have an immediate effect on the colour and clarity of the water, which can persist to a degree for days and even weeks afterwards, as countless ditches continue to leach their soil-laden drainage into the main stream.

After continuous heavy rain it will come into spate and be bank high and the colour of cocoa, and often take considerable time to settle down to a normal flow; after weeks of drought it will become so thin and clear that one wonders where the fish that one knows to be there can find to hide themselves.

Open stretches of bank on the smaller rain-fed rivers – or the higher reaches of larger ones – are normally few and far between, most are well bushed to a greater or lesser degree, and a few are almost impossibly so from the point of view of the fly-fisher: this is probably because the land through which they flow, being less rich, is not so intensively cultivated as that along the chalk streams and big rivers of the plains; also a healthy binding of tree roots is essential to the banks to lessen the effect of scouring during spates.

Casting is therefore rarely as described in most of the text books: the side cast is probably the one most frequently employed, together with flicks, switches and all manner of extemporary expedients to which formal names have never been given.

In width our rain-fed stream can vary from broad, shallow rippling stickles to narrow, deep pools – often very deep indeed where overhanging tree roots have been undercut; the unevenness of the bottom engendered by these variations is often increased by the presence of large stones or even boulders. The effect of all this is a surface in constant movement in all directions varying from a gentle rippling to downright turbulence; only in broad pools or long slow glides is anything approaching a smooth surface encountered.

The presence of a fish is usually only recognised by the appearance of a rise form on the water; fish are rarely seen in the water except in conditions of unusual clarity when the light and the observer's position are just right; unless, of course, the fish are leaving hurriedly!

The larder available to the fish in a rain-fed stream is far from being as comprehensive or as super-abundant as that at the disposal of his chalk stream cousin; the size of the former is in consequence proportionately very much less, though size-for-size his fighting qualities must earn him every respect. Except on exceptional and possibly carefully preserved waters a three-quarter pound trout is noteworthy, a pounder exceptional and anything above that something to boast about for the rest of the season. Where they are encountered the grayling tend to be larger – often much larger – than the trout, although not often seen by purely trout fishermen not actually looking for them.

The diet of fish in such streams is catholic in the extreme, and most of it is obtained off the bottom: wash-in worms and grubs, aquatic nymphs and larvae, drowned terrestrial insects, berries in season, shrimps, snails and crayfish if they are fortunate enough to live in a stream containing them; small fish of their own and other species, and also the eggs of their own and other species are all fair game. On the comparatively rare occasions when they are tempted to come up and feed off the surface it will often prove to be on terrestrial insects which have got there inadvertently; every sort of land-based fly gets onto the water at some time, and most are acceptable to the trout and grayling in a rain-fed stream. I once caught a trout of above average size for the water which was stuffed to the gills with wasps. Small caterpillars of the variety which lower themselves on threads, and who have misjudged the length of their threads, are always prized, as are the ones which just tumble in, and also spiders.

Specific species of insects which interest the rain-fed fish are primarily the smaller kinds of stone fly (and the very large ones in some rivers, particularly in the North Country where they are known as mayflies), various sedges, and, in my experience a very poor third (excepting the true mayfly, where it occurs), various up-winged flies of the *Ephemeroptera*.

The number of times on which I have encountered a general and sustained rise to a specific insect on a rain-fed stream I could count on the fingers of my two hands. I have only once seen a truly selective rise (to the sherry spinner) during which the fish would look at nothing but the specific natural insect.

It follows from the foregoing that it is the exception rather than the rule for a fisherman on a rain-fed stream to be able to cast to a regularly rising fish: he will often cast to where he has seen a fish rise (not the same thing at all); or he may cast to where he thinks there may be a fish and "bring it up". (This is an occurrence, fortunately very common on our sort of water, which I have discovered is quite beyond the comprehension of friends whose only experience is of chalk streams.) He may also fish the likely spots with an upstream nymph, or on wider streams fish the water generally with downstream wet flies.'

ROUGH STREAM TROUT FLIES
S. D. (Taff) Price (1976)

Rough Stream Trout Flies is a book about fly patterns for turbulent water – of which plenty can be found in the Welsh Borderlands and which, according to Michael Leighton, contained at the time of publication, the best listing of flies for use on Welsh Borderland streams. There are three introductory chapters and then details of fly patterns.

The first chapter, *On Streams and Rivers*, opens bemoaning the fact that chalkstream fishing is far too expensive, and then goes on to state: 'What is left for us less well-endowed mortals? Waters that tumble their way through woodland and mountain; waters that sing in quiet valleys and streams that add a kind of music to a still and lovely moor.' What better description of Welsh Borderlands fishing haunts do you need? The chapter concludes by stating that 'river reading and insect observation are the two most important factors for successful fishing on smaller waters.'

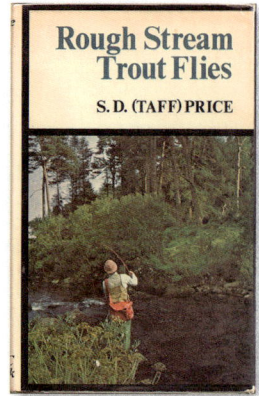

In the chapter *On Artificial Flies*, we are informed that 'each area of the country has its own favourite patterns … many of these localised patterns have proved their worth on waters far away from their birthplace … probably due to an accident of re-birth. The dressing styles of artificial flies vary, depending on which part of the country they hail from. The further north one travels the more sparse becomes the dressing.' There follows an interesting account of the importance of the size of artificial fly often for the benefit of the flyfisher's eyesight rather than that of the fish's!

The brief chapter *Insect Life* introduces the major groups of insect which concern the flyfisher and then subsequent chapters look at each one in greater detail with a selection of appropriate artificial flies. Specific reference to the Welsh Borderlands is found in a few of the chapters, for example *Stoneflies*, where mention is made of the February Red as a Welsh Dee pattern and the Yellow Sally as a Welsh Border pattern.

In *Beetles*, naturally reference is made to the Coch-y-bonddu, the Welsh name for the beetle that is 'red with a black belly.' The Welshman's Button features as a June bug imitation and the dressings of John Henderson's Beetle 'A' and Beetle 'B' patterns also feature – devised for use on Talybont-on-Usk Reservoir.

In *Moths* there is a delightful description of Jack Hughes-Parry's Feather Duster complete with its cork underbody.

In *Grubs and Caterpillars* there are details of Francis Francis's Grasshopper and Wasp Grub patterns, whose origins probably lie somewhere in the Teme valley.

The chapter *Flies for Welsh Waters* opens with 'The rivers of Wales can be likened to great trees, with streams as twisting branches, and all the little brooks like small twigs … they are as numerous as that. All contain trout; small trout in most cases.' The dressings of ten Borderlands flies are contained within this chapter which concludes with Terry Griffiths's selection of flies for the River Alyn, a tributary of the Dee.

The chapter on *Grayling Flies* contains the details of a few patterns that have their origins in the region – Red Tag, Green Insect, Brookes' Fancy and Orange Otter.

The final chapter *Fly-dressing Notes and Sketches* has some remarkably useful advice for those who dress their own flies which is as relevant today as the day it was written.

FLY PATTERNS
FOR THE RIVERS AND LAKES OF WALES
Moc Morgan (1984)

Fly Patterns for the Rivers and Lakes of Wales must rank as the definitive work of the time for Welsh fly patterns for trout, sea-trout and salmon.

The Foreword by Lynn Hughes, *The origins and background of fly-fishing in Wales*, is a six-page masterpiece on the history of the sport within the country. We're told at the outset that fly dressing, 'that rare combination of intensely practical and instinctive artistry, has a thoroughly absorbing historical development in Wales.' Also that there is literary evidence from the great Welsh poet Dafydd ap Gwilym from the period 1320 to 1380 that salmon were known to be *gylionwr* or 'catcher of flies.' Much later in history the Coch-y-bonddu* is thought to have its origins in the Drop Fly described by Scotcher in 1820 for use on the Usk. He records that fishing on the Wye and Usk was not without its problems since the landowners of the nineteenth and early twentieth centuries imported keepers and gillies from Scotland and the North of England to work on their large estates 'in order to impose an alien, disciplined policing on a rural society that was steeped in tribal loyalties and prejudices.' However with the arrival of these keepers came 'foreign' fly patterns, which in time became local currency, hence the noticeable similarities between old Usk patterns and Scottish flies. (Since the end of the Second World War many of the large estates have been fragmented and the waters sold to syndicates and alternative methods of management implemented). Hughes goes on to say 'local knowledge is what counts in fly-fishing … to lose track of some of the traditional local patterns is a loss to angling and the cultural life of a nation.'

The introduction to the book itself is a short section, *Materials*, in which the author stresses the importance of using well-sourced and good quality natural feathers, skins and fur for fly-dressing.

The bulk of this book is devoted to giving details of fly patterns in separate sections for *Sewin; Salmon; Trout – Wet Fly; Trout – Dry Fly; Nymphs* and *Grayling*. In the introduction to *Trout – Wet Fly* we are told that the writings of Dame Juliana Berners, Scotcher and Hansard confirm that flyfishing has been practised in Wales since the Middle Ages and that 'flies

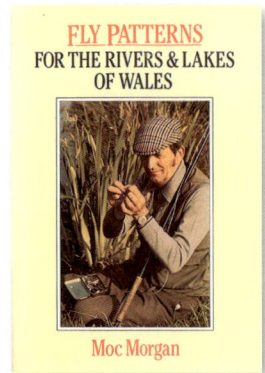

that could be fished wet were fully evolved by the beginning of the nineteenth century.' There is also mention of the early flies of the Usk as being 'flies with very slender bodies and very little hackle … divided wings … set low over the hook with concave sides together … dun wings and hackle … no tails and body of wool or hare's ear fur.' In general Welsh wet flies have always been streamlined ensuring good entry into the water and have liveliness or 'kick' achieved by the setting of the wings and hackle.

In the introduction to *Trout – Dry Fly* we are told that this style of flyfishing could well have its origins in Cardiganshire and not the Southern Counties of England. This method 'is the most pleasureable and satisfying method … often the most productive.' Early Welsh dry flies needed to have good floatability and visibility and well established wet flies such as Coch-y-bonddu and March Brown 'were tied with two or three cock hackles and were used as floaters.'

Nymph fishing in Wales 'originated with the traditional wet fly being cast downstream and worked in a teasing, rhythmic manner.' Reference is made to the fact that in more recent times, Oliver Kite, originally from Monmouth, presented the correct image of nymph fishing. The quality of grayling fishing, we are told, has improved over the years, with the rivers of the Dee, Severn and Wye catchments being top class grayling waters.

This book is very well illustrated with photographs of many of the important innovators of the sport in Wales, copies of etchings and items of equipment. A second edition, newly entitled *Trout and salmon flies of Wales*, (1996) is in a larger format and has improved colour plates of flies.

---

*Citing expert Welsh etymologists, Morgan explains that he feels the spelling 'coch-a-bon-ddu' is correct. This is the spelling he uses throughout. Coch-y-bonddu and coch-a-bon-ddu are alternative spellings of the same word and refer to the same fly.

TROUT FLIES OF SHROPSHIRE
AND THE WELSH BORDERLANDS
Michael Leighton (1987)

Trout Flies of Shropshire and the Welsh Borderlands is a masterpiece in flyfishing detective work: no less than 105 patterns are described in the text and the reader is given a great deal of historical information about fly-tying, flyfishing and the people of the Borderlands.

T. Donald Overfield suggests in his Foreword that this book is 'a work of considerable scholarship which will become a much sought after classic.'

The section *A Brief History of the Region as it Appears in Angling Literature* makes reference to fifteen key books which have in turn formed the framework for my own research, and reviews of all are included within this chapter.

In a chapter called *The Patterns* we learn about the secrecy that surrounds some of them (especially wet fly patterns) and how certain localities are notorious for this. He bemoans the fact that the reluctance of some originators to share the knowledge makes collecting and selecting flies for inclusion in a book an incredibly difficult task. The River Tanat, we are told, 'is still shrouded in secrecy.'

The wider appeal and popularity of some of the Border patterns outside the region is mentioned with reference to Courtney-Williams's belief that the Grey Duster, Dogsbody, Welsh Partridge and Paragon would in time become household names (which indeed they have) together with Michael Leighton's appeal for the Tanat Dun, Grizzly Bourne, Coltman's Duster and the William Rufus to go the same way.

With regard to the entry for each fly there is a description

of its history and information relating to its inventor followed by the precise details for dressing the pattern.

SOUNDS OF RUNNING WATERS:
LLANGOLLEN AND THE WELSH DEE REVEALED
D. J. Maybury (1988)

This personal story of a Llangollen man is written in a lilting style rather reminiscent of Dylan Thomas's *Under Milk Wood*.

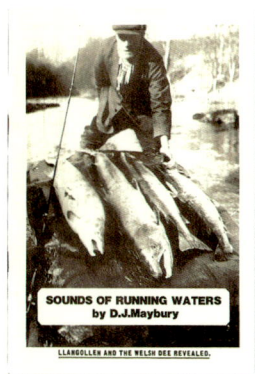

There is a brief account of stream fishing on the Fedw Stream (a small tributary of the Dee) at an early age using crude makeshift equipment in challenging locations. There follows a description of coracle use on the Dee ('a vessel for delight or disaster') of which there are two types, one-man and two-man versions.

Whilst most of the booklet is devoted to salmon fishing there are some passages relating to trout. The River Ceiriog has a mention as 'a fruitful and very pleasant tributary to fish that is said to be the fastest flowing river in Wales (which) … runs through a magnificent valley and its scenery is a joy to behold.'

The dearth of small trout in the Dee, Maybury considers to be the result of a combination of acid rain, pollution and predation by birds and coarse fish. Llangollen Angling Association tried to compensate for these factors and has restocked the river but the real beneficiaries of this have been those that fish the river upstream, in the Corwen area.

Even so Maybury recalls that 'by far the most gratifying type of fly fishing is to be had by fishing the mountain streams around Llangollen … as the water fined down after a spate … I don't suppose anyone does it now.' Bags of forty fish, some up to a pound in weight, were recorded and on the technical front we are told that an un-spooked brook trout will tolerate several attempts at fly presentation but that the 'angler must not allow himself to be seen' – crouching and kneeling are the order of the day. Furthermore: 'The brook trout is probably one of the most successful species in the survival game, being able to tolerate drought conditions … and also extremely high waters following heavy rain storms. These fish gorge themselves and then seek cover only to be replaced by another fish.' Caddis grubs abound in these streams and the fish devour them – case and all – after nudging them off their rock base.

The closing account in this little booklet recalls monks rearing trout at the Abbey (now a ruin) beside the Eglwyseg Stream, which is primarily 'fed from the outfall from a lake inside the mountain at World's End.'

GRAYLING: THE FOURTH GAME FISH
Ronald Broughton (1989)

This is a most important text on grayling. It has contributions from acknowledged experts from around the world, one of whom is the Wrexham-based fishing guide, Louis Noble, whose chapter *Of Stillwater and Welsh Rivers* gives the reader an insight into grayling fishing on Llyn Tegid (Bala Lake), as well as a very thorough examination of the fishing possibilities on the Dee, Severn and Wye and some of their tributaries.

We learn that Llyn Tegid is Wales' largest natural sheet of water and has the Dee flowing through it. Some of its trout are

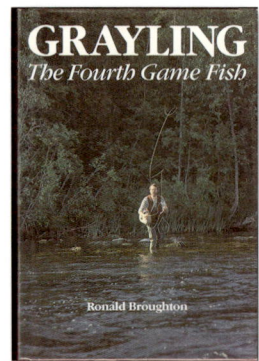

huge and you might even catch a rare gwyniad (a member of the whitefish family). The lake also holds a population of grayling (*crothell* in Welsh) that are best fished using an intermediate line with wet flies in the shore zone. Grayling are thought to be indigenous to the Dee, Severn and Wye systems.

The Dee is sluice controlled and therefore does not fall to very low levels in dry conditions. Reference is made to Huet's classification of European rivers into species-related zones with trout, grayling and coarse fish as biotic indicators. It is no wonder that the region abounds with so many rivers suitable for flyfishing since so many fit into the trout and grayling zones. The main stem of the Dee is no exception and between Bala and Bangor-on-Dee are numerous fine locations. Fly patterns created on the Dee include the Grey Duster, and Y Diawl Bach (Little Devil), a wet fly invented by Dewi Evans of Bala.

The Severn has a reputation for its coarse fishing and grayling are principally found between Llanidloes and Llandinam where shoals seem to stay in the shallower runs. Some of the tributaries are worth a visit, especially the Vyrnwy with characteristics similar to the parent Severn. The Banwy, Cain and Tanat all hold respectable populations. Further south the smaller rivers, the Onny, Clun and Corve have small grayling populations and the Teme is a major consideration and is steeped in literary and famous fly-tying history. The Ludlow area is the home of a number of significant fly-dressers whose patterns are justly important and the river hereabouts is known to be a 'white fly river.'

The main stem of the Wye has a proportion of its length within Huet's trout and grayling zones, especially between Rhayader and Glasbury, and even down to Hay-on-Wye. Many of the Wye's tributaries fit into Huet's zones especially the Ithon and Irfon in the upper reaches and the Lugg, Arrow and Monnow in the lower reaches.

A later revised and enlarged edition was published in 2000 under the new title, *The Complete Book of the Grayling*.

A GUIDE TO RIVER TROUT FLIES
John Roberts (1989)

This is a worthy successor to Courtney-Williams' *Dictionary*, keeping up-to-date with new designs and materials. There are over 400 fly patterns listed and illustrated in this book. The average flyfisher usually carries between six and twelve patterns in a season – so there is plenty of choice between these covers.

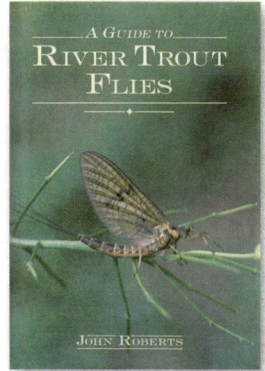

For convenience the flies are divided up into sections – *Dry flies, Subsurface flies, Aquatic flies, Sedges or caddisflies, Terrestrials* and *Grayling flies*.

For those flyfishing the region attention is naturally drawn to the Welsh Border flies within the *Dry Flies* section, however it is significant that the first and third flies shown in the book have their origins there too, namely the Grey Duster and John Storey.

The eight selected patterns in the *Welsh Border flies* section give a true flavour of the type of fly to be expected and interestingly are derived from a variety of originators with only one repeat. The patterns are:

Borderer	W. M. Gallichan
Tanat Dun	Ted Painter
Dogsbody	Harry Powell
Barrett's Bane	Cosmo Barrett
Doctor	Rev. Edward Powell
Baby Sunfly	Rev. Edward Powell
Grizzly Bourne	Michael Leighton
Coltman's Duster	F. H. Coltman

Elsewhere in the book we find seven other Welsh Borderland flies:

General dry flies:	Coch-y-Bonddu	trad. Welsh origin
Aquatic flies	Dark Stone	Alan Hudson
	March Brown	Cyril Hancock
	Medium Olive Dun	Alan Hudson
	White Ermine Moth	Rev. Edward Powell
Grayling flies	Orange Otter	Rev. Edward Powell
	Red Tag	Thomas Flynn

TROUT AND SALMON FLIES OF WALES
Moc Morgan (1996)

This is a revised edition of Morgan's earlier *Fly Patterns for the Rivers & Lakes of Wales*. There is very little new material in this book but the *Nymphs* section of the previous edition has been absorbed into an enlarged *Wet Flies* section. The earlier book's black and white illustrations have been omitted, and the colour plates, newly photographed by Terry Griffiths, are a vast improvement on those of the first edition.

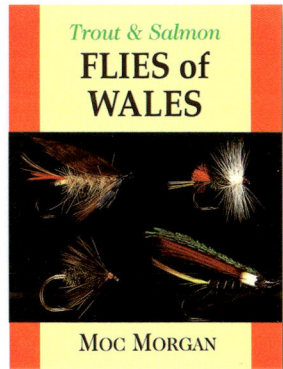

GONE FISHING:
ADVENTURES IN PURSUIT OF WILD TROUT
Jon Beer (2002)

Gone Fishing: Adventures in Pursuit of Wild Trout is a collection of amusing and eventful articles originally published in The *Daily Telegraph* and *Trout & Salmon* magazine; two of the articles are of particular interest to the region.

The Passing of the Peugeot or *Farewell to the Wagon* (Trout &

Salmon Magazine: November 1995) is the tale of a September fishing trip, in an old car on its last journey into the heart of Welsh Borderlands before its MOT certificate ran out, 'west along the Teme, crossed the Lugg and followed the Arrow to Kington ... where England suddenly stops and Wales unmistakably begins.' The journey continues up the Wye beyond Rhayader and eventually reaches Llanidloes on the banks of the Severn. The original intention was to fish the Severn but low water levels in the main river made the reservoir-fed Clywedog tributary a more appetising proposition, albeit showing the characteristics of a springtime river – cold water, high flow rate and little in the way of fly-life. The 'dry-fly-and-weighted-nymph' option brought a fish after three or four casts then nothing for three hours, after which it was time to sample the Severn. It ends with an extraordinary story of a twice-hooked grayling and a flurry of fly activity in the closing hour of daylight. Needless to say the car failed its MOT; 'Thank God they don't have MOTs for old fishermen.'

A River Runs Through It is the cunningly interwoven histories of a number of 'institutions' of the Usk valley; of how the Brabner family became involved with the Gliffaes Hotel near Crickhowell, now being run by the third generation of the family; how Harry Powell, the barber of Dogsbody fly fame, started to retail fishing gear, employed Molly Salter who married Lionel Sweet who in turn took over the fishing business and moved it to a side street in the market town of Usk. More recently they employed Jean Williams who is now the owner of the shop. Nowadays nearly all transactions are accompanied by a cup, or mug, of tea!

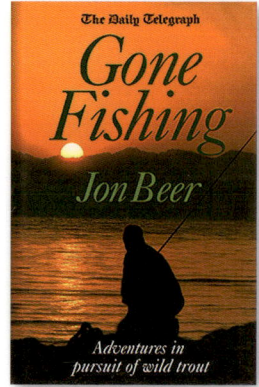

THE TROUT & I:
MORE ADVENTURES IN PURSUIT OF WILD FISH
Jon Beer (2003)

Jon Beer's second collection of amusing and anecdotal articles in which flyfishing in the Welsh Borderlands features in no less than five, three of which comprise the trilogy *The Border Years*. As with all his writing, all the waters described are accessible on a day ticket.

In *Monnowphil* he writes primarily of fishing the home beat of Kentchurch Court on the River Monnow many years ago when he rented a cottage there and, more recently, as day ticket water. The river is charmingly described as it 'slips gently through deep countryside, hidden below high banks of red sand eroded from the old sandstones of the Welsh Borders.' He recalls that in the past numerous large fish were taken in mayfly time 'under the bosky banks.'

The Border Years: '94 – Teme Spirit relates the story of a visit to the Teme valley above Leintwardine where a fruitful morning spent calling at farms and pubs thereabouts yielded numerous opportunities for fishing, and after a liquid lunch at the Lion Hotel in Leintwardine the afternoon was very successfully spent fishing for feisty Teme trout.

The Border Years: '95 – Stitched up by Doctors describes a frustrating morning spent looking for opportunities to fish on the Lugg, each time being told that the water was let to a syndicate of doctors from Worcester, Birmingham or somewhere similar. By the afternoon, attention moves from the Wye to the Severn River catchment and to the Horseshoe Inn at Llanyblodwell beside the River Tanat. Here the remainder of a pleasant afternoon is spent leap-frogging upstream on the mile-and-a-half of water owned by the pub.

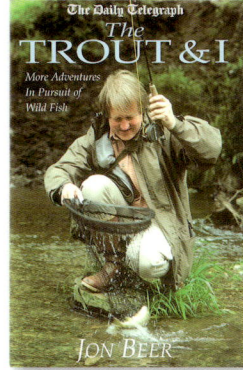

The Border years: '96 – Lugg at Last or Beside the Bridge at Aymestry (*Trout & Salmon*: June 1996) describes the antics in a scout camp in 1962 beside the river and the fortunes of fishing the recently acquired stretch of river now belonging to the Riverside Inn at Aymestry. Interwoven with these themes is a story of a jeweller and an upholsterer from neighbouring Presteigne – Peter Flint and Cosmo Barrett respectively. The chapter concludes with a graphic description of the dry-fly-and-weighted-nymph method of fishing identical to what we call the Duo system today.

A Day on the Dee relates an early start on an October day in order to fish the Welsh Dee, 'almost certainly the finest grayling water in England and Wales, possibly the British Isles.' The Llangollen Angling Association has seven miles of the river hereabouts all of which is available on a modestly priced day ticket.

ORANGE OTTER
Christopher Knowles (2006)

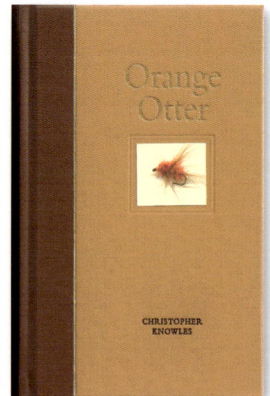

Orange Otter is a brilliant portrayal of the life and times of the Rev. Edward Powell, skilfully interwoven with anecdotal material regarding many other anglers of his acquaintance. To the Welsh Borderlands flyfisher this is an essential title, each of the twenty-one chapters has material of direct interest and relevance since they record 'an era of fishing theory and practice which was in danger of disappearing.' The book covers many facets of Powell's life – the Eagles/Powell family links; the rivers close to the vicarage at Munslow, the Corve, Onny and Teme; rivers further afield, the Ithon,

Irfon and Teifi; the extraordinary influence of Dai Lewis, the wizard of Tregaron.

Details of the dressing of 26 of Powell's flies are given within the text set against his statement that 'fly-tying is a form of self-expression – in the higher sense of the word, an art' and his belief that the smaller the stream the larger the fly.

Within the book are numerous original quotations from Powell's personal diary, the writing of which he kept to faithfully and formed an integral part of his fishing process. Of fishing he records it to be 'the insatiable in pursuit of the incalculable' and that 'fishing the water upstream, with one or two dry flies, is of all forms of fishing the most remunerative.'

THE ANGLE OF THE CAST
Gwilym Hughes (2009)

Gwilym Hughes privately published this autobiographical account of his life as an angler. He outlines how he spent his early years on the Lleyn Peninsula assisting his water bailiff father; his life as a Police Officer in Wrexham; fishing competitions for the Police and the Welsh National Teams; the 1990 World Championships of the Dee. In 1994, after suffering a heart attack, he left the force and turned to professional flyfishing. His company, Game Angling, is based in the Dee valley at Corwen where he could well be described as the 'doyen of the Dee.' He describes the development of his Cul de Canon fly as well as the successful use of the New Zealand method with a dry fly and a lightweight nymph being tied in tandem. In the section *River Flies* he enthuses about the Rev. Powell's Baby Sunfly and his pearly-thoraxed

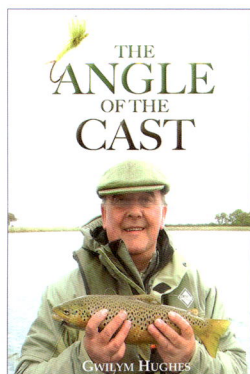

variation of the same.

The book concludes on a more salutary note by looking at the current environmental situation and he suggests that 'we should make the most of what we have presently and try not to damage it too much … farming methods have changed, modern man's methods and thinking is not all that great … unfortunately… to the detriment of Nature. We need to think.'

FISHING IN TIME
(THE HISTORY OF THE LEINTWARDINE FISHING CLUB)
Barney Rolfe-Smith (2011)

Fishing in Time is the story of The Leintwadine Fishing Club, one of the oldest and most exclusive fishing clubs in the country and situated in the heart of Welsh Borderlands. It is a meticulous piece of historical research that traces trout and grayling fishing on the River Teme in the vicinity of the village of Leintwardine on the Harley Estate, at Bampton Bryan, and the Downton Estate.

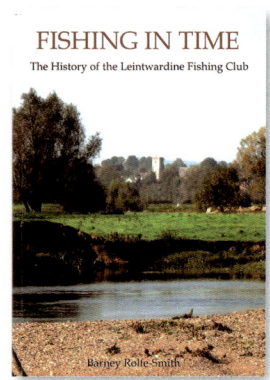

In the chapter *The Developing Reputation of the Leintwardine Fishery* the author makes reference to sections of Richard Bowlker's *The Art of Angling* and to Sir Humphry Davy's masterpiece, *Salmonia*.

The rather convoluted manner in which the club was formed is admirably covered in the chapter on *The Origins of the Club*. The foundation of the club is believed to have been somewhere between 1836 and 1855, and 1848 is given as the official date. Initially the fishing was solely on the Downton Estate water, but by 1855 the club also had also secured access to the Harley Estate water. The club originally comprised 25 members of whom eight were 'local,' eight were from

London and nine from elsewhere in the country.

The remainder of the book outlines in detail the problems the club has faced with the conjoining estate landowners, whose successive heirs have tried to modify the legal aspects of the fishing leasehold arrangements with the club. The major result of these upheavals has been the near closure and reforming of the club in 1870 and its reconstitution 1912 in order to comply with riparian needs. In the 1920s the club needed to move to a more business-like style of management and in more recent years it has managed to purchase the fishing rights of the Downton water and has a very stable lease of the Harley Estate water. The book concludes with the events of the club's history up to 1967, but there is a short *Postscript* covering the period 1967 – 2010. The last word comes from the current Chairman, Daniel McDowell: 'As I write the club has a sound financial basis and a long waiting list; we are blessed in both the quality of fishing and the beautiful and largely unchanged landscape in which it takes place. There will be new challenges and problems but little that an old and well organised club cannot resolve.'

Chapter 6

A poetic view of fishing the region

There are a number of stanzas, verses and poems that are featured in the books reviewed in the previous chapter that deserve a chapter of their own. They epitomise the sport of flyfishing within the Welsh Borderlands and make a fine collection. Reference is given to the source of each entry and they are listed in chronological order of the date of publication.

1) From *Barker's Delight*, first edition 1651:

A Brother of the Angle

A Brother of the Angle must always be sped
With three black Palmers, & also two red,
And all made with Hackles: in a cloudy day,
Or in windy weather, angle you may:
But morning and evening, if the day be bright,

And the chief point of all is to keep out of sight.
In the moneth of May, none but the May-flye;
For every month one, is a pitiful lye:
The black hawthorn flye must be very small,
And the sandy hogs haire is sure best of all
For the Mallard wing'd May-flye; and the Peacocks train
Will look like the flesh-flye to kill Trout amaine.
The oak flye is good, if it have a brown wing,
So is the Grasshopper that in July doth sing,
With a green body, make him on a middle siz'd hook;
But when you have catcht fish, then play the good Cook.
Once more my good brother, Ile speak in thy eare,
Hogs, red Cows, & Bears wooll, to float best appear,
And so doth your fur, if rightly it fall;
But alwayes remember, make two and make all.

2) From *Barker's Delight*, second edition 1659, in appreciation of the first edition:

Cards, Dice, and Tables pick thy purse;
Drinking and Drabbing bring a curse.
Hawking and Hunting spend thy chink;
Bowling and Shooting and in drink.
The fighting-Cock, and the Horse-race
Will sink a good Estate apace.
Angling doth bodyes exercise,
And maketh soules holy and wise:
By blessed thoughts and meditation:
This, this is Anglers recreation!
Health, profit, pleasure, mixt together,
All sport's to this not worth a feather.

Nagrom Notpoh
Armiger

3) From *Art of Angling*, Richard Bowlker, (c. 1746):

Preface to the section on *Fly Fishing*. Preface to the section on Fly Fishing. This fragment is from *Spring* from *The Seasons* by James Thomson (1700-1748). Thomson is best-known for writing the lyrics to the anthem *Rule Britannia*.

> *When, with this lively ray, the potent sun*
> *Has pierced the streams and roused the finny race,*
> *Then, issuing cheerful, to thy sport repair.*
> *Chief should the western breezes curling play,*
> *And light o'er aether bear the shadowy clouds.*
> *Just in the dubious point, where with the pool*
> *Is mix'd the trembling stream, or where it boils*
> *Around the stone, or from the hollow'd bank*
> *Reverted plays in undulating flow,*
> *There throw, nice judging, the delusive fly;*
> *And as you lead it round in artful curve,*
> *With eye attentive mark the springing game.*
> *Straight as above the surface of the flood*
> *They wanton rise, or urg'd by hunger leap,*
> *Then fix, with gentle twitch, the barbed hook.*
>
> James Thomson

This stanza, also from *Spring*, appears after the section which ends 'at the clearing of rivers after they have been disturbed by heavy rain.'

> *Now, when the first foul torrent of the brooks,*
> *Swell'd with the vernal rains, is ebb'd away;*
> *And, whit'ning down their mossy tinctured stream*
> *Descends the billowy foam: now is the time,*
> *While yet the dark brown water aids the guile,*
> *To tempt the trout. The well-dissembled fly,*
> *The rod, fine tapering, with elastic spring,*

Snatch'd from the hoary steed, the floating line,
And all thy slender wat'ry stores prepare.

James Thomson

This stanza appears as the Preface to the section *Materials for making Artificial Flies*

To frame the little animal provide
All the gay hues that wait on female pride;
Let nature guide thee. Sometimes golden wire
The shining bellies of the fly require;
The peacock's plumes thy tackle must not fail,
Nor the dear purchase of the sable's tail.
Each gaudy bird some slender tribute brings,
And lends the growing insect proper wings;
Silks of all colours must their aid impart,
And every fur promote the fisher's art.

John Gay (1685-1732)
Gay's Rural Sports

4) From *A Series of Letters on Angling, Shooting & Coursing*, Robert Lascelles (1815). This stanza, once again from *Spring*, appears in the fifth letter following a delightful section describing the process of hand-tying flies in great detail.

But should you lure
From his dark haunt, beneath the tangled roots
Of pendent trees, the monarch of the brook,
Behoves you then to ply your finest art.
Long time he, following cautious, scans the fly;
And oft attempts to seize it, but as oft
The dimpled water speaks his jealous fear.
At last, while haply o'er the shaded sun
Passes a cloud, he desperate takes the death,
With sullen plunge. At once he darts along,

Deep struck, and runs out all the lengthened line;
Then seeks the farthest ouze, the sheltering weed,
The cavern'd bank, his old secure abode ;
And flies aloft, and flounces round the pool,
Indignant of the guile. With yielding hand,
That feels him still, yet to his furious course
Gives way, you, now retiring, following now
Across the stream, exhaust his idle rage:
Till floating broad upon his breathless side,
And to his fate abandon'd, to the shore
You gaily drag your unresisting prize.

James Thomson

5) From *The Fly Fisher's Legacy*, George Scotcher (1820)

This stanza appears in the section entitled *Some account of aquatic insects* and is from *Summer* from *The Seasons.*

To sunny rivers some
By fatal instinct fly; where on the pool
They, sportive, wheel; or sailing down the stream,
Are snatch'd immediate by the quick-ey'd trout,
Or darting salmon.

James Thomson

6) From *Trout and salmon fishing in Wales*, George Agar Hansard (1834)

Found at the conclusion of the section on *The Common Trout*

The generous trout, to make the angler sport,
In deep and rapid streams will oft resort,
Where if you flourish but a fly, from thence
You hail a captive, but of fish the prince.

Found at the conclusion of the section on *The Grayling*

> *Umber or grayling in the streams he'll lie*
> *Hovering his fins at every silly fly;*
> *Fond of a feather; you shall see him rise*
> *At emmets, insects, hackles, drakes, and flies.*

Preface to the section on *Radnorshire*

> *Oh, sylvan Wye! Thou wanderer through the woods,*
> *How often has my spirit turn'd to thee!*
> *Once again I see these hedge-rows, hardly hedge-rows,*
> *Little lines of sportive wood run wild; these pastoral forms*
> *Green to the very door; and wreaths of smoke*
> *Sent up in silence from among the trees!*
> *With some uncertain notice, as might seem,*
> *Of vagrant dwellers in the houseless woods,*
> *Or of some hermit's cave, where by his fire*
> *The hermit sits alone.*

William Wordsworth

7) From *A Book on Angling*, Francis Francis (1867).

This old rhyme gives the angler some very sound advice and is found in the section on *The Weather*:

> *When the wind blows from the west,*
> *It blows the hook to the fish's nest;*
> *When the wind blows from the south,*
> *It blows the hook to the fish's mouth;*
> *When from the north and east it blows,*
> *Seldom the angler fishing goes.*

8) From *A Shropshire Lad*, A. E. Housman (1896).

These extracts from Housman's nostalgic verses make specific reference to the Welsh Borderland:

Verse XXVIII: The Welsh Marches

In my heart it has not died,
The war that sleeps on Severn side,
They cease not fighting, east and west,
On the marches of my breast.

Verse LII: Western Brookland

Far in a western brookland
That bred me long ago
The poplars stand and tremble
By pools I used to know

Verse XXVII: Other Rivers of the Region

The land where I shall mind you not
Is the land where all's forgot.
And if my foot returns no more
To Teme nor Corve nor Severn shore,

Verse L: Reference to Places and Rivers

Clunton and Clunbury,
Clungunford and Clun,
Are the quietest places
Under the sun.

In valleys of Springs of rivers,
By Ony and Teme and Clun,

The country for easy livers,
The quietest under the sun.

9) From *An Old Man's Holiday,* E. Marston (*The Amateur Angler*).

This poem was written by Percy Bysshe Shelley in about 1811 when he was staying at Nantgwillt House in Cwm Elan, sadly now lost to view lying beneath the waters of Caban Coch reservoir! It was written at a time just after he had been expelled from Oxford and after breaking off his engagement to his sixteen-year-old cousin, Harriet Grove.

When mountain, meadow, wood, and stream
With unalloying glory gleam,
And to the spirit's ear and eye
Are unison and harmony.
The moonlight was my dearer day,
Then would I wander far away,
And, lingering on the wild brook's shore,
To hear its unremitting roar,
Would lose in the ideal flow
All sense of overwhelming woe;
Or, at the noiseless noon of night,
Would climb some heathy mountain's height,
And listen to the mystic sound
That stole in fitful gusts around.

Percy Bysshe Shelley

10) From *Fishing for Pleasure and Catching it,* E. Marston (*The Amateur Angler*) (1906).

Preface to Chapter 1: *May Fly Fishing in Herefordshire in 1903.*

We plunge and strive from spot to spot,
But not a fish will rise;

In wonderment at our ill lot,
Turn up our wistful eyes.

Robert Blakey
Historical Sketches of the Angling Literature of All Nations

11) From *Clear Waters*, A.G. Bradley (1915).

A poem from Welsh poet Dafydd ap Gwylim which may have lost a little through translation into English:

Sweet Wye

Sweet Wye, with thy waters as white as the snow,
Now dark as the thunder-cloud's banner of woe.
Oh why should we wander beyond thy wild stream,
From the land of the harp and the bard and his dream!
The streams of the Saxons are languid and dead,
Like the mist on the mountain when summer is fled.
With thy wild, thronging billows, now softened, now shrill,
Like the laugh of fair children that sport on the hill,
Now all glowing with light and all snowy with foam,
Like the maids of the land of my heart and my home.

12) From *Down along Temeside*, Richard Holding (1963).

The following four poems, *The Song of the 'Red Tag'; Trout Season; The Trout;* and *Border Monnow*, are among fifteen which appear in the second edition (1989) of this book of flyfishing reminiscences.

The Song of the 'Red Tag'

My body it is tied with the finest peacock herl,
Some two or three strands twisted, with copper in the twirl;
Neck feathers of the game-cock complete my heady hackle,

My tail of bright red ibis shines gaily through the tackle.
Bright 'Red Tag.'

We met one sunny August in Alfred Housman's Teme,
With father's borrowed fly-rod, Bare-legged to the stream,
And there in plashy shallows, two-handed cast about,
Until at last we landed, together our first trout.
Bright 'Red Tag.'

Proud as any cockerel, he bore me off to school;
Then boyhood's legs grew stronger, and cricket was the rule,
But when the games were over, and evening light was failing,
He bore me to the riverside in search of trout and grayling.
Bright 'Red Tag.'

We fished this Island's rivers North, East and South, and West,
Though Clun, and Teme, and Monnow, were those we loved
the best.
In search of 'Salmo Trutta' we even went to Spain,
But always Offa's Marches called us home agin.
'Ubique Tagus Rufus.'

Now sixty summers later, denying the decline,
We persevere more finely far off, with nylon line.
The ageing legs now wadered, may sometimes feel the cold,
For though he won't admit it, I think he's growing old
Dear 'Red Tag.'

Trout Season
(*Piscator non solum piscator)

When the cold grey windy days of March
Give way to April sun,
And the blossom on the cherry tree
Proclaims that winter's gone,

When the primrose shines on the river bank,
And the plaintive curlew cries –
Then the March brown hatch goes sailing by,
And the fish take up their lies;
It is time for the angler's early outing,
The time the old writers called 'spring trouting'.
When the scent of the blossom fills the air,
And the earth revives from the winter rains,
When buttercups powder the waders with gold,
And cow parsley laces the leafy lanes;
Then the foam-flecked river sparkles and boils,
Alive with eagerly rising trout,
And still, as the daylight fades in the west
One may fish 'till the evening star shines out,
For these are the heady days of June,
The day when the May-fly calls the tune.

Late summer brings family holidays,
Thyme-scented walks in the August sun,
Lazy hours on the sandy beach,
Endless nights when the sea-trout run;
Then beneath golden September skies
Jealous summer lingers on,
Though trout still rise to the grayling flies,
The angler knows that the season's done;
And cold mist rises in gathering gloom,
As reluctant headlight turns for home.

(*There is more to fishing than catching fish)

The Trout
(A Fishy Moral Story)

He used to lie above the bridge,
For which young John O'Kent
Foreswore his soul, to covenant

The ancient road to Gwent
A robust Monnow trout he was,
Of most unusual size,
With quite uncanny predudice
Of artificial flies.

The syndicate all tried for him,
Read all the books to prosper,
From Halford, Skues, and Carter-Platts,
Right down to Konrad Vospar.

He knew the contents of each box,
From 'Tups' to 'Greenwell's Glory'
Some poachers tried the 'local Lure,'
(But that's another story).

But still he lay above the bridge,
Indifferent to all.
But trout have pride, and so at last
There came a mighty fall.

For on a day, from far upstream,
With noise and hearty shouting,
Came thrashing through the placid runs,
Unfeeling for our trouting.

A shoal of youths, in bright canoes,
And psychodelic gear,
Who met just protestation, with
'As much right to be here.'

Offensively they splashed downstream
Until they reached the place
Where lay our trout; and there set up
A sort of slalom race

I watched in abject impotence
Until at last they went
Down through the ancient masonry
That takes the road to Gwent.

And not until the turbulence
Had slowly petered out,
Did I perceive, within his lie,
A most indignant trout.

He thrashed around and in and out
Among the teenage fry,
I shared his mood! And when I cast
He took the proffered fly.

He fought as never trout before,
Unwilling to be slain …
I held his proud resplendent form,
Then slipped him back again.

So still he lies above the bridge,
Before admiring eyes,
And so remains defiantly,
A tantalising prize.

And if you cross the Kentchuch Bridge,
Whatever your intent,
Just pause to look; before you take
The ancient road to Gwent.

Border Monnow

How sweet are the springs of the sheep-trodden hills,
Where the Monnow brook rises, and chatters, and trills
From the border Black Mountains that lie above Hay,
Gath'ring Olchron and Escley brooks on its way.

By the stone farms of Crasswell it hurries on down,
Past the old mills and church of scattered Longtown,
'Til at Pandy the Honddhu comes hastening in
From Llanthony, where so many found peace hard to win.

Now the Monnow flows deeper, the speckled foam sails
Beside the old railway that runs down to Wales;
Under the road bridge, where the name 'Monmouth Cap'
Remembers Fluellen and Prince Hal perhaps.

By Pontrilas village three streams add their tally,
From Dulas, and Wormbrook, and Dore's Golden Valley;
Through cornfield and pasture, to where John of Kent
Had his bridge built that thwarted the Devil's intent.

'Neath the castle at Grosmont, where Owain Glyndwr
Met his march with King Henry's men garrisoned here;
Down to Skenfrith's castle, trim church, and cold mill
Where the water-wheel creakingly grinds its corn still.

Under willow and alder it runs in and out,
With mallard and wagtail, shy grayling and trout,
Past the cricket at Rockfield, and the Hendre of Rolls,
And the medieval bridge where the turnpike took tolls.
'Til at time-honoured Monmouth, its school field nearby
At last is embraced in the waters of Wye.

Chapter 7

Where to fish today

Within each of the river catchments there are numerous opportunities for flyfishing, either through day tickets or by club membership. The following information has been gleaned from a variety of sources and was up-to-date at the time of publication. However circumstances can change and it is always advisable to thoroughly check the availability of fishing before visiting the area. The opportunities within each river catchment are listed in a progression from the mouth of the main river to its source, following up each tributary system in its entirety before continuing up the main river.

River Dee

The lower reaches of the River Dee are predominantly mixed fishing and the first notable wild trout and grayling fishing opportunities are on the first major tributary, the River Alyn.

Warrington Anglers' Association has, among many other river beats, two stretches on the Alyn. Refer to website for season ticket details: www.warrington-anglers.org.uk

Rossett & Gresford Flyfishers' beats have increasing stocks of trout and grayling above Rossett. Membership only, refer to website: www.rossett-flyfishers.co.uk.

Returning to the main River Dee:

Bangor on Dee Salmon Anglers' Association has some excellent wild trout and grayling fishing with day tickets available from Middle Shop, Royal Oak or Buck Hotel in the village. Refer to website also: www.bodsaa.org.uk

Bryn-y-Pys AA have water below Overton Bridge at Erbistock down to Bangor-on-Dee. Day tickets from Deggy's Fishing Tackle, 2 Ruabon Road, Wrexham, LL13 7PB. Tel: 01978 351815. See website for further details: www.bryn-y-pys.webs.com

The Prince Albert Angling Society controls stretches on the main river at Llandderfel, Cynwyd, Newbridge, Erbistock and Bangor-on-Dee but issue no day tickets. There is currently a five year waiting list for membership. See website: www.paas.co.uk

The next tributary upstream is the River Ceiriog, which is believed to be the river with the steepest gradient in Wales, and has some fine wild trout and grayling fishing.

Ceiriog Fly Fishers at Chirk have eight miles of fishing on some of the lower stretches of the Ceiriog and offer day and season tickets. Tel: 01691 773632.

Cul de Canon

Back on the main river:

The Maelor Angling Association has three miles of excellent water near Trevor. Membership available at www.maelorangling.co.uk. Day tickets are available from Derek's Cycles, Well Street, Cefn Mawr. Tel: 01978 821841.

Llangollen Angling Association has several miles of fishing in the area. and now incorporates what was previously Maelor A.A. water. Day tickets are available, see website: www.llangollenangling.net and www.maelorangling.co.uk. Tickets from Watkin & Williams, Ironmongers, 4, Berwyn St, Llangollen, LL20 8ND. Tel: 01978 860652. Open 7 days a week. also from Derek's Cycles, Well Street, cefn Mawr. tel: 01978 821841. Additionally, Ty Mawr Country Park issue tickets, but only in summer.

Wirral Game Fishing Club has beats at Erbistock, Overton and Chirk as well as a mile-and-a-half stretch at Corwen. Membership only. Refer to website: www.wirralgame.org.uk

Midland Fly Fishers Ltd has four miles of excellent water from Glyndyfrdwy downstream. Day tickets are available from Watkin & Williams, Ironmongers, 4 Berwyn St, Llangollen, LL20 8ND Tel: 01978 860652, open 7 days.

Capenhurst Angling Club has water below Carrog. Membership only. Details from Mr A.T. Howden, Secretary, 24 Saughall Hey, Saughall, Chester CH1 6EJ. Tel: 01244 880621.

Corwen & District Angling Club has water on the main river and on tributaries (Alwen and Ceirw) in the Corwen area. No day tickets but membership available. Refer to website: www.cadac.org.uk or contact Club Secretary David Wooldridge, Ty Isa, Tan-y-Fron, Bylchau, Denbigh, Denbighshire, LL16 5NP. Tel: 01745 870115.

Ty Isaf Farm, Bala, has water between Llanfor and Llandderfel. Tel: Mr Evans 01678 520574.

Bala & District Angling Association has excellent wild trout and grayling possibilities on the Dee, from Bala Lake downstream to Llandderfel, and in the lake itself. There is also trout fishing available on the Tryweryn, Llafar and Lliw. Membership available, refer to website: www. balaangling.co.uk. Day tickets and permits are available from a number of outlets in Bala:

Derwen Stores, High Street, Bala.Tel: 01678 521084
Post Office, High Street, Bala.Tel: 01678 520317
Sbanner a Hanner, Tegid Street, Bala.Tel: 01678 520382
Tourist Information Centre, Bala.Tel: 01678 521021
Bryntirion Inn, Llandderfel.Tel: 01678 530205

River Severn

The River Severn, at over two hundred miles long, is the longest river in the UK. Its lower two-thirds is primarily a coarse fishing river, but in the upper reaches, above Welshpool, and in many of the tributaries, there are populations of wild trout and grayling.

At the time of writing, the Severn Rivers Trust is in the process of establishing a series of beats on a number of tributaries that will be accessed through a passport scheme similar to those in operation elsewhere in the country. Details of these beats and the scheme of operation are posted on the Severn Rivers Trust
Visit www.severnriverstrust.org.uk for particulars.

As one progresses up the Severn from its estuary, the first trout fishing of interest lies on the first tributary where the Gloucester Angling Club holds the rights to seven miles of the River Leadon near Upleadon and Durbridge Mill. This is principally a mixed fishery but there are some trout. Membership only. Details on the club website:
www.wix.com/daddyruffe/gloucester-angling-club

The next tributary of interest is the River Teme which itself has many important tributaries containing some excellent wild trout and grayling fishing.

The first tributary of the Teme itself is the Leigh Brook with the Cradley Brook at it head. The Gamefishers Club has a stretch on each. Membership only. Details from website:
www.gamefishersclub.org.uk

Further upstream on the River Teme, The White Swan Piscatorials have stretches at Bransford Bridge, Ham

Bridge, Shelsley Beauchamp, Orleton Court and Stanford Bridge. Membership only. Details from website: www.whiteswanpiscatorials.org.uk

The Prince Albert Angling Society has several beats on the River Teme from Ham Bridge up to Ashford Carbonell. Membership only. See website: www.paas.co.uk

The next tributary of note is the River Rea on which The White Swan Piscatorials have beats at Cleobury Mortimer, Hopton Court and Detton Bridge. Membership only. Details from website: www.whiteswanpiscatorials.org.uk

The Gamefishers Club has a stretch on the River Rea at Mawley Hall. Membership only. Details from website www.gamefishersclub.org.uk

Tenbury Fishing Association has about four and three-quarters of a mile on the River Teme and Ledwyche Brook. Membership and day tickets are available. See website for details: www.teme-valley.co.uk

The White Swan Piscatorials have a stretch of the Lower Ledwyche Brook. Membership only. Details from website: www.whiteswanpiscatorials.org.uk

Returning to the River Teme:

There are two stretches of free fishing in Ludlow: one from Dinham Bridge to Ludford Bridge, known as the Breadwalk, and the other from the Horseshoe Weir downstream for a quarter of a mile to the large pipe over the river. Details available from Ludlow Tackle, Bromfield Road, Ludlow, SY8 1DW Tel: 01584 875886. www.ludlowtackle.co.uk

Ludlow Angling Club controls a two-mile stretch of the River Teme as well as its tributary, the River Corve. Day tickets can be purchased at East Hamlet News, 8 New Road, Ludlow, Tel: 01584 872575 or the Cliff Hotel, Dinham, Ludlow, Tel: 01584 872063 or from the Club Membership Secretary, who can also give information. Tel: 01584 876997.

The next tributary upstream is the River Onny where day tickets are available at Halford Farm, Halford, Craven Arms, Shropshire. For details phone Mr J Edwards Tel: 01588 672382.

The Plowden Estate has syndicate fishing on the West Onny. For particulars Tel: 01588 68040.

Back on the River Teme we next come to Leintwardine where there are two fishing clubs.

The Leintwardine Fishing Club which was founded towards the end of the nineteenth century. There is a long waiting list for membership of this exclusive club. The Club allows residents of Leintwardine and their guests to fish the first 200 metre stretch of the river below the bridge on condition that they obey the usual protocols of fishing.

A short distance upstream from Leintwardine village the River Clun joins the River Teme and has some fine trout and grayling possibilities.

The Pheasant Tail Fly Fishers have a number of beats on the rivers Clun, Redlake and Kemp close to Clungunford, and Aston on Clun. Membership only. Details on the website: www.thepheasanttailflyfishers.co.uk

The Salopian Fly Fishers have one mile of the River Clun

Orange Otter

near Clungunford. Membership only. Details on the website: www.salopianflyfishers.co.uk

Returning to the River Teme above its confluence with the River Clun there are possibilities at the following locations.

Bucknell House has approximately three quarters of a mile of the river which is available to those using the Caravan Club CL site. Tel: 01547 530640. Or through the Wye and Usk Foundation. www.wyeuskfoundation.org

Milebrook House Hotel has approximately three miles of water, which is available to residents, from Bucknell upstream to Knighton. For details Tel: 01547 528632 or visit www.milebrookhouse.co.uk

Above Knighton the river has a habit of disappearing under-ground and resurfacing further downstream as it passes through limestone strata. However when there is water in the river fishing is possible!

Lower House Farm has approximately one mile of fishing available to those who call. Tel: 01547 528670.

Monaughty Poeth near Llanfair Waterdine, LD7 1TT, has about 500 metres of double bank fishing as well as a Caravan Club CL site. Tel: 01547 528348.

Returning to the River Severn, a short distance upstream from Worcester at Hawford, the River Salwarpe enters from the north-east.

The White Swan Piscatorials have a stretch of the River Salwarpe at Hawford. Membership only. Details from website: www.whiteswanpiscatorials.org.uk

A short distance upstream of Bridgnorth the River Worfe joins the Severn from the north-east.

The Salopian Fly fishers have some fishing on the River Worfe. Membership only. Details on the website: www.salopianflyfishers.co.uk

Further up the main river the Cound Brook enters from the west.

The Gamefishers Club has stretches on the Cound Brook close to Eaton Mascott, Cantlop Bridge and Berrington. Membership only. Details on the website: www.gamefishersclub.org.uk

A little further upstream the River Tern joins from the north-east.

The Environment Agency has one of its free fisheries on the River Tern. Details from website: www.dofreefishing.co.uk/england/free-fishing-shropshire.html

The Nantwich Angling Society has a stretch at Waters Upton near Hodnet. Membership only. See website for details: www.nantwichangling.co.uk

The Prince Albert Angling Society has a couple of beats on the River Tern near Upton Magna. Membership only. Details on website: www.paas.co.uk.

The Rea Brook joins the Severn in Shrewsbury and the Shropshire Anglers' Federation (website can be found at: www.shropshireanglersfederation.in) has approximately three miles available on season or day tickets which can be obtained from Frankwell Post Office or Total Angling, Units 18-20 Vanguard Way, Battlefield, Shrewsbury Tel: 01743 46269.

A short distance upstream from Shrewsbury the River Perry joins the Severn from the north. Warrington Anglers' Association has a short stretch at Ruyton XI Towns. Membership only. Details on website: www.warrington-anglers.org.uk

The next major tributary is the River Vyrnwy which, with its own tributaries, has some very fine wild trout and grayling fishing.

Montgomeryshire Angling Association at Llanymynech has about half a mile of double bank fishing. Membership and day tickets available Tel: 01938 554971. Details on website: www.montgomeryshireanglingassociation.co.uk. The Prince Albert Angling Society controls several stretches. Membership only. Details on website: www.paas.co.uk

Blue-winged Olive (Powell)

Crewe Pioneer Anglers has a stretch in the lower reaches. For details & permits Tel: 01270 214859.

Close to Four Crosses the **Warrington Anglers' Association** has a short stretch. Membership only. Details on website: www.warrington-anglers.org.uk.

The first tributary of size to join the River Vyrnwy is the River Tanat on which there are the following possibilities.

The Horseshoe Inn at Llanyblodwel has about one mile and issues day tickets. Tel: 01691 828969.

The Gamefishers Club owns a stretch on the River Tanat upstream of Llanyblodwel. Membership only. Details from website: www.gamefishersclub.org.uk.

The Green Inn at Llangedwyn has a stretch of fishing on the River Tanat and supplies day tickets. Tel: 01691 828234.

The Upper Tanat Fishing Club has approximately seven miles of fishing on the upper reaches of the River Tanat extending upstream from Carreghofa weir, located between Llanyblodwell and Llanymynech. Membership only. Details from website: www.tanatfishing.com.

Back on the River Vyrnwy near Llansantffraid the Bryn Vyrnwy Caravan Park issues day tickets. Tel: 01691 828252.

The next tributary is the River Cain.

Green Hall in Llanfyllin offers a small but good stretch of the river. Tel: 01691 648364.

Then comes the River Banwy on which there are a number of possibilities.

The Prince Albert Angling Society controls three stretches on the River Banwy. Membership only. Details on website: www.paas.co.uk

At Llanfair Caereinion the Montgomeryshire Angling Association has about half a mile of fishing on the River Banwy. Membership and day tickets available. Tel: 01938 554971 for details or website:
www.montgomeryshireanglingassociation.co.uk

Llysun Farm, Llanerfyl has a mile of double-bank fishing on the River Banwy. Tel: 01938 820347

Cann Office Hotel, near Llangadfan has a fine stretch of the River Banwy. Day tickets from the hotel. Tel: 01938 820202.

Back on the River Vyrnwy the Glyndwr Fishery near Dolanog controls two and a half miles of excellent fishing but only season tickets available. Visit website for details. www.glyndwr-fishery.co.uk

Lake Vyrnwy has plenty of brown and rainbow trout. Tickets and information from Lake Vyrnwy Hotel. Tel: 01691 870692 or website: www.lakevyrnwy.com

Returning to the River Severn above its confluence with the River Vyrnwy.

Montgomeryshire Angling Association has nearly two miles of single bank mixed fishing. Membership only. Website: www.montgomeryshireanglingassociation.co.uk

Warrington Anglers' Association has one mile of single bank fishing east of Welshpool. Membership only. Details from website: www.warrington-anglers.org.uk

Further up the main river the next tributary is the River Camlad – the only river to flow from England into Wales!

Montgomeryshire Angling Association has a short stretch of the river near Forden. Membership and day tickets available. Tel: 01938 554971 or visit:
www.montgomeryshireanglingassociation.co.uk

A short distance up the main river the River Rhiw enters from the north-west.

Near Berriew, the Montgomeryshire Angling Association has a short stretch of the river near Forden. Membership and day tickets available. Tel: 01938 554971.
Website: www.montgomeryshireanglingassociation.co.uk

Further up the River Severn at Newtown there is a very good free stretch below the new bridge. Water in and above the town is controlled by Severnside and Newtown Angling Club. Day tickets are available from Newtown Angling, Severnside Centre, Short Bridge Street, Newtown. Tel: 01686 624044.

Caersws Angling Association controls several miles of the River Severn around Caersws and Llandinam. Day tickets available from the Spar Shop and Newsagent in Caersws and Post Office in Llandinam.
Website: www.caersws-aa.co.uk

The Llanidloes and District Angling Association have water on the River Severn below and above the town. They also have stretches on the Dulas and Clywedog.
Website: www.llanidloes.com

In Llanidloes itself, there is free fishing on the River Severn at the Environment Agency Fishery, an 800 metre stretch below the sewage works. Further details from Environment Agency. Tel: 01743 272828.

Llyn Clywedog is situated at the head of the River Clywedog. Day tickets available from Woosnam and Davies Newsagents, Llanidloes, Tel: 01686 412263 and The Traveller's Rest, Llanidloes. Tel: 01686 412329.
Website: www.llanidloes.com/angling_club

River Wye

The River Wye offers rich and diverse opportunities for trout and grayling fishing both on the main river upstream from Bredwardine and on its notable primary tributaries, the

Monnow, Lugg, Llynfi, Edw, Irfon, Ithon, and Elan. Many of these primary tributaries support important secondary and even tertiary tributaries of which the Dore, Honddu, Arrow, Hindwell Brook and Cammarch are the most significant. In total there are about forty rivers in the catchment, most of which hold populations of trout and grayling.

Progressing up from the mouth of the river at Chepstow the first notable trout and grayling fishing is to be found in the River Trothy close to Monmouth. The Monmouth & District Angling Society has two stretches on the Trothy, giving a total of around three-and-a-half miles. Day tickets available from Bridge Cycles in Monmouth.
Website: www.monmouthfishing.co.uk

Above the confluence of the Rivers Monnow and Wye in Monmouth, the Monmouth & District Angling Society also has three stretches on the Monnow. Day tickets available from Bridge Cycles in Monmouth.
Website: www.monmouthfishing.co.uk

The Monnow Fisheries Association has water on the Monnow and Trothy. For further information contact the Secretary on 01989 770667. Website: www.monnow.org

The Cwmbran Angling Association has two miles of fishing on the Monnow above Osbaston weir. Tickets (season and day) and information about the association on 01633 874472.

Garway Flyfishers have a stretch of the Monnow at Kentchurch and issue season tickets. Tel: 01873 811230.

On the upper Monnow and its tributaries the Dore, Dulas Brook, Olchon, Escley and Honddu, the Wye and Usk

Shuttlecock Suspender

Foundation offers a range of day ticket fishing. Tel: 01982 560788. Website: www.wyeuskfoundation.org

The Gamefishers Club has short stretches on the Monnow and Honddu close to their confluence. Membership only. Website: www.gamefishersclub.org.uk

It is possible to access some fishing on the Garren Brook through the Wye and Usk Foundation. Website: www.wyeuskfoundation.org

The Hereford and District Angling Association has fishing on the lower Lugg and a few trout and grayling have been recorded hereabouts. Website: www.hdaa.blogspot.com

The Rivers Lugg and Arrow Fisheries Association in conjunction with the Wye and Usk Foundation have a number of beats available on highly productive waters. The Lugg and Arrow rivers have substantial trout and grayling populations and are situated in magnificent countryside, and the Hindwell (tributary of Lugg) has wild brown trout. Notable beats on the River Lugg are those at Eyton and Lyepole and on the River Arrow are The Leen and Court of Noke. Website: www.wyeuskfoundation.org

The Pheasant Tail Fly Fishers have a couple of beats on the Lugg between Leominster and Presteigne. Membership only. Website: www.thepheasanttailflyfishers.co.uk

Above Presteigne the Gamefishers Club has two stretches on the Lugg. Membership only.
Website: www.gamefishersclub.org.uk

Returning to the main river, The Red Lion Hotel at Bredwardine has four miles of water known as The Moccas Fishery. Primarily this is a salmon and coarse fishery but it is worth noting that a number of trout and grayling have been caught hereabouts. Realistically this beat marks the downstream limit of trout and grayling on the river. Website: www.redlion-hotel.com

At Hay-on-Wye there is free fishing on the Town Water downstream of the bridge to the Pump Station.

Between Hay-on-Wye and Builth Wells there are some magnificent beats, such as Abernant, available on the main river through the Wye and Usk Foundation. They also have some superb stretches of small stream wild trout fishing on tributaries: Llynfi, Dulas, Clettwr, Edw and Duhonw. Website: www.wyeuskfoundation.org

At Builth Wells, The Groe Park and Irfon Angling Club have fishing on the main river and the Irfon. Tickets are available from Nibblets, the ironmonger's shop in Builth Wells.

In the vicinity of Builth Wells there are many possibilities for trout and grayling on the main river as well as the tributaries, the Irfon, Cammarch, Ithon and Clywedog, which are also accessible through the Wye and Usk Foundation. Website: www.wyeuskfoundation.org

Hendre Farm, Builth Wells has three miles on the Irfon. For tickets and information, telephone 01982 551070.

Permits are available for the Cammarch Hotel water on the Irfon from the hotel. Website: www.cammarch.com

Permits are available for the Lake House Country Hotel water on the Irfon from the hotel.
Website: www.lakecountryhouse.co.uk

Upstream of Builth Wells the River Ithon enters the Wye. The Llandrindod Wells Angling Association has fishing on approximately four miles of the River Ithon in the vicinity of the town. Information and permits from their secretary. Tel: 01597 823539, or the Tourist Information Centre. Tel: 01597 822600, or Disserth Farm Caravan Park. Tel: 01597 860277.

Further upstream towards Penybont day tickets for about two miles of fishing on the River Ithon are available from Bryn Thomas Farm, Penybont. Tel: 01597 851315.

The Severn Arms Hotel, Penybont issues day tickets for a few stretches of the River Ithon which are mainly upstream

Claret Coch-y-bonddu

from Penybont. Tel: 01597 851224.
Website: www.severn-arms.co.uk

Back on the River Wye and upstream of Builth Wells is
the Doldowlod beat which is especially well-known for its
grayling fishing. This beat is available from The Wye and
Usk Foundation. Website: www.wyeuskfoundation.org

There are beats on the Upper Wye, Elan and Marteg
tributaries around Rhayader which are accessible through
the Rhayader & Elan Angling Association – website at
www.rhayaderangling.co.uk. Permits available from Daisy
Powell's Newsagents, West Street, Rhayader. Tel: 01597
810451 or from The Wye and Usk Foundation.
Website: www.wyeuskfoundation.org

Glaslyn Estate near Rhayader, has superb fishing for
holiday guests but no day tickets. Tel: 01597 810258.
Website: www.glaslynestate.co.uk

River Usk

The River Usk is acclaimed as one of the best wild brown trout rivers in the UK and has opportunities throughout most of its length. It is interesting to note that grayling for some reason are absent from the whole river catchment.

Much of the water is in private ownership but there are opportunities for the visiting angler. The Wye and Usk Foundation has numerous beats on the main river and on some of its tributaries and there are some other possibilities.

Working up river from its mouth at the confluence with the River Severn near Newport the lower limit of trout fishing is just below the town of Usk and there is some good trout fishing available hereabouts.

Usk Town water is available on a season, week or day ticket basis. Fishing is situated on both banks above and below Usk town. Fishing is located two miles from Llanbadoc Church to one-and-a-half miles above town with the exception of some private gardens. Flyfishing only and bag limits are imposed. NB. Thigh waders only, Chest waders are not permitted. For all types of permit and assistance contact Jean Williams at Sweet's Fishing Tackle in Porthcarne Street, Usk. Tel: 01291 672552.

Pantygoitre Farm, Llanfair Kileddin (close to Abergavenny) has luxury self-catering cottages and a mile of fishing on the river. Tel: 01873 840207. Website: www.swanmeadow.co.uk

The next stretch of accessible fishing is on the Abergavenny Town Water which is double bank fishing that extends for just over a mile. Season and day tickets are available at the Town Hall in Abergavenny or at the garage on the Merthyr road out of town or telephone 01873 857737.

Gwent Angling Society manages a total of four miles of the Usk on beats below Glangwrny and Chainbridge as well as fishing on the Sirhowy. Membership only.
Website: www.gwentanglingsociety.co.uk.
A short distance downstream from Crickhowell is the Dan-y-Parc beat which arguably has some of the best trout fishing on the river. It is possible to fish this water through the office at The Wye and Usk Foundation.
Website: www.wyeuskfoundation.org

Crickhowell Angling Club owns or rents nine-and-a-half miles on the Usk from Crickhowell downstream to Pantygoitre Bridge as well as some on the Grwyne. Membership only. Membership Secretary. Tel: 01873 832204.

Between Crickhowell and Talybont-on-Usk there is some outstanding brown trout fishing much of which is available through the office at The Wye and Usk Foundation.
Website: www.wyeuskfoundation.org

The following beats are also available directly:

The Glanusk Estate has four miles of fishing on the river and also offers accommodation and self-catering cottages.
Website: www.glanuskestate.com

Gliffaes Hotel owns a mile or so of double bank fishing for residents in a beautiful setting. The hotel water is available to non-residents on a day ticket basis. Tel: 01874 730371.
Website: www.gliffaeshotel.com

Talybont Reservoir is a wild trout fishery which is stocked on an annual basis to supplement the native brown trout population. Fly and bank fishing only. Tickets from machines at car park beneath the dam.

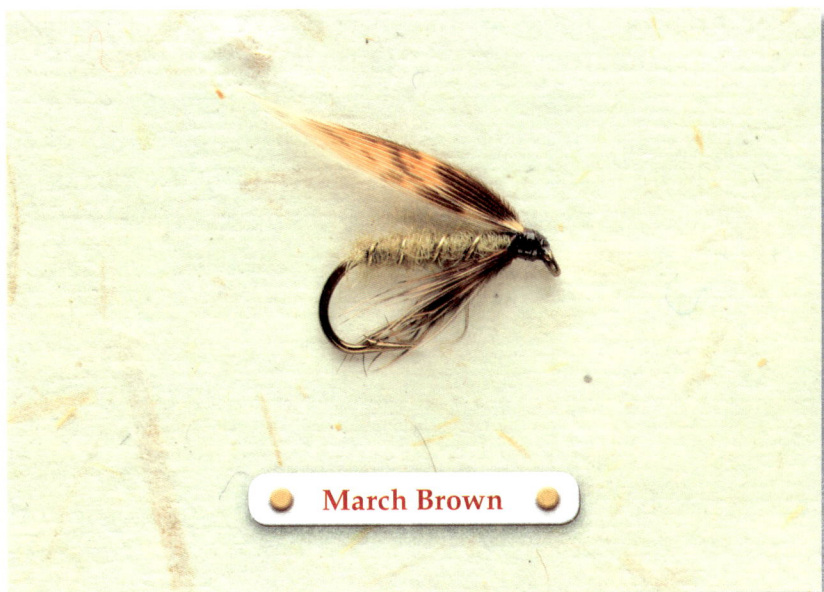

March Brown

From Talybont to Brecon there are some high quality beats available through the Wye and Usk Foundation. The Dinas and Abercynrig beat is of special note hereabouts.
Website: www.wyeuskfoundation.org

Brecon Town Council has water extending from Llanfaes Bridge in the centre of the town for just over a mile to the Welsh Water works. Tickets are available from the Town Clerk's Office at the Guildhall; the Post Office; Edwards' Newsagents and HM Supplies, The Wotton, Brecon.

On the main river upstream from Brecon, as far as Pont-ar-Hydfer, the Wye and Usk Foundation has a number of beats on the main river offering some outstanding trout fishing (especially the Fenni Fach beat) as well as a few beats on some of the tributaries e.g. the Honddu, Cilieni and Crai. Website: www.wyeuskfoundation.org

The first 350 metres of the river flowing out of the Usk Reservoir are free fishing courtesy of Welsh Water.

Usk Reservoir itself is a remote upland reservoir set in moorland and forest. The wild brown trout population is supplemented by stocking with brown and rainbow trout. Permits are available at the reservoir car park.

BIBLIOGRAPHY

BARKER, Thomas.
The Art of Angling. 1615.
Barker's Delight, Or The Art of Angling. Wherein are discovered many rare secrets. 1659 (This is the second edition of *The Art of Angling*).

BEER, Jon.
Gone Fishing. Aurum Press, London, 2002.
The Trout and I. Aurum Press, London, 2006.

BENNION, Bertie. ("B.B." of the "Field").
The Trout are Rising in England and South Africa. A book for slippered ease. John Lane, London, 1920.

BERNERS, Dame Juliana.
The Treatyse of Fysshynge with an Angle; printed in the Book Of Saint Albans by Wynkyn De Worde, 1496.

BOWLKER, Richard.
The Art of Angling. Ludlow, c. 1746.

BRADLEY, A.G.
In the March and Borderland of Wales. Constable, London, 1905.

Clear Waters: Trouting days and trouting ways in Wales, the West Country and the Scottish Borderland. Constable, London, 1915.

FLY-TIERS FROM THE BORDERLANDS

Cosmo Barrett

BROUGHTON, Ron.
Grayling: The Fourth Game Fish. Crowood Press, 1989.
The Complete Book of the Grayling. Hale, London, 2000.

DAVY, Sir Humphry.
Salmonia. John Murray, London, 1828.

EVANS, Emrys.
Plu Stiniog: Trout Flies for North Wales. Coch-y-Bonddu Books, Machynlleth, 2010.

EVANS, James.
Small River Fly-Fishing. A. & C. Black, London, 1972.

FRANCIS, Francis.
A Book on Angling; being a complete treatise on the art of angling in every branch, with explanatory plates, etc. Longmans Green & Co., London, 1867.

GALLICHAN, Walter Matthew.
Fishing in Wales. A guide to the angler. F.E. Robinson, London, 1903

The Trout Waters of England, a practical guide to the fisherman for sea trout, brown trout and grayling. T.N. Foulis, Edinburgh & London, 1908.

Fishing Waters and Quarters in Wales. A practical guide to fishermen with costs of fishing accommodation, etc. Heath Cranton, London, 1916.

Fishing in Mid-Wales; a practical guide. Brecon, 1939.

GIBBINGS, Robert John.
Coming down the Wye.
Dent, London, 1942.

GREY, Sir Edward.
Fly Fishing. Dent, London, 1899.

FLY-TIERS FROM THE BORDERLANDS

Walter Gallichan

FLY-TIERS FROM THE BORDERLANDS

E.C.COOMBES.
BOOTMAKER
& FISHING TACKLE

Ted Coombes

HANCOCK, CYRIL V.
East and West of Severn. Faber, London, 1956.
Rod in Hand. An angler's moods and memories. Phoenix House, London, 1958.
The Land of Teme and Gleam. An 8 pp contribution to Maurice Wiggin's excellent collection, *The Angler's Bedside Book*.

HANSARD, George Agar.
Trout and Salmon Fishing in Wales. Longman, Rees, Orme, Brown, Green and Longman, London, 1834.

HARVEY, Norman K.
The River Dee (Afon Dyfrdwy) from Source to Sea. Countryvise, Birkenhead, 2007.

HOLDING, Clifford Richard
Down Along Temeside. Privately published, Halesowen, 1963.
Down Along Temeside. Second edition, revised, privately published, Halesowen, 1989.

HOUSMAN, A.E.
A Shropshire Lad. Kegan Paul & Co., London, 1896.

HUGHES, Gwilym.
The Angle of the Cast. Published by the author, 2009.

HUGHES-PARRY, Jack.
Fishing Fantasy: A Salmon Fisherman's Note-Book. Eyre & Spottiswoode, London, 1949.
Second edition retitled *A Salmon Fisherman's Note-Book: A Fishing Fantasy*. Same publisher, 1955.

JOHN, David.
Fly Fishing on the Usk: An historical approach. Brecknock Museum, 1968.

JONES, P. Thoresby.
Welsh Border Country. Batsford, 1938.

KNOWLES, Christopher.
Orange Otter. Medlar Press, Ellesmere, 2006.

LASCELLES, Robert.
Angling: being the first part of a series of familiar letters on sporting. J. Cornes, London, 1815.

LAWRIE, W.H.
English and Welsh Trout Flies. Muller, London, 1967.

LEA, Archdeacon William.
Fishing Reminiscences. The Shuttle Office, Kidderminster, 1892.

LEIGHTON, Michael.
Trout Flies of Shropshire and the Welsh Borderlands. Published by the author, Shrewsbury, 1987.

MANSFIELD, Kenneth (Editor).
The Art of Angling. The Caxton Publishing Company, London, 1957.

MARSTON, Edward, F.R.G.S. ("AMATEUR ANGLER").
An Old Man's Holidays, by the Amateur Angler. Sampson Low, London, 1900.

Fishing for Pleasure and Catching it [with] two chapters on angling in North Wales by R.B. Marston. Werner Laurie, London, 1906.

MAYBURY, D.J.
Sounds of Running Waters: Llangollen and the Welsh Dee revealed. Published by the author, Llangollen, 1988.

MORGAN, Moc.
Fly Patterns for the Rivers and Lakes of Wales. Gomer Press, Llandysul, 1984.

Trout and Salmon Flies of Wales. Merlin Unwin Books, Ludlow, 1996.

PRICE, Taff.
Rough Stream Trout Flies. A. & C. Black, London, 1976.

FLY-TIERS FROM THE BORDERLANDS

Rev. Powell

PRYCE-TANNATT, T.E.
  Trout-Fly Dressings. An 8-page leaflet produced by the Welsh Fly-Fishing Association about 1965.

ROBERTS, John.
  A Guide to River Trout Flies. Crowood Press, 1989.

ROLFE-SMITH, Barney.
  Fishing in Time: The history of the Leintwardine Fishing Club. Stonebrook Publishing, Ludlow, 2011.

ROLT, H.A.
  Grayling Fishing in South County Streams. Sampson Low, London, 1901.

SALTER, Robert.
  The Modern Angler. Oswestry, 1800.

SCOTCHER, George.
  The Fly Fisher's Legacy. M. Willett, Chepstow, 1820.

STEPHENS, Wilson.
  The Severn. Muller, Blond & White Rivers of Britain Series, London, 1986.

TAYLOR, Samuel.
  Angling in all its Branches. 1800.

THRELFALL, Richard Evelyn.
  Notes on Trout Fishing in Lake Vyrnwy and the Upper Vyrnwy River. Mark & Moody Ltd., Stourbridge, 1947.

VENIARD, John.
  Reservoir and Lake Flies. A. & C. Black, London, 1970.

FLY-TIERS FROM THE BORDERLANDS

Canon Eagles

WIGGIN, Maurice Samuel.
  The Passionate Angler. Sylvan Press, London, 1949.
  Troubled Waters. Hutchinson, London, 1960.
  Editor. *The Angler's Bedside Book.* Batsford, London, 1965.

WILLIAMS, Alfred Courtney.
   Trout Flies: A discussion and a dictionary. A. & C. Black, London, 1932.

   A Dictionary of Trout Flies; and of flies for sea trout and grayling. A. & C. Black, London, 1949.

WARD LOCK RED GUIDE.
   Guide to Hereford and the Wye Valley; including Llandrindod Wells and the spas of Central Wales. Special sections for motorists and anglers. Ward, Lock & Co., London, 1959 14th edition. (First published in 1896).

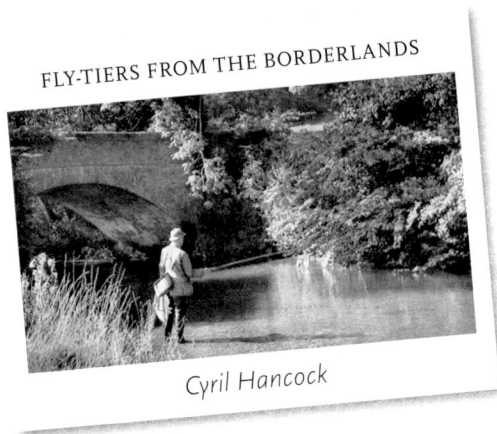

FLY-TIERS FROM THE BORDERLANDS

Cyril Hancock

Note: The date given is that of the first edition. In several instances there have been later reprints. Second-hand copies of almost all of these books are available from Coch-y-Bonddu Books.

Website at www.anglebooks.com

INDEX

FLIES

Colour plates in bold type

OTHER IMPORTANT FLY-FISHING BOOKS
AVAILABLE FROM
THE FLYFISHER'S CLASSIC LIBRARY

————— ↻ —————

A Salmon Fisher's Odyssey – John Ashley-Cooper
The Flyfisher's Guide – G. C. Bainbridge
The Art of Fly Making – William Blacker
An Angler's Paradise – F. D. Barker
Sunshine and the Dry Fly – J.W. Dunne
Brook & River Trouting – Edmonds & Lee
Fly-Tyer's Masterclass –Oliver Edwards
The Book of the Salmon – Ephemera
Going Fishing – Negley Farson
A Book on Angling – Francis Francis
Golden Days – Romilly Fedden
Fly Fishing – Sir Edward Grey
The Essential Kelson – Terry Griffiths
An Angler's Autobiography – F. M. Halford
The House the Hardy Brothers Built – J. L. Hardy
A Summer on the Test – J. W. Hills
My Sporting Life – J. W. Hills
River Keeper – J. W. Hills
Autumns on the Spey – A. E. Knox
Salmon and Sea Trout – Sir Herbert Maxwell
Fly-Fishing: Some New Arts and Mysteries – J. C. Mottram
Fishing in Eden – William Nelson
Grayling Fishing – W. Carter Platts
The Book of the Grayling – T. E. Pritt
Yorkshire Trout Flies – T. E. Pritt
Rod and Line – Arthur Ransome
Flies for Snowdonia – Plu Eryri – William Roberts
The Frank Sawyer Omnibus – Frank Sawyer
Days and Nights of Salmon Fishing on the Tweed – W. Scrope
Nymph Fishing for Chalk Stream Trout – G. E. M. Skues
Silk, Fur and Feather: The Fly Dresser's Handbook – G. E. M. Skues
Side-lines, Side-lights and Reflections – G. E. M. Skues
The Way of a Trout with a Fly – G. E. M. Skues
The Practical Angler – W. C. Stewart
Jones's Guide to Norway – F. Tolfrey
Grayling and How to Catch Them – F. M. Walbran
The Rod and Line – H. Wheatley
River Angling for Salmon and Trout – J. Younger
Three in Norway by Two of Them

The Flyfisher's Classic Library – Coch-y-Bonddu Books
Machynlleth, Mid-Wales
01654 702837
www.ffcl.com   www.anglebooks.com